VIRGINIA WOOLF AND THE VICTORIANS

Criticism of Woolf is often polarised into viewing her work as either fundamentally progressive or reactionary. In *Virginia Woolf and the Victorians*, Steve Ellis argues that her commitment to yet anxiety about modernity coexists with a nostalgia and respect for aspects of Victorian culture threatened by radical social change. Ellis tracks Woolf's response to the Victorian era through her fiction and other writings, arguing that Woolf can be seen as more 'Post-Victorian' than 'modernist'. He explains how Woolf's emphasis on continuity and reconciliation related to twentieth-century debates about Victorian values, and he analyses her response to the First World War as the major threat to that continuity. This detailed and original investigation of the range of Woolf's writing attends to questions of cultural and political history and fictional structure, imagery and diction. It proposes a new reading of Woolf's thinking about the relationships between the past, present and future.

STEVE ELLIS is Professor of English Literature at the University of Birmingham.

VIRGINIA WOOLF AND THE VICTORIANS

STEVE ELLIS

CAMBRIDGE UNIVERSITY PRESS
Cambridge, New York, Melbourne, Madrid, Cape Town, Singapore, São Paulo, Delhi

Cambridge University Press
The Edinburgh Building, Cambridge CB2 8RU, UK

Published in the United States of America by Cambridge University Press, New York

www.cambridge.org
Information on this title: www.cambridge.org/9780521882897

© Steve Ellis 2007

This publication is in copyright. Subject to statutory exception
and to the provisions of relevant collective licensing agreements,
no reproduction of any part may take place without
the written permission of Cambridge University Press.

First published 2007

Printed in the United Kingdom at the University Press, Cambridge

A catalogue record for this publication is available from the British Library

Library of Congress Cataloguing in Publication data
Ellis, Steve, 1952–
Virginia Woolf and the Victorians / Steve Ellis.
        p.   cm.
Includes bibliographical references and index.
ISBN-13: 978-0-521-88289-7 (hardback)
ISBN-10: 0-521-88289-3 (hardback)
1. Woolf, Virginia, 1882–1941 – Criticism and interpretation. 2. Woolf, Virginia, 1882–1941 – Political and social views. 3. Social values in literature. 4. Sentimentalism in literature. I. Title.
PR6045.O72Z62678 2007   823'.912 – dc22   2007016483

ISBN 978-0-521-88289-7 hardback

Cambridge University Press has no responsibility for
the persistence or accuracy of URLs for external or
third-party internet websites referred to in this book,
and does not guarantee that any content on such
websites is, or will remain, accurate or appropriate.

To Patrick

'I say Ethel what a happy life you had – in the very cream and marrow of the 19th Century. I had a glimpse too, but not a long look.'

Letter to Ethel Smyth, 14 April 1939

Contents

Acknowledgements	*page* viii
List of editions and abbreviations used in the text	x
Introduction: Post-Victorian Woolf	1
1 Reclamation: *Night and Day*	12
2 Synchronicity: *Mrs Dalloway*	43
3 Integration: *To the Lighthouse*	78
4 Disillusion: *The Years*	110
5 Incoherence: the final works	140
Conclusion: reclaiming the shadows	171
Notes	181
Index	207

Acknowledgements

First and foremost I thank my colleagues at the University of Birmingham with whom I have discussed and, in organising together the sixteenth Annual International Conference on Virginia Woolf held in June 2006, practically 'lived' Woolf over the last few years: Anna Burrells, Deborah Parsons and Kathryn Simpson. Thanks also to, among other colleagues, Andrzej Gasiorek and Marion Thain. Papers relating to earlier stages of this research were given at the twelfth and thirteenth Annual Woolf Conferences held at Sonoma State University and Smith College in 2002 and 2003 respectively – I am grateful to the conference organisers for allowing me to develop and test ideas by these means, also to Emily Blair, Joe Kreutziger, Patricia Moran, Elizabeth Shih and Nick Smart (and other delegates) for helpful suggestions and conviviality at these events, likewise to Christine Rauer and John Drakakis for inviting me to speak to research seminars at the Universities of St Andrews and Stirling. I am indebted to the advice and support of Jane Goldman, Laura Marcus, Susan Sellers and Stan Smith. I should also like to thank the staffs of the Birmingham Central Library, the British Library and the libraries of the Universities of Birmingham and Sussex (Monk's House Papers) for unfailingly helpful and considerate support, and, in the latter case, for permission to quote from unpublished material. Every effort has been made to secure necessary permissions to reproduce copyright material in this work, though in some cases it has proved impossible to trace copyright holders. If any omissions are brought to our notice, we will be happy to include appropriate acknowledgements in any subsequent edition of this book. Thanks also to Barbara Blumenthal at Smith College for providing me with the cover-image for this book. To the Arts and Humanities Research Council I am indebted for a Research Leave Award that supported this work in its latter stages, and to Ray Ryan, Maartje Scheltens, Rosina Di Marzo and Caro Drake at Cambridge University Press, and to the Press's anonymous readers, for their encouragement and advice. As always, I'd like to thank my wife, children and friends, who made sure I continued to live many things besides Virginia Woolf; if I have not always achieved that 'wholeness' that Woolf herself complained is generally sacrificed to specialised study, the dedication of this book to my younger son signals fulfilling periods spent away from its pages.

List of editions and abbreviations used in the text

Place of publication here and in the notes is London unless otherwise stated.

BA	*Between the Acts*, ed. Stella McNichol, introd. Gillian Beer (Penguin, 1992)
CDB	*The Captain's Death Bed: and Other Essays* (Hogarth, 1950)
CSF	*The Complete Shorter Fiction*, ed. Susan Dick, rev. edn (Hogarth, 1989)
D	*The Diary of Virginia Woolf*, ed. Anne Olivier Bell, 5 vols. (Penguin, 1979–85)
DM	*The Death of the Moth: and Other Essays* (Hogarth, 1942)
E	*The Essays of Virginia Woolf*, ed. Andrew McNeillie, 6 vols. (Hogarth, 1986–)
F	*Flush: a Biography*, introd. Margaret Forster (Hogarth, 1991)
JR	*Jacob's Room*, ed. and introd. Sue Roe (Penguin, 1992)
L	*The Letters of Virginia Woolf*, ed. Nigel Nicolson and Joanne Trautmann, 6 vols. (Hogarth, 1975–80)
LS	*The London Scene: Five Essays* (Hogarth, 1982)
M	*The Moment: and Other Essays* (Hogarth, 1947)
MD	*Mrs Dalloway*, ed. Stella McNichol, introd. Elaine Showalter (Penguin, 1992)
MOB	*Moments of Being*, ed. and introd. Jeanne Schulkind, 2nd edn (Hogarth, 1985)
ND	*Night and Day*, ed. and introd. Julia Briggs (Penguin, 1992)
O	*Orlando*, ed. Brenda Lyons, introd. Sandra M. Gilbert (Penguin, 1993)

P	*The Pargiters: the Novel-Essay Portion of 'The Years'*, ed. and introd. Mitchell A. Leaska (Hogarth, 1978)
PA	*A Passionate Apprentice: the Early Journals 1897–1909*, ed. Mitchell A. Leaska (Hogarth, 1990)
RF	*Roger Fry: a Biography* (Hogarth, 1940)
RO, TG	*A Room of One's Own [and] Three Guineas*, ed. and introd. Michèle Barrett (Penguin, 1993)
TL	*To the Lighthouse*, ed. Stella McNichol, introd. Hermione Lee (Penguin, 1992)
TY	*The Years*, ed. and introd. Jeri Johnson (Penguin, 1998)
VO	*The Voyage Out*, ed. and introd. Jane Wheare (Penguin, 1992)
W	*The Waves*, ed. and introd. Kate Flint (Penguin, 1992)
W & W	*Women and Writing*, introd. Michèle Barrett (The Women's Press, 1979)

INTRODUCTION

Post-Victorian Woolf

On 22 September 1925 Woolf noted in her diary that she had been approached by her cousin Herbert Fisher to write a book 'for the Home University Series on Post Victorian' (*D* III. 42). Though she turned the offer down for reasons we shall return to – 'To think of being battened down in the hold of those University dons fairly makes my blood run cold' (*D* III. 43) – it is worth speculating on why she was thus approached, and on what she (or Fisher) would have understood by the term 'Post Victorian' (or 'Post-Victorian' as it is used in this present book) in 1925. Did Fisher see Woolf as a writer in the vanguard of a modern movement that had definitively moved on from the Victorian, the stress thereby falling on the sense of 'Post' to mean 'after'? Or did he (which is rather more unlikely) have a sense of Woolf's position as I investigate it in the following pages, that is, as a writer whose modern and innovatory practice coexists with a powerful nostalgia for various elements of Victorian culture and the desire to proclaim these in her work? In this sense, 'Post' has more of the value it carries in expressions like Post-Impressionism or post-modernism, a complex relationship of difference and debt that is the subject of this study.[1]

There are several occurrences of the term 'Post-Victorian' that predate the OED's first citing of it (in 1938), and already in 1918 Herbert Asquith is projecting a 'post-Victorian' era that will be unable to rival the achievements of the Victorian age.[2] This sense of rivalry between a period and its successor characterises *The Post Victorians*, an anonymous compilation of short biographies published in 1933 with an introduction by W. R. Inge, the Dean of St Paul's, who stoutly defends his right, as one born between 1850 and

1870, to be seen as a Victorian proper and thus as belonging to a 'finer' age than that of the present.[3] Several of the contributors to the volume, however, take the opposite view, crying up those whose careers, spanning the later nineteenth and earlier twentieth centuries, declare their rejection of Victorian 'rigidity' and intolerance.[4] Although in this oppositional sense 'Post-Victorian' is used synonymously in the volume with Edwardian, or Georgian, the occurrence of the term itself, in its differential self-definition, suggests the importance of the period being rejected, while the volume as a whole shows the consistent use of such period labels in a spirit of partisanship.

Woolf's Post-Victorianism is, as remarked, a much more complicated affair, comprising affiliation with and dissent from her Victorian past, which reciprocally and necessarily signifies affiliation with and dissent from her modern present. T. S. Eliot argued in his *Horizon* obituary notice that Woolf could be seen as maintaining 'the dignified and admirable tradition of Victorian upper middle-class culture' in her relationship with her readers, where 'the producer and the consumer of art were on an equal footing', a claim we return to in considering Woolf's aloofness from the increasing professionalisation and specialisation that she saw overtaking modern letters, and her alarm at modern forms of publicity.[5] Eliot's statement indicates how much Woolf clung to models of writing and reading she was brought up with, and how far a Woolfian piety towards these modified her embrace of modernism's proclamation of the 'new'. When in his enthusiasm for Joyce's *Ulysses* Eliot told her that it 'destroyed the whole of the 19th Century', Woolf resisted such a claim (*D* II. 203), and her frequently expressed admiration for the 'giants' of Victorian writing indicates how little, unlike some of her contemporaries, she was dismissive of the English nineteenth century. Elizabeth French Boyd has suggested that 'Bloomsbury' more generally 'was rebelling against the Victorian world, but it was also rooted in it and unable to escape wholly being the transmitters of its traditions and its legacies'.[6] The apologetic note here ('unable to escape wholly') is now somewhat obsolete as an increasing number of critics has recognised how deep and prolonged Woolf's attachment to aspects of the 'Victorian world' was, though it remains under-acknowledged how far this distinguishes her even from other members of Bloomsbury itself, such as her husband, Leonard, whose outlook was informed by a much more forthright 'battle', in his own words, against 'what for short one may call Victorianism'.[7] We shall see more than once in this study how Woolf's own supposedly fundamental anti-Victorianism is sustained as a position by critics refusing to recognise key differences between her and 'Bloomsbury', and indeed how adopting the latter as an umbrella category often means in effect ceasing to talk about Woolf altogether as she becomes subsumed within the coterie term.

'With hindsight', as Jane Wheare has remarked, 'we can see that [Woolf] has as much in common with her Victorian predecessors as with modernist writers.'[8] Hermione Lee's biography of Woolf returns frequently to a similar assessment:

Virginia Woolf was 'modern'. But she was also a late Victorian. The Victorian family past filled her fiction, shaped her political analyses of society and underlay the behaviour of her social group. And it was a powerful ingredient, of course, in her definition of her self.[9]

Lee indeed uses the term 'Post-Victorian' a few times in her biography to summarise Woolf's complex relation to her familial past, unlike other critics who on occasion use the term merely in the rather inert sense, noted above, of 'no longer Victorian'. If this present book attempts to reclaim the Woolfian retrospect in more positive terms than is often accorded it, resisting thereby what has been called the 'Great Victorian Myth', or belief that Victorian domestic life was exclusively one of 'thwarted motherhood, tyrannical husbands and fathers, and spiritual frustration in dark, rambling houses', I have no desire to run to the opposite extreme and convert Woolf into a simple neo-Victorian, so to speak.[10] Thus the reactionary figure found in the pages of Quentin Bell's biography – 'She belonged, inescapably, to the Victorian world of Empire, Class and Privilege' is not only a simplification in itself,[11] but has encouraged the extreme reaction, of which Jane Marcus has been the principal spokesperson, of producing an entirely progressive, democratic and even 'socialist' Woolf that turns this very formulation of Bell's precisely on its head.[12] Marcus's insistence on Woolf's 'passionate hatred for the Victorian patriarchal family' and on her 'utopian vision of social equality for women and working-class men' suggests antithetical positions in Woolf's work between a past to be fled and a future to be embraced, whereas the obsessive Woolfian retrospect, even when it considers the patriarchal family, is much more uncertain than this (the term 'utopian', as I shall argue, is also practically the last that should be applied to her).[13] And although we can hope that such extreme readings of Woolf now belong to an outmoded polemic, there are plenty of current responses to her still upholding, if more indirectly, an essentially conservative or radical Woolf which precisely obscures what I represent as her Post-Victorian position.[14]

This position is more than a Victorianism that 'combines fascination with critique', in Victoria Rosner's words, if that fascination is merely seen as something Woolf was in helpless throes to, and would repudiate if she could.[15] It can also be misrepresented as part of a traditionalism that, in Jane de Gay's welcome and persuasive emphasis on a 'less sweepingly radical' and more retrospectively orientated Woolf, committed her to the 'prizing of past literature over contemporary writing' or the simple 'denigration of writings by her contemporaries'.[16] If the former comment ignores Woolf's constructive and purposeful retrieval of the past, which I consider in the following pages, the latter tells only half the story of how contemporary writing, while indeed disturbing and upsetting Woolf, also excited and enthralled her. If Woolf at times looked back at the Victorian era with 'passionate hatred' in Marcus's phrase, we also frequently find an attitude of admiration, which indicates not a desire to 'return' to the past, but the recognition of an inheritance that can be serviceable to modernity in various ways. This is perhaps nowhere better summarised than in Woolf's 1928 obituary on Lady Strachey, who, mother, wife and member of the upper middle class, was also 'the type of the Victorian woman at her finest – many-sided, vigorous, adventurous, advanced':

Last summer, though too weak to walk any more, she sat on her balcony and showered down upon the faces that she could not see a vast maternal benediction. It was as if the Victorian age in its ripeness, its width, with all its memories and achievements behind it were bestowing its blessing. And we should be blind indeed if we did not wave back to her a salute full of homage and affection. (*E* IV. 573, 576)

It is the blindness of a self-regarding, self-sufficient modernity that Woolf accosts here, plus the refusal to pay homage to the Victorian at its 'finest' — significantly embodied in a 'maternal' figure in a gendered recognition we shall return to. But such blindness continues in much writing on Woolf herself with regard to her Post-Victorian positioning, confirmed as it seems by much better known and notorious (for my purposes) statements like 'on or about December 1910 human character changed' (*E* III. 421), a declaration that it is frequently argued puts Woolf at the forefront of the modernist 'call for rupture'.[17] Taken in isolation even from positions in the same essay ('Mrs Brown is eternal, Mrs Brown is human nature, Mrs Brown changes only on the surface', p. 430), such a proclamation (often linked to the occurrence of the first Post-Impressionist exhibition in the same year) announces, it would seem, Woolf's unreserved embrace of the new. Thus we find it blazoned at the head of the opening paragraph of Pedersen's and Mandler's *After the Victorians* as the starting-point for the modern disowning of the recent past which their volume seeks to challenge.[18]

Indeed, it is difficult to find any of the recent spate of re-evaluations of the Victorian period, occasioned by our arrival at the new century and the centenary of the Queen's death in 1901, that does not take Woolf (generally hanging onto the coat-tails of Lytton Strachey) as bête noire in the attempt, as Matthew Sweet puts it, to 'liberate the Victorians' from modern prejudices.[19] Scholarship that holds no such pro-Victorian brief has likewise been unable to resist the lure of Woolf's 'December 1910' as definitive watershed, from the cultural history of Peter Stansky to specialised Woolfian studies like that by Ann Banfield, concerned, respectively, to ignore the pervasive Woolfian insistence on historical continuity or wishing to define what *is* modern in Woolf through merging her work unreservedly with Roger Fry's Post-Impressionism.[20] While Banfield explores in meticulous detail the antecedents of Fry's aesthetics and Woolf's response to Fry in a tradition of (Cambridge) philosophical realism that encompasses Woolf's own father, she argues that this intellectual affiliation yet involves a radical break with the past in the social sphere. Thus in the space of two pages (pp. 14–15) she brings together what have become practically the three clichés of Woolfian criticism in its positing her identification with modernity: the December 1910 comment, the words on the 'Georgian cook' from the same essay ('a creature of sunshine and fresh air' compared with the Victorian cook who 'lived like a leviathan in the lower depths', *E* III. 422) and the 'revelation' of the light and air of 46 Gordon Square after the 'rich red gloom' of 22 Hyde Park Gate, described in Woolf's 'Old Bloomsbury' memoir (*MOB*, p. 184). Although Banfield doesn't go quite as far as claiming the second of these instances as key evidence for Woolf's democratic or Labourite affiliation, as some critics have done, she uses such statements as foundational support for a general Woolfian positioning where 'sunshine and fresh air are also a new ethos, one which substitutes free exchange for the "prison" – "the cage" – of the old social relations' (p. 15).

While no-one would deny the importance of these 'moments' in Woolf and what they might signify, the cost of uprooting them from the matrix of Woolf's pervasive preoccupation with the relationship between Victorian and modern culture and its sense of loss and gain, of desire and rejection, is that such well-worn 'landmarks' offer false certainties, aid misrecognition and obscure the ambivalence, including that about social class issues, that is precisely the keynote of Woolf's writing. My study brings alongside such 'landmarks' many other comments by Woolf that have been under-represented in the criticism and even at times, one is tempted to say, suppressed, instanced by that on Lady Strachey above, which we rarely find quoted. This comment is also of importance in showing how willing Woolf always was to use the term 'Victorian' as a designation with no misgivings that such labels might be reductive in encompassing broad and very varied historical periods; she is here happy moreover to personify the period in one individual. In short, Woolf needed the idea of the Victorian, and with it that of the modern, to structure her sense of history, even though at the same time a scepticism about the use of such periodisation runs counter to this through her work, a complication that intensifies the 'Post-Victorian' as an increasing site of conflict for her. The debate over periodisation is investigated towards the end of this book, but before this we consider in a series of chapters her repeated worries that the qualities embodied in Lady Strachey and other Victorians of adventure, energy, non-specialisation (or 'width') and 'ripeness' are lacking in a cautious, narrow and in many ways debilitated modernity which in its iconoclasm, scepticism, self-importance and desire for immediate gratifications threatens to throw over the claims of the past. At the same time, there are many ways in which 'we' moderns (as she states in discussing Hemingway) 'steal a march upon the Victorians', as in our lack of prudery (E IV. 451). This book explores these ambiguities in Woolf's Post-Victorian stance primarily through a reading of her fiction, but it also attends to her essays, letters and diaries, considering overt statements about past–present relations alongside a detailed examination of textual structure, imagery and diction. I should make plain that this is not a study of the Victorian literary influence on Woolf, along the lines of Perry Meisel's work on Woolf and Pater or Alison Booth's on Woolf and George Eliot;[21] rather I offer an analysis of the comparison and evaluation of the Victorian and the modern that Woolf constantly undertakes in her work, as she considers the place of sentiment, romance and individualism in the modern world, together with questions relating to science, politics, social duties, gender, fashion, sexual relations and the practice of reading. It may come as a surprise how often Woolf's commentary on the 'contemporary', for all its frequent exhilaration and sense of emancipation, is accompanied by anxiety, insecurity and a sense of regret that feeds off the nostalgia informing her Victorian retrospect.

As a foretaste of the discussion, one might take what is her earliest explicit assessment of the Victorian–modern distinction in a 1916 review of a study of Samuel Butler, where Butler himself is seen as promoting the situation whereby 'today we are less ambitious, less apt to be solemn and sentimental, and display without shame a keener appetite for happiness' compared with the Victorians (E II. 37). If this sounds like the note of modern emancipation, Woolf's writing as it later situates itself in the post-War world offers a series of contradictions to this statement with regard to the issue of sentimentality in particular.[22] Her constant worries about the 'sentimentality' of her own writing – 'I dont feel sure what the stock criticism [of *To the Lighthouse*] will be. Sentimental? Victorian?' (*D* III. 107) – are partly occasioned by the recognition of how vulnerable her retrospective susceptibilities might make her to such a charge, especially when these come up against characteristic modern efficiencies in fields ranging from love-making (as with the behaviour of Alan and Phoebe in chapter 6 of *A Room of One's Own*) to literary criticism. Thus in reviewing *Scrutinies*, 'a collection of critical essays by various writers' in 1931, she asks herself in 'turning over the honest ... and unsentimental pages', 'where is love? ... where is the sound of the sea and the red of the rose; where is music, imagery, and a voice speaking from the heart?' (*CDB*, pp. 114, 117). Her reference to Wyndham Lewis's charge of sentimentality against her (*D* IV. 308) indicates, as Leslie Hankins has suggested, how deeply affected Woolf was by the masculinist 'interdiction against sentimentality' in modern culture, and how she thereby 'found herself in a vulnerable position in the emotional minefield of modernist aesthetics'.[23] Often in celebrating such things as love, roses and 'a voice speaking from the heart', the Woolfian retrospect specifically invokes Tennyson, and the poet of *In Memoriam* in particular, himself asserting the rights of the 'heart' to an audience busy with ideas of public and scientific progress.[24] And her keenest vision of Victorian (marital) romance in the final pages of Part I of *To the Lighthouse* also gives us the fullest evocation in her writing of 'happiness' – supposedly a modern 'appetite' – in the emotion of Mrs Ramsay, which 'nothing on earth can equal' (*TL*, p. 136).

In its sense of both the losses and gains that characterise modernity, Woolf's work frequently attempts to communicate with, retrieve and proclaim a heritage that should not override what has succeeded it but will act as a resource for the present day in the problems it faces, as well as help allay its excesses, if possible through a dovetailing, or partnership, between the best qualities of the old and the new. The search is for 'a ... helpful relationship between the generations', to adapt a phrase she used in a review of 1919 while criticising a book of heavily biased pro-Victorian memoirs, returned to below, that impeded such a relationship (*E* III. 64). My study begins with Woolf's novel of the same year, *Night and Day*, as an act of 'reclamation' in the face of the vigorous pro- and anti-Victorian debate unleashed at the end of the First World War, before it examines in two subsequent chapters the strategies of 'synchronicity' and 'integration', which represent more complex methods of reclamation in the face of a modernity that is by now pressing its (justifiable) claims far more strongly. These various modes of retrieval inform the writing of the 1920s, and climax in *To the Lighthouse*, a kind of Woolfian consummation, which then opens the way for a more critical, though by no means dismissive, understanding of the Victorian legacy in the writing of the 1930s. In this decade Woolf develops a markedly conflicted and openly ambivalent, though no less obsessive, retrospect, leading to an 'incoherence' that leaves former devices of retrieval under great strain, as discussed in my two final chapters. The sequence of Woolf's responses is traced using the key texts announced in my chapter headings, but works like *The Voyage Out*, *Jacob's Room*, *Orlando* and *Flush* also receive attention in what follows.

Throughout her life, Woolf remained deeply attentive to the era into which she had been born, for good and ill, and this study uses the term 'Post-Victorian' as a new way to approach the blend of conservatism and radicalism that informed her outlook. Her characteristic search for continuity and conciliation results in many narratives in which the present is 'backed' by the past, as she put it in *A Sketch of the Past* (*MOB*, p. 98); I also consider how Woolf responded to the two world wars as the major interruptions and threat to these ideas of continuity and historical 'backing'. A recurrent concern is to show how both Woolf's welcome and her resistance to the new era is regularly couched in images of light, as already seen in the comments on the sunshiny Georgian cook and the interior of Gordon Square quoted above. It is a fact, however, that the new climate of light is by no means wholly synonymous with enlightenment, just as the shadows left behind have a much more extensive significance than that of simple oppression. Whatever the complexity of Woolf's relation with the Victorian period, it remained a major presence to her throughout her writing career, the inseparable 'shadow' of a modernity inevitably seen in relation to it; a starting-point that can only be returned to in a trajectory for which the term 'Post-Victorian' seems the apt designation, and in this sense more appropriate for her and arguably more serviceable to us than the customary term 'modernist'.

And here there seems a clear distinction with other modernist writers to be emphasised. Thus in Eliot and Pound modernism found spokesmen who advanced the new by frequently proclaiming their disdain for the Victorians, even if it has long been accepted that such a dismissal conceals important literary debts, such as Pound's to Browning, or Eliot's to Tennyson or Arnold.[25] The 'tradition' both poets formulated found little to approve in the English nineteenth century, for Pound 'a rather blurry, messy sort of a period, a rather sentimentalistic, mannerish sort of a period', while the writing and art of other periods, notably the Middle Ages, offered 'that precision which I miss in the Victorians'.[26] Eliot too will frequently contrast the 'bright, hard precision' of earlier writing (in this case Marvell), with a Victorian 'mistiness' and 'vagueness', or complain of the 'ruminations' of Tennyson and Browning, or lambast Swinburne for the cloudy 'hallucination of meaning' his poetry provides.[27] Such literary judgements are aspects of a wider cultural disapproval: 'cheerfulness, optimism, and hopefulness ... these words stood for a great deal of what one hated in the nineteenth century'.[28] Woolf's retrospect, though just as concerned to posit a 'tradition' and a sense of literary continuity within which modern writing takes its place, shows marked differences, to begin with in the extent of its geographical and historical range. If *The Common Reader* volume of 1925 embodies such a tradition, it does not go back as far as 'the rock drawing of the Magdalenian draughtsmen' or attempt to encompass 'the mind of Europe' in the (over-reaching) way that characterises Eliot's practice or Pound's.[29] In particular it shows no desire to celebrate the Dantean Middle Ages, as so many of her contemporaries did, and what Pound enthused over as the 'medieval clean line' — which informed the 'precision' of Imagism and other instances of his and Eliot's theory and practice — smacked to Woolf of that ruthless modern masculinism that was inimical to lyricism and romance: indeed the celebration of 'bright, hard precision' and attack on 'mistiness' is repeatedly undermined in her writing.[30] The key tradition Woolf excavates is not that of the European 'centre' to which English writing must be related, but that which lies effaced within the latter tradition itself, the records of the 'lives of the obscure' and, of course, the ancestry of women's writing in particular.

Victorian novelists had a key place in that ancestry, but beyond considerations of gender Woolf's investment in the nineteenth century would always be conspicuous compared with that of many of her contemporaries. Eliot's perception of 'the dignified and admirable tradition of Victorian upper middle-class culture' she perpetuated posited her as 'the centre, not merely of an esoteric group, but of the literary life of London', labelling this 'a kind of hereditary position in English letters' (pp. 315–16). The complex social and cultural network that descended to Woolf from the Stephen family line and from that of Leslie Stephen's two wives veritably embedded Woolf in the Victorian past, knitted the literary and the familial together in an imposing 'pedigree' she was keenly conscious of, and enabled her, through the 'social side' she 'inherited' from her mother (*D* II. 250), to make full use of it. Lines of communication with figures like James, Meredith and Hardy ran back through her father, and with Thackeray through his first wife; other lines ran back through Stephen's second wife to Julia Margaret Cameron, Watts, Tennyson and all the Freshwater circle. These communications, as we see from documents like Stephen's *Mausoleum Book*, were enforced by close relationships between the various lines, as in the 'ardent friendship' Cameron enjoyed with Anne Thackeray Ritchie.[31] Not only were Woolf's Victorian forebears numerous and eminent, but they all knew each other in a consolidated network that effected Woolf's 'hereditary position', and that she would spend the lengthy Post-Victorian portion of her life continually remaking.

CHAPTER I

Reclamation: Night and Day

Before one can become a Post-Victorian one has to establish what the 'Victorian' itself represents, and it is not until 1916 that Woolf's writings start to do this to any degree. In July of that year she reviewed a study of Samuel Butler, referred to in my introduction, that had advanced propositions about the Victorian age – one of 'false values and misplaced enthusiasms', with more in a similarly critical vein – that encouraged Woolf in her own generalisations: 'The Victorian age, to hazard another generalisation, was the age of the professional man' (*E* II. 35).[1] By 1916 this age had receded sufficiently to acquire definition and difference from the present: 'the eminent men appear ... already strangely formal and remote from us in their likes and dislikes' (p. 36); 'today we are less ambitious, less apt to be solemn and sentimental, and display without shame a keener appetite for happiness', differences which 'we owe ... very largely to Butler's example' (p. 37). Woolf's sense of having definitively moved on from the Victorians is repeated in a review appearing a month after the Butler piece, where the novel *The Park Wall* (1916), by the 'landmark' writer Elinor Mordaunt, is considered alongside 'old novels of great reputation' to show 'how far we have travelled and in what respects we differ' (*E* II. 42). Thus an angry family scene in a Bloomsbury hotel shows Mordaunt 'attempting something that the Victorians never thought of, feeling and finding expression for an emotion that escaped them entirely' (p. 44). This raises a distinction Woolf will make throughout her work between a modern openness in dealing with the emotions and Victorian 'suppression', the fact that her parents' generation 'would sit talking till 2 am – but what about? So many things could never be said, & the remaining ones coloured by the abstinence' (*D* II. 89 – though the note of Victorian 'energy' is here also apparent). At the same time, the all-seeing, all-speaking candour of modern writing caused Woolf some discomfort, and the discretion of the Victorians is by no means always to be despised, as we shall see. The scene Woolf refers to in Mordaunt's novel concerns a woman who has deserted her husband, who is filing for divorce, and the anger of her 'respectable' family, who are trying to make her go back to him ('If Ralph wishes to divorce me, he can; I want to be free. That's all I want – to be free!'), but it is significant that nowhere in her fiction will Woolf use the new freedoms to espouse a similar sensationalism.[2] Marriage, for good or bad, remains her primary theme in contrast to adultery or divorce.

From 1916 onwards in Woolf's writing remarks about and judgements on the Victorians appear frequently, and her own novels become immersed in a Victorian–modern debate, whereas before 1916 the term 'Victorian' is used very sparingly, and usually with a qualifier – 'early Victorian' in 1905 and 1910, 'mid-Victorian' in the latter year (*E* I. 19, 334, 341). Though Woolf's early essays frequently discuss and centre on Victorian writers, these are not categorised by means of the period term; see for example the 1907 review of the diary of William Allingham (1824–89), which is peppered with the customary names, Tennyson, Carlyle, Dickens, George Eliot, or the 1908 article that considers the 'great age' of *The Times* under the editorship from 1841 of John Delane (*E* I. 154–6, 188–94). Whereas Woolf's two essays from 1919 and 1924 on Anne Ritchie see her specifically in relation to a period context – 'She will be the unacknowledged source of much that remains in men's minds about the Victorian age' (*E* III. 18), and was 'always escaping from the Victorian gloom and dancing to the strains of her own enchanted organ' (*E* III. 399) – the 1908 piece on the same writer has no such emphasis and indeed stresses rather Ritchie's interest in eighteenth- and earlier nineteenth-century writing (*E* I. 228–9).

The major stimulus in Woolf's consideration of the Victorian as a cultural and historical entity (and in its 'eminent' figures) in the years during and after the First World War was the writing by Lytton Strachey that came to be published as *Eminent Victorians* in 1918.

Woolf had read Strachey's unpublished lives of Cardinal Manning and Florence Nightingale in 1915–16 (*L* II. 58, 91), and her reactions anticipate the 'astonishing interest' the book caused on its publication, 'even though a European war was raging' (*DM*, pp. 121–2). 'Taking stock of the Victorians is undoubtedly the literary game of the moment', the *Athenaeum* noted as the consequence of Strachey's book, and Woolf reviewed several items published at the end of the War that took stock accordingly.[3] Crucially, her own second novel, *Night and Day* (1919), is deeply concerned with the Victorian retrospect, and it is no surprise that such retrospective evaluation is widespread at the end of the War, as if the Victorian ceased definitively with this event rather than with the Queen's death in 1901. Katherine Mansfield's dismissive review of *Night and Day* – 'We had thought that this world was vanished for ever, that it was impossible to find on the great ocean of literature a ship that was unaware of what has been happening ... we had never thought to look upon its like again!' – ignores how far Woolf was well aware of what had 'been happening', if not obviously with regard to the War itself, in terms of the Victorian debate, an awareness which makes *Night and Day* very much of its historical moment.[4] In this, it differs significantly from Woolf's first novel, *The Voyage Out* (1915), which like the rest of Woolf's early work is of interest here in showing how little at this stage 'the Victorian', and with it the Victorian–modern comparison, had yet to become explicit in Woolf's thinking. Many of the works treating this comparison predictably found it difficult to resist adverse comparisons between the old and the new, either discussing Victorian idealism and morality from a critical or sceptical viewpoint, as with Strachey, or upholding a traditionalism that can only watch resignedly as the modern world goes to ruin. The latter stance, adopted by the eighty-eight-year-old Frederic Harrison in his *Obiter Scripta*, another book of retrospect Woolf reviewed in 1919, is criticised by her for its conviction of the 'truth' of the mid-Victorian world-view and consequent 'matter of course ... ironies about Cubism and morality and the manners of young women in omnibuses'. 'A less helpful relationship between the generations it would be difficult to conceive', Woolf notes (*E* III. 64).[5]

Reclamation: Night and Day

The search for this 'helpful relationship' informs *Night and Day*, a work that had been meditated since near the beginning of the War, was under way by mid-1916, and was finished shortly after Armistice Day in November 1918. The intimate personal and literary relationship Woolf enjoyed with Strachey during this period is fraught with a sense of rivalry and some jealousy over the extraordinary success of *Eminent Victorians* (*D* I. 238; II. 110), and *Night and Day* can be seen as a riposte to it. There has been a tendency to see the two writers as sharing the same iconoclastic outlook, what Phyllis Rose has called Woolf's 'Stracheyan hatred of Victorianism', a tendency illustrated as early as an *Athenaeum* review of November 1919 where the destruction and shrinkage of the 'great figure' to 'entirely average proportions' is claimed as their common endeavour.[6] Woolf can certainly turn her hand to the Stracheyesque, as 'The Soul of an Archbishop', published in the same magazine the previous May, shows, with its mockery of the contradictions between the spiritual and the worldly shown in the career of William Thomson, Archbishop of York, who died in 1890 (*E* IV. 204–8). Indeed, Woolf's 'Memoirs of a Novelist', written in 1909 but not published till 1985, pre-Stracheys Strachey in its unveiling of its subject, Miss Willatt, as a 'restless and discontented woman, who sought her own happiness rather than other people's' behind the sanctified portrait of the official biography (*CSF*, p. 75). But Woolf and Strachey had had in fact a long history of differing about the Victorians, indicated as early as 1912, where in an exchange of letters Strachey refers to his hatred of them as 'a set of mouthing bungling hypocrites', eliciting Woolf's reply 'I don't suppose I altogether agree'.[7] When Woolf in the same letter defended the previous century with the remark that 'It's a good deal hotter in the head than the 18th', Strachey answered in clarification, 'It's the Victorians I hate – not the nineteenth Century' (*Letters*, pp. 45, 48). While Strachey seems rather keen to promote a modern–Victorian antagonism in Woolf herself, praising *The Voyage Out* on the grounds of its '18th century' and modern values of 'absence of folly' and 'amusement', and summing this up in the statement 'it's very, very unvictorian!', and even dedicating his *Queen Victoria* (1921) to her on the grounds that 'you're more unlike

Old Vic than anyone else in the world' (*Letters*, pp. 56, 89), this ironically ignores how important it was for her to keep the lines of communication between the two periods open, in that search for generational continuities emphasised in *Night and Day*.[8]

However much *Eminent Victorians* was a stimulus to the novel's completion, *Night and Day* owes a good deal more to a work memorialising the Victorians that could hardly be less Stracheyesque, Henry James's book of reminiscences, *The Middle Years*, which Woolf reviewed in October 1917 under the title 'The Old Order'. Strachey's clinical manner of inspection, in which the historian will 'row out' over the vast ocean of documentary material the Victorians have left behind and 'lower down into it ... a little bucket, which will bring up to the light of day some characteristic specimen, from those far depths, to be examined with a careful curiosity', contrasts with James's rapturous tribute to the 'old order' which Woolf greets with an equal rapture in the longest review she wrote in the period 1912–18.[9] The London of the 1870s is lovingly preserved in the Jamesian 'atmosphere', she argues, which differs entirely from Strachey's exposing 'light of day' (or 'searchlight', to use another metaphor from the Preface to *Eminent Victorians*, p. 3); it is indeed 'the half light in which [James] sees most, and sees farthest':

The mellow light which swims over the past, the beauty which suffuses even the commonest little figures of that time, the shadow in which the detail of so many things can be discerned which the glare of day flattens out, the depth, the richness, the calm, the humour of the whole pageant ... (*E* II. 168)[10]

'The old world of London life which [James] brings out of the shades' (that is, both resurrects and tenderly illuminates) 'provides a picture that many of us will be able to see again as we saw it once perhaps from the perch of an obliging pair of shoulders' (*E* II. 168–9). It is a world whose inhabitants are characterised by an 'unquenchable optimism', 'energy', 'personal exuberance' and 'personal beauty' – 'if they had merely to stand and be looked at, how splendidly they did it!' Society ladies like Mrs Greville and Lady Waterford, writers like Tennyson and George Eliot, all pursue in James's pages 'the beautiful, the noble, the poetic ... lend[ing] their lives in retrospect a glamour of adventure, aspiration, and triumph such as seems for good or for evil banished from our conscious and much more critical day' (*E* II. 171–2). Here the comparison between 'our day' and the Victorian is phrased in terms that will recur frequently in Woolf, and indeed such comparison features centrally in the review, as in the further observations that intellectual society was more coherent and 'representative ... than anything of the sort we can show now', and that 'Undoubtedly the resources of the day – and how magnificent they were! – were better organised' (*E* II. 170). James's 'act of piety' towards the past, 'a superb act of thanksgiving' (*E* II. 173), clearly strikes a resonant chord in Woolf, and his memoirs 'afford us the greatest delight that literature has had to offer for many a year'. Woolf continues significantly, 'The mere sight is enough to make anyone who has ever held a pen in his hand consider his art afresh in the light of this extraordinary example of it' (*E* II. 168).

The pen in Woolf's hand at this time was mainly engaged with *Night and Day*; indeed, a month after the James review we have the first reference in her diary to it – 'I want to get on with my novel' (*D* I. 76), and we are justified in responding to what is practically Woolf's invitation to consider her novel 'in the light' of the James volume. Or rather, in the light of what Woolf says of it, since after reading *The Middle Years* it is difficult to account for the extent of Woolf's enthusiasm without accepting that a good deal of it is made up by the 'glamour' of her own retrospect rather than by James's.[11] Woolf's respect for a vanished energy and commitment is anticipated in a diary entry of 1915, where she is pondering *The Third Generation* (the work which was to develop into *Night and Day*):[12]

> read[ing] about 1860 – the Kembles – Tennyson & so on; to get the spirit of that time ... They were immensely scientific – always digging up extinct monsters, & looking at the stars, & trying to find a Religion. At this moment, I feel as if the human race had no character at all – sought for nothing, believed in nothing, & fought only from a dreary sense of duty. (*D* I. 19)

Woolf's salute to Victorian initiative, and the individualism that characterises it, recurs in essays on, for example, her 'indefatigable' great-aunt Julia Margaret Cameron and the Freshwater circle of the 1860s (*E* IV. 280–1, IV. 375–86), a circle preserved above all for Woolf in the memoirs of her aunt Lady Ritchie, but of a sufficiently legendary status to figure in many other memoirs known to Woolf by, for example, Ethel Smyth, Jane Harrison and Laura Troubridge. Woolf reviewed the latter's *Memories and Reflections* in 1925 under the title 'Pattledom', which effectively compresses the interest of Troubridge's life into its earliest experiences (and first three chapters) alone, in focussing on the 'energy' and 'vitality' of Cameron and her sisters and circle – in Troubridge's words on 'their superabundant energy, their untempered enthusiasms, their strangle-hold on life, their passionate loves and hates'.[13] The remaining ten chapters of the memoir are but a pale aftermath for Woolf (*E* IV. 281). In a letter of 1919, discussing George Eliot, she suggests 'Whatever one may say about the Victorians, there's no doubt they had twice our – not exactly brains – perhaps hearts. I don't know quite what it is; but I'm a good deal impressed' (*L* II. 391). This contrast was, doubtless, something of a commonplace, echoed by an *Athenaeum* reviewer in 1920 for whom 'the Victorians often displayed an energy and courage ... which extorts the respect of a comparatively debilitated generation'.[14] In Woolf the 'heart' – representing courage, passion, sentiment, romance – becomes iconic of the Victorian in contrast to a modern rationalism and scepticism, thus contributing to an antithesis that Woolf will frequently pursue in her writing. The idea that the Victorians had 'twice' our hearts is an instance supporting Gillian Beer's remark that 'Woolf's writing ... everywhere suggests that hyperbole was the principal stylistic and psychological mode of Victorian experience'.[15]

It is the qualities of vitality and passion that Woolf perhaps intends in her remark to Strachey about the nineteenth century being 'hot[] in the head'; in Mrs Hilbery's words on her father's generation in *Night and Day*, 'It's the vitality of them! ... That's what we haven't got! ... my father wasn't in bed three nights out of the seven, but always fresh as paint in the morning' (*ND*, p. 96). Of course, the hyperbolic can provoke both respect and ridicule, and Freshwater and its affairs also elicited a comic response from Woolf, as in her play on the subject that the Bloomsbury circle acted in 1935.[16] *Night and Day* also takes a more complicated approach than simply duplicating the enthusiastic retrospect that informs Woolf's James review. Undiluted enthusiasm in the novel, proceeding in large measure from the mouth of Mrs Hilbery, is often treated ironically:

> she would lament the passing of the great days of the nineteenth century, when every department of letters and art was represented in England by two or three illustrious names. Where are their successors? she would ask, and the absence of any poet or painter or novelist of the true calibre at the present day was a text upon which she liked to ruminate, in a sunset mood of benignant reminiscence. (*ND*, p. 27)

If the scene from chapter 9 set in Mrs Hilbery's study, where she is struggling to write the biography of her father, strongly echoes the James review in her tribute to the vitality, individuality and beauty of her father's generation, it is to Katharine herself, who is rather less of an enthusiast, that we should look for a piety towards the past that does not itself become comically exaggerated. The struggle towards a more balanced retrospect is indeed one of the major themes in the novel, with Katharine's being constantly seduced by the past in terms that echo the appeal of the 'mellow light' and the 'depth, the richness, the calm' it exudes in the James review, as in this same scene:

> Katharine could fancy that here was a deep pool of past time, and that she and her mother were bathed in the light of sixty years ago. What could the present give, she wondered, to compare with the rich crowd of gifts bestowed by the past? (*ND*, pp. 91–2)

At times this attitude leads to a parroting of her mother's position:

> she glanced up at her grandfather [that is, his portrait], and, for the thousandth time, fell into a pleasant dreamy state in which she seemed to be the companion of those giant men, of their own lineage, at any rate, and the insignificant present moment was put to shame. (*ND*, pp. 8–9)

This position is tested at the outset of the novel in the encounter with the energetic meritocrat Ralph Denham, who is not of the Alardyce lineage:

> 'Nobody ever does do anything worth doing nowadays', she remarked ... '... as for poets or painters or novelists – there are none ...'

'No, we haven't any great men', Denham replied. 'I'm very glad that we haven't. I hate great men. The worship of greatness in the nineteenth century seems to me to explain the worthlessness of that generation'. (*ND*, p. 12)

It is clear that the novel sees the dangers in Katharine's inclination towards ancestor-worship, showing her suffering 'moments of despondency' when 'the glorious past, in which men and women grew to unexampled size, intruded too much upon the present, and dwarfed it too consistently' (*ND*, p. 29), or when she feels 'so closely attached' to these giants that 'she very nearly lost consciousness that she was a separate being, with a future of her own' (p. 92). The intrusion of the past is particularly represented by the incubus-like biography of Alardyce the two women are producing, and Katharine's claim to her own future by the relationship with Ralph Denham. But it would be far too simple a reading to believe that the novel rejects that past in Katharine's discovering her future – on the most obvious level, the resolution of marriage is extremely traditional – or that Denham, with his attack on the nineteenth century, is the voice of a modernity rescuing Katharine from the past. If Katharine is seen foundering on an antithesis,

sometimes she felt that it was necessary for her very existence that she should free herself from the past; at others, that the past had completely displaced the present, which ... proved to be of an utterly thin and inferior composition. (*ND*, p. 32),

then the basic position of the novel, indeed somewhat predictably, is neither to free nor to immure oneself, but comes in the words of Katharine's realisation that 'she must join the present on to this past' (*ND*, p. 95). This anticipates the declaration in *Orlando* a decade later that 'the most successful practitioners of the art of life' manage to ensure that 'the present is neither a violent disruption nor completely forgotten in the past' (*O*, p. 215).

This emphasis on continuity upholds a respect for the past that is frequently expressed in the novel in religious terms; thus the room holding the Alardyce relics is described as 'something like a chapel in a cathedral' (*ND*, p. 8), and Katharine remembers as a girl laying flowers on her grandfather's tomb during services in Westminster Abbey, or being 'brought down into the drawing-room to receive the blessing of some awful distinguished old man, who sat, even to her childish eye, somewhat apart ...' (*ND*, p. 28). This last memory draws on Woolf's own sense of ceremonial linkage through her parents with figures like Meredith and Henry James, meetings with whom as a child she recalled years later at the end of *A Sketch of the Past* in phrases that echo *Night and Day*, noting that 'Greatness still seems to me a positive possession; booming; eccentric; set apart; something to which I am led up dutifully by my parents', and which 'never exists now'. 'I cannot remember ever to have felt greatness since I was a child', she adds (*MOB*, p. 158). The action of being 'led up dutifully' is here described in the present tense, as if the ritual of generational piety is undying.[17] In *A Sketch* Woolf also talks of the optimum relationship between past and present, in which the latter 'runs so smoothly that it is like the sliding surface of a deep river':

Then one sees through the surface to the depths. In those moments I find one of my greatest satisfactions, not that I am thinking of the past; but that it is then that I am living most fully in the present. For the present when backed by the past is a thousand times deeper than the present when it presses so close that you can feel nothing else ... (*MOB*, p. 98)

If this is a fuller version of Katharine's desire to 'join the present on to this past' it is important that both past and present are beneficiaries in the process. It is not simply a question of dutiful retrospect, but of how the life of the past, resurrected in the memory or the memoir, can invigorate the present. Katharine's true moment of communion with her grandfather comes when she realises that, rather than 'flowers and incense and adoration', a 'gift of greater value' would be 'some share in what she suffered and achieved': 'The depth of her own pride and love were not more apparent to her than the sense that the dead asked neither flowers nor regrets, but a share in the life which they had given her, the life which they had lived'. Here the 'mysterious kinship of blood' flows in a two-way transfusion, enabling the dead to 'look with us upon our present joys and sorrows', thus reviving Katharine's grandfather more as 'her brother' and, as with Henry James, bringing figures of the past 'out of the shades' (*ND*, pp. 271–2). There is here an echo of the blood-libation ritual by which Odysseus revives the shades in Book XI of the *Odyssey*, a reference that Elena Gualtieri has also detected in Woolf's delving into the 'lives of the obscure' in the first *Common Reader* essays (E IV. 118ff.), bringing with her an 'infusion of life' represented by the reader's attention.[18] Woolf's sense of blood-kinship is a powerful force allaying the threat of either World War (*Night and Day* and *A Sketch* were written during the first and second of these respectively) to create a chasm with the past.[19] If there were those who felt that by the end of the First World War the Victorian period was now more 'remote' and incomprehensible than 'almost any other period in history', this was never the case with Woolf.[20] In *A Sketch* she notes how moments from her childhood 'can still be more real than the present moment' (*MOB*, p. 67), and it is indeed this continuing presence of the past that enables her, in works like *To the Lighthouse* and *The Years*, to produce fictional accounts of it that never need resort to the 'period' trappings that we customarily find in the 'historical' novel, Woolf's quarrel with which we shall return to.

In the competing claims of past and present and in Katharine's quest to harmonise these in *Night and Day*, there is a glamorising of the past that replicates the glamour Woolf salutes in the Jamesian retrospect. To begin with, although the 'heads of three famous Victorian writers' preside over the Hilbery dining-room (*ND*, p. 79), the pressure of the past hardly takes the form of a stifling tradition: if the presence of such heads recalls the opening scene of Forster's *A Room with a View* (which Woolf both reviewed and drew on for *The Voyage Out*) with its 'portraits of the late Queen and the late Poet Laureate', Katharine is no Lucy Honeychurch hemmed in by the pressures of middle-class respectability.[21] She is able to form her own friends and attachments, is free to roam London at any hour of the day or night largely unchaperoned, and is generally given a great deal of liberty by her parents (particularly her laissez-faire father), including the liberty to marry a man from a much poorer background. Even at the crisis point when Mr Hilbery 'no longer felt that he could ultimately entrust [Katharine] with the whole conduct of her own affairs after a superficial show of directing them' (*ND*, p. 399), his intervention is ineffectual and easily side-stepped by

Katharine. In fact, Woolf's own familial biography has been much 'improved' in passing into the novel, even if, as Woolf noted in a letter to Janet Case, this was its starting-point: 'try thinking of Katharine as Vanessa, not me; and suppose her concealing a passion for painting and forced to go into society by George [Duckworth] – that was the beginning of her; *but* as one goes on, all sorts of things happen' (*L* II. 400). It is true that Katharine needs to conceal her passion for mathematics from her father, but the absence of any bullying (far less incestuous) half-brothers in the household points up how far the novel departs from any painful autobiography, and how completely different in many respects the Hilbery house is from 22 Hyde Park Gate. The crowded household of the latter, with the masculine exactions that intensified after the deaths of Woolf's mother and half-sister, could hardly differ more from the spacious (literally and metaphorically) environment that surrounds a doted-on only child, a household under the sway of what is presented as an endearingly eccentric mother. In this sense *Night and Day* is a spectacular act of compensation, and shows how far Woolf is willing to rewrite the past in the interests of a Jamesian 'act of piety'. This also explains the puzzlement she expresses to her sister in confessing she was 'a little surprised that [*Night and Day*] gives you the horrors' (Vanessa was still in the process of reading it). Woolf continued, 'When I was writing it, I didn't think it was much like our particular Hell – but one never knows' (*L* II. 393).

The retrospective filter Woolf adopts in *Night and Day* is not, of course, totally rosy, and there are things like the social duties of the tea-table and acting as guide to the Alardyce shrine that Katharine is required to perform which lead her to express frustration at the limits to her freedom – 'I want to have a house of my own' (*ND*, p. 162). Even so, the domestic environment is presented as benign in many ways, and the novel's telling finale sees Katharine crossing the threshold not into her own marital house but back into 'the friendly place' of the parental (and grand-parental) abode (*ND*, p. 432). Nor is Katharine's life outside the home presented as a round of arduous social duties, and on only one occasion do we see her performing a philanthropic 'task' of taking flowers to a widow living in the

Cromwell Road (a task surprisingly lightly carried out, *ND*, pp. 264–7). There are indeed reminders elsewhere in the novel of women being sacrificed to patriarchal tyranny, as in the Otways' house in Lincolnshire, where Euphemia's 'prime of . . . life was being rapidly consumed by her father' in his dictating to her the memoirs of his service in India that were going to 'avenge his memory' (*ND*, p. 173). Katharine's envious thoughts on Mary Datchet, the independent modern woman, anticipate Woolf's famous argument of a decade later – 'in such a room one could work – one could have a life of one's own' (*ND*, p. 229), and show that the awareness of a new world emerging around Katharine in the person of Mary troubles her retrospective mentality. But if Mary and the work she performs are treated respectfully in the novel, their limitations are also expressed in a significant metaphor: 'a world entrusted to the guardianship of Mary Datchet . . . seemed to [Katharine] a good world, although not a romantic or beautiful place or, to put it figuratively, a place where any line of blue mist softly linked tree to tree upon the horizon' (*ND*, p. 304).[22] The comment expresses, as we shall see, several of Woolf's own reservations about a world that might be emerging.

The contrast between Mary Datchet, efficient, practical, hard-working and dedicated to 'the truth' (*ND*, p. 384), and the discourse of romance, dream and 'imagination' which largely invests Katharine, is fundamental to the way the novel conceptualises modernity on the one hand and the nineteenth century and its legacy on the other. Although Ralph notes 'Two women less like each other could scarcely be imagined' (*ND*, p. 74), the novel is eager to find ways of mediating between past and present that will avoid such an antithesis developing into an irreparable breach, in the quest for the 'helpful relationship between the generations'. In working this out, however, *Night and Day* tends not towards finding some halfway house between opposites but prioritises the claims of the imaginative or 'figurative' engagement with the world. That both Ralph and Katharine are emphatically dreamers, possessors of a 'persistent imagination' which constantly invests the other with a visionary status that has to be tested against 'the cold light of day' in their meetings (*ND*, p. 196), causes Katharine to worry that, as she confesses to her mother, 'when we think we're in love we make it up — we imagine what doesn't exist' (*ND*, p. 412). Mrs Hilbery effects the marriage between them by stilling Katharine's fears with her insistence that 'We have to have faith in our vision' (*ND*, p. 412). This vision is equated with the 'night' of the novel's title, as opposed to the 'cold light of day'; 'night' signifying not pitch blackness but a kind of sublime chiaroscuro that invests the intimacy between its protagonists, a repeated discourse of muted light and shadow that practically inundates the novel:

But he persuaded her into a broken statement, beautiful to him, charged with extreme excitement as she spoke of the dark red fire, and the smoke twined round it, making him feel that he had stepped over the threshold into the faintly lit vastness of another mind, stirring with shapes, so large, so dim, unveiling themselves only in flashes, and moving away again into the darkness, engulfed by it. (*ND*, p. 430)

Love and union are constantly described in such figures:

Quietly and steadily there rose up behind the whole aspect of life that soft edge of fire which gave its red tint to the atmosphere and crowded the scene with shadows so deep and dark that one could fancy pushing farther into their density and still farther, exploring indefinitely. (*ND*, p. 420)

It is this world of shadow, mist and 'haze' which Mary, in ceasing to be in love with Ralph, emerges from into the daytime 'truth' (*ND*, p. 384). The limitations of such 'truth', however, are made evident, as we shall see.

The Hilbery house itself, representing the familial legacy of the past, functions as an appropriate site of this lustrous 'atmosphere' ('Ralph received an impression of a room full of deep shadows, firelight, unwavering silver candle flames ...' *ND*, p. 119), and in this respect it contrasts with the lower middle-class Denham house ('blazing with unshaded lights ... reveal[ing] more ugliness than Katharine had seen in one room for a very long time', *ND*, pp. 316–17), and with the suffrage office where Mary works: 'The unshaded electric light shining upon the table covered with papers dazed Katharine for a moment ... life in this small room appeared extremely concentrated and bright' (*ND*, p. 68). Woolf will later compare that epitome of modernity, Joyce's *Ulysses*, to 'being in a bright and yet somehow strictly confined apartment' (*E* III. 34), a comment we shall return to. The final words of the novel are the climax of the symbolic scheme of lighting that *Night and Day* emphasises, where Katharine and Ralph, strolling on the Embankment in the 'enchanted region' of their love,

> turned and found themselves opposite the house. Quietly they surveyed the friendly place, burning its lamps . . . Katharine pushed the door half open and stood upon the threshold. The light lay in soft golden grains upon the deep obscurity of the hushed and sleeping household. For a moment they waited, and then loosed their hands. 'Good night', he breathed. 'Good night', she murmured back to him. (*ND*, pp. 432–3)

The scene embodies not only the idea of the welcoming house as a figure of intimacy with the other ('he had stepped over the threshold into the faintly lit vastness of another mind', above) but the commitment to a familial past that will be 'joined' with a present and a future deriving from the lovers' union. The golden light mingling with 'deep obscurity' offers its chiaroscuro blessing on such a union, and the final words, 'Good night', once more pick up the novel's title in a celebration of night over day, even if we are reminded at several points that the higher realm of dream and 'vision' has to be combined with the everyday world of society, 'the hours of work' (*ND*, p. 104) and so forth.[23]

Throughout her work Woolf instances the development of strong, usually electric, lighting as a feature of an alienating modernity that contrasts with the lights and shadows of the past, so that retrospect is frequently equated with the enticing chiaroscuro described above. We shall return a good deal to this opposition, and its relevance to Woolf's response to a range of issues including contemporary literature and painting, politics and the operations of modern publicity. The contrast has already been suggested in the review of Henry James ('The mellow light which swims over the past, the beauty which suffuses even the commonest little figures of that time, the shadow in which the detail of so many things can be discerned which the glare of day flattens out'), but the *locus classicus* occurs with the description in *Orlando* of the advent of the twentieth century:

> At a touch, a whole room was lit; hundreds of rooms were lit; and one was precisely the same as the other. One could see everything in the little square-shaped boxes; there was no privacy; none of those lingering shadows and odd corners that there used to be; none of those women in aprons carrying wobbly lamps which they put down carefully on this table and on that. At a touch, the whole room was bright. (*O*, p. 205)[24]

Although there is a reference to this advent in *Night and Day* in the 'bright' setting of the suffrage office, with its 'unshaded electric light', the novel strives, as we have argued, to seek continuity rather than historical rupture. It is significant, therefore, that the Hilbery house itself is lit by electricity, even in the innermost sanctum of the Alardyce room, but here an electricity that is not an exposing glare but is seen as contributing to 'the mellow light which swims over the past':

> As Katharine touched different spots, lights sprang here and there, and revealed a square mass of red-and-gold books, and then a long skirt in blue-and-white paint lustrous behind glass ... and, finally, a square picture above the table, to which special illumination was accorded. When Katharine had touched these last lights ... the eyes looked ... out of the mellow pinks and yellows of the paint with divine friendliness ... The paint had so faded that very little but the beautiful large eyes were left, dark in the surrounding dimness. (*ND*, p. 8)

It is thus of no significance whether the house's 'burning ... lamps' referred to above that feature at the end of the novel (*ND*, p. 432) are fuelled by oil or gas, or as is more probable by an electricity that still draws on the traditional vocabulary ('burning') of lighting.[25] This insistent figuration of light and lighting throughout the novel also applies to Mary Datchet, as in her moment of revelation about a future in socialist politics:

> She did not love Ralph any more ... her eyes rested upon the table with its lamp-lit papers. The steady radiance seemed for a second to have its counterpart within her; she shut her eyes; she opened them and looked at the lamp again; another love burnt in the place of the old one ... (*ND*, p. 381)

At the end of the novel Katharine and Ralph pay obeisance to the 'light burning' up in Mary's room, and the progressive movement it signifies.

It is significant, however, that Mary and the work she performs are honoured not in relation to 'daytime' activity within the society she works for but through the use of the romantic image of a solitary 'burning' lamp, like that of a mage in a tower. The novel may be aware of a world that is changing in the period 1910–12, when it is set, and may acknowledge the worth of change, but it proceeds to gather the modern back within traditional tropes, to retraditionalise it. This is further shown in the depiction of Ralph Denham, who enters the novel, as we have seen, in a spirit of iconoclasm that confronts Katharine's traditional views ('I hate great men') and who is initially cast by Katharine as her opponent – 'You said you liked modern things. I said I hated them' (*ND*, p. 119). But, for all his determination as a self-made meritocrat, Ralph never joins any radical political group, and though like Katharine he is sympathetic to Mary he is in effect swallowed up by the institution of the Hilberys, acceding at the end of the novel to the idea of marriage in Westminster Abbey 'near the very spot where [Mrs Hilbery's] father lay quiescent with the other poets of England' (*ND*, p. 416).[26] No less than Katharine, he allows Mrs Hilbery to preside over his destiny, seeing her 'from the distance of her age and sex ... hailing him as a ship sinking beneath the horizon might wave its flag of greeting to another setting out upon the same voyage' (*ND*, p. 362). Mrs Hilbery's description of the beauties of her youth, evoked by a portfolio of old photographs she is poring over, 'sweeping over the lawns at Melbury House ... so calm and stately and imperial ... like ships, like majestic ships ... like ships with white sails' (*ND*, p. 94), duplicates Woolf's own romance of Little Holland House (situated in what is now Melbury Road in Kensington) and the 'six lovely [Pattle] sisters' (including Woolf's maternal grandmother) who presided over it, a setting for 'the vision' of beauty embodied in her mother in *A Sketch* (*MOB*, pp. 86–7).[27] Katharine in her physical appearance perpetuates this line, as in Ralph's sighting of her at Kew:

Distance lent her figure an indescribable height, and romance seemed to surround her from the floating of a purple veil which the light air filled and curved from her shoulders.

'Here she comes, like a ship in full sail', he said to himself . . . (*ND*, p. 280)

Ralph's very susceptibility to Katharine's neo-Victorian beauty, and to what she calls his 'romantic' delusions (*ND*, p. 323), thus confirms the limits to his up-to-dateness; it is no accident that in the law firm where he works he is 'an authority upon our mediaeval institutions' (*ND*, p. 394).

The resort to the Victorian inheritance in *Night and Day* takes the form of not simply traditionalising emerging forces of the modern but by indeed presenting a surprisingly limited version of modernity. Cassandra Otway's introduction to the cultural delights of London, hearing Brahms and Beethoven, visiting the National Gallery and the Wallace Collection (*ND*, p. 309), reflects the tastes of the novel's protagonists in general – '"We have been seeing old masters in the Grafton Gallery", said Katharine' (*ND*, p. 143) – and it would be difficult to identify in *Night and Day* any of the aesthetic ferment which members of the Bloomsbury group were involved in and promoting before the War. The Grafton Gallery was of course the venue of the two Post-Impressionist exhibitions of 1910 and 1912, and writers Woolf had already identified as challenging the Victorian world-view – Samuel Butler, Bernard Shaw – seem to be on scarcely anyone's reading-list in the novel. The former is indeed mentioned, along with Ibsen, in chapter 8, a chapter written at the time when Woolf was working on the review that enthused over Butler, referred to earlier, but solely as a mentor in the life of the hapless Cyril, living out of wedlock with the mother of his children (*ND*, pp. 89, 85), a state of non-marriage ('those ugly thoughts') the novel is careful to reject for Katharine and Ralph themselves (*ND*, p. 412). Ralph, who supposedly likes 'modern things', shows no taste for the avant-garde: even Belloc and Chesterton are less to his liking than De Quincey (*ND*, p. 123).

In a telling moment from Woolf's diary, in March 1923, she records an evening spent with Strachey and others when 'We had the photographs out. Lytton said "I don't like your mother's character.

Her mouth seems complaining" & a shaft of white light fell across my dusky rich red past' (*D* II. 239).²⁸ Strachey's phallic 'exposure' of Woolf's past, ruthless, anti-romantic, an instance of the 'solar light of masculinity' in Jane Goldman's phrase,²⁹ exemplifies 'our conscious and much more critical day' and is described using images of light and dusk consistent with the scheme of *Night and Day*, and with the Preface to *Eminent Victorians* and its 'searchlight'. Opposed to this is a respect for the shades of the past, the reverse procedure that Woolf adopts in *Night and Day*. It is significant that Mrs Hilbery, who for all her eccentricity acts as the 'equally wise and equally benignant' (*ND*, p. 410) *dea ex machina* in the novel, was inspired by Woolf's aunt (through Leslie Stephen's first marriage), Anne Ritchie (*L* II. 406), Thackeray's daughter, whose reminiscences of the Victorian age invest it in a light very different from Strachey's: 'Seen through this temperament ... the gloom of that famous age dissolves in an iridescent mist which lifts entirely to display radiant prospects of glittering spring, or clings to the monstrous shoulders of its prophets in many-tinted shreds' (*E* III. 399–400). Similar phrasing is found in Woolf's 1919 obituary on her aunt: 'She will be the unacknowledged source of much that remains in men's minds about the Victorian age. She will be the transparent medium through which we behold the dead. We shall see them lit up by her tender and radiant glow' (*E* III. 18).³⁰ In *Night and Day* Woolf views the Victorians through the Henry James/Ritchie 'medium' or filter rather than that provided by Strachey, who, in bringing up to 'the light of day' figures from 'those far depths', as his Preface puts it, commits an act of depredation upon the past, a stark critical presentism which contrasts with Woolf's stance of looking *down* into the 'deep pool of past time' (*ND*, p. 91), or seeing *through* 'the surface to the depths' (*A Sketch, MOB*, p. 98); an activity that allows full scope to a creative imagination that plays among the shadows rather than seeks to put them to flight. This heralds the important issue of the value of 'obscurity' to Woolf, and the way this comes to represent an increasingly valuable aesthetic and political resource.

There is of course no looking down into the depths that can avoid seeing the past through the 'surface' of the present – 'this past is much affected by the present moment' as Woolf notes in writing *A Sketch*, (*MOB* p. 75) – and Woolf is aware in the James review of the power of 'retrospect' precisely to glamorise (*E* II. 171). In a review of Ethel Smyth's memoir *Streaks of Life* she notes how the past *qua* past has an 'enkindling effect', which implies that someone in the future looking back on 'this very year 1921' could find 'going on in our midst . . . this brave, bustling, important, romantic society' that those actually living in it are unaware of (*E* III. 299–300). But no mendacity is involved here, given that the present can never claim a full self-knowledge: 'the past is beautiful because one never realises an emotion at the time. It expands later, & thus we don't have complete emotions about the present, only about the past . . . That is why we dwell on the past, I think' (*D* III. 5). Woolf's admiration for the beauty of the past as revealed in James's memoirs does not avoid the inevitable condition of retrospect but actively embraces it; it is indeed inseparable from her admiration of the writer's power to arrange and set off that beauty to the best effect, like a curator displaying his 'dexterity', 'his consummate knowledge of how best to place each fragment' (*E* II. 168). Thus enthusiasm for James's 'treasure' is inseparably an enthusiasm for his connoisseurship and creativity. Whereas Strachey's examining the past 'with a careful curiosity', did mean that 'at last it was possible to tell the truth about the dead', as Woolf later put it in 'The Art of Biography' (*DM*, p. 121), such 'truth' is in fact a limited mode of apprehension compared with what she called the 'greater intensity and truth of fiction' (*E* IV. 395). In *Night and Day* Mary Datchet emerges from the hazy delusions of love into a world of 'truth' which makes her feel that Katharine, who 'did not know the truth . . . was immensely to be pitied' (*ND*, p. 384). But such truth is itself a half-truth, a 'daytime' disillusion associated with a modern critical scepticism that the novel makes defer to its nostalgic night vision, synonymous with the elevation of romance and the figurative imagination.

The fact that the stance towards the past in *Night and Day* makes use of the 'medium' of Lady Ritchie does not mean that Mrs Hilbery's 'sunset mood of benignant reminiscence' does not have its excesses (*ND*, p. 27), and Woolf can be satirical elsewhere about retrospective 'sunset reflections', to quote the title of a review she published in 1917 (*E* II. 198–200). For such reflections to have their full force an expert in the genre of memoir, like Henry James, is required, and Mrs Hilbery's incompetence as a writer perhaps raises questions about her critical estimations. Nevertheless, her belief in the Victorians as a race of giants, and its corollary, which Katharine inherits – 'Nobody ever does do anything worth doing nowadays' – tallies with Woolf's own stance about the vacuum of talent that characterised the Edwardian period, at the end of which *Night and Day* is set, as spelt out most clearly in her essay of 1922, 'On Re-reading Novels'. Here she discusses 'the failure of the Edwardians', and 'how the year 1860 was a year of empty cradles; how the reign of Edward the Seventh was barren of poet, novelist, or critic . . .' (*E* III. 336). The absence or scarcity of giants continues into the post-War period, as in the essay 'How It Strikes a Contemporary' (1923), where a lack of great writers – 'our age is meagre to the verge of destitution' – and the resultant absence of any 'great critic' – 'where is even the very tall man . . .?' (*E* III. 355), chime with remarks in her review of Smyth's memoirs ('the men and women of those times appear about five inches taller than those of the present day', *E* III. 299), and with the late accolade to Henry James *et al.* in *A Sketch of the Past*: 'I cannot remember ever to have felt greatness since I was a child' (*MOB*, p. 158). At the same time, the 'courage', 'sincerity' and 'widespread originality' of modern writers in their need to find new modes of expression is saluted by Woolf (*E* III. 357), and we shall explore further how Woolf negotiates the relationship between past and present in the early 1920s, by which time the claims of a modernist movement in literature have become much more pressing. Suffice it to remark here that in a series of well-known essays Woolf wrote at that time she seeks to establish relations between contemporary writers and the great Victorians across the 'barren' interval of the Edwardian years. Katharine's communing with the portrait of her grandfather discussed above emerges as a figurative anticipation of the 'solace and guidance' the Georgians can find in their literary 'grandparents', thus appeasing that 'breach between the generations' occasioned by the Edwardian failure ('On Re-reading Novels', *E* III. 336).

The retrospective fidelities and format of *Night and Day*, summed up in Katherine Mansfield's review — 'We had thought that this world was vanished for ever ...', have resulted in its being frequently dismissed by critics who note the very different type of fiction Woolf was developing in her short stories even as she was completing the novel, as if it belongs entirely to an outmoded past that Woolf herself consigned to oblivion as she moved into her modernist production. Those who wish to retain its 'true' Woolfian credentials, however, in the face of Mansfield's charge of outdatedness, argue not only for a more emphatic canvassing of the new in the novel than Mansfield (or I) would recognise, but also for Woolf's identification with its progressive elements, reading it as a critique of traditional institutions such as the family and marriage. Janis M. Paul, in her *The Victorian Heritage of Virginia Woolf*, goes so far as to call Katharine Hilbery 'a Modernist spirit trapped in a Victorian novel', which among other things seriously exaggerates Katharine's moments of restiveness when weighed against the fidelity to the ancestral previously discussed.[31] Paul argues that the Victorian 'trap' is represented in the Hilbery house itself, a 'suffocating setting', which with its 'stuffy, overcrowded rooms ... cages in the impulses for natural freedom' (p. 88). This characterisation may owe something to Woolf's description of the 'gloom' of 22 Hyde Park Gate in her memoir on 'Old Bloomsbury', but the point should be reiterated that the Cheyne Walk house is precisely not Hyde Park Gate in location, design or habitation — indeed, its situation in Chelsea might well suggest a distance from both Kensington and Bloomsbury that figures mediation, rather than confrontation, between old and new in the manner we have argued for. The house in *Night and Day* is constantly evoked through images of soft lighting, spaciousness (*ND*, p. 19) and welcoming comfort, as in the opening of the final chapter: 'The lamps were lit; their lustre reflected itself in the polished wood; good wine was passed round the dinner-table ...' (*ND*, p. 427); in the frequent use of terms like 'lustrous' and its avoidance of vulgarity the house and its furnishings might indeed be said to be positively Jamesian. To see the house as hostile to Katharine, or to set it up in antithesis to the streets of

London where she roams at leisure, works against the novel's project of conciliation between interior and exterior that is part of the broader conciliation between past and present it embodies, even if it does this, as I suggested, by minimising the impact of the 'modernist spirit'.[32]

If the war years and the end of the First World War brought the Victorian debate to a head, it is worth going back to the novel Woolf was writing before the War, *The Voyage Out*, to see how, correspondingly, it features little of such debate. There is a glimpse of it in chapter 16, where Rachel, at Hewet's prompting, considers her life in Richmond in her spinster aunts' house from the exotic distance of Santa Marina. The house, 'a little dingy – dull I should say', is described by Rachel as 'full of old furniture, not really old, Victorian', a base from which her aunts, who 'visit the poor a good deal', continue the tradition of Victorian philanthropy – 'Aunt Clara has what they call a G[irls'] F[riendly] S[ociety] meeting in the drawing-room on Wednesday' (*VO*, pp. 198–9). Rachel is led to realise her frustrations with such an existence, 'with its four meals, its punctuality, and servants on the stairs at half-past ten', a world that she wanted 'to smash to atoms'. At the same time, she repeats her assertion that 'there's a sort of beauty in it', and in answer to Hewet's question 'Were you happy?', remarks 'I was both ... I was happy and I was miserable' (*VO*, p. 202). Rachel's situation as an only child in a household of Victorian elders anticipates that of Katharine in *Night and Day*, but here any explicit discussion of the relation between the Victorian past and the present is a barely realised interlude in this one chapter, with Rachel's home life only briefly sketched in. When the novel was revised for publication in America in 1920 Woolf's only major change was to shorten chapter 16 considerably, leaving out most of Rachel's assessment of Richmond life and her reactions to it, as if Woolf indeed felt this to be an excursus; by then, however, she had devoted an entire novel to examining the relationship between a young woman and the domestic traditions of the past. It might be clear from *The Voyage Out* that this is a subject waiting to be addressed – we are told earlier in the novel that Rachel has a kind of fixation with 'the characters of her aunts, their views, and the way they lived' (*VO*, p. 28) – but *The Voyage Out* it seems is not the place to do it.

One might emphasise the fact that it was written during a period when the 'Victorian' had not fully realised itself in Woolf's thinking, just as in other early texts. Thus 'Memoirs of a Novelist' from 1909, which as noted above strikingly anticipates the approach of *Eminent Victorians*, does so without ever seeing its subject, Miss Willatt (whose dates are given as 1823–84), in an explicitly Victorian context, and never makes use of the period term. In 1908 Woolf reviewed Forster's *A Room with a View*, which Louise DeSalvo has argued was an influence on the early version of *The Voyage Out* known as *Melymbrosia* (in progress until 1912).[33] In Forster's novel, however, the Victorian context is used as a starting-point in tracing the heroine's passage from confinement to freedom, the opening page establishing this context in the dining-room of the Pensione Bertolini sporting its 'portraits of the late Queen and the late Poet Laureate that hung behind the English people' (p. 23). Lucy Honeychurch's arrival in Florence, accompanied by a chaperon of impeccable respectability, her cousin Charlotte Bartlett, occasions an encounter between old and new values represented by the dutiful first morning visit to Santa Croce, as enjoined by Ruskin in *Mornings in Florence*, into which blow the winds of change in the shape of the Emerson family (pp. 35–49).[34] Although the landscapes and climate of Woolf's trips to Greece (in 1906) and Florence (1909) obviously contributed to the setting of Santa Marina in *The Voyage Out*, Woolf clearly chose a location for her own novel which would be free of the cultural appropriations of the English, and one less well trodden by culture wars between the old and the new.[35]

The idea of voyaging to a 'new world' clearly permits nonetheless the allegorical suggestion that Phyllis Rose sees in the novel, whereby Rachel's 'pilgrimage' is 'a fictionalised presentation of Virginia Woolf's own "journey" from Hyde Park Gate to Bloomsbury' (*Woman of Letters*, p. 58), as if the period themes *Night and Day* explores might here be given a geographical expression. The new world of blue skies and bright colours the voyagers travel to is certainly suggestive of freedom and enlightenment, as in the letter Rachel's aunt Helen writes home:

> The earth, instead of being brown, was red, purple, green. 'You won't believe me', she added, 'there is no colour like it in England'. She adopted, indeed, a condescending tone towards that poor island ... She went on to deride the islanders themselves ... 'When have you ever encouraged a living artist? Or bought his best work? Why are you all so ugly and so servile? Here the servants are human beings. They talk to one as if they were equals. As far as I can tell there are no aristocrats' (*VO*, pp. 85–6)

The letter goes on to indicate Helen's progressive ideas on female education in sexual matters, and her determination to put this into effect with Rachel, as well as addressing 'her ignorance upon other matters as important' (*VO*, p. 86). The role of chaperon here could hardly contrast more markedly with that of the backward-looking Charlotte Bartlett; indeed, we might say Helen possesses a Post-Impressionist mentality, emphasised by her reference to encouraging living artists, as well as her enthusiasm for the bright colours of the landscape.[36] But as we have also seen with *Night and Day*, the 'new' can hardly be said to triumph in *The Voyage Out* given that the world left behind still exercises its potency on the main protagonists Rachel and Hewet, whose nostalgia for a John Constable-like England shows them to be less aesthetically 'advanced':

> there would be English meadows gleaming with water and set with stolid cows, and clouds dipping low and trailing across the green hills ... 'look at the stony red earth, and the bright blue sea, and the glaring white houses – how tired one gets of it! ... I'd give anything for a sea mist'. (*VO*, p. 283)

Rachel, seen as oddly vague and hesitant, with 'nothing hard, permanent, satisfactory' about her in her aunt's first impression, and whose very features show a 'lack of colour and definite outline' (*VO*, p. 13), literally embodies an aesthetic contrary to her aunt's throughout the novel. Her pleasure in 'mist' above, in autumn dusk (*VO*, p. 200), in English rain 'falling against the windows' (*VO*, p. 284), in the smoke of London (*VO*, p. 284), anticipates her outcry, 'What's so detestable in this country ... is the blue – always blue sky and blue sea. It's like a curtain – all the things one wants are on the other side of that' (*VO*, p. 285). In this reaction she is again anticipated by Hewet (*VO*, p. 227).

This debate over landscape and atmosphere, between a new world and an old expressed respectively in terms of brightness and dusk, glare and mist, is later transformed in Woolf into that between modern and Victorian as we have seen, but in *The Voyage Out* it awaits this formulation. In Woolf's Cornwall journal of 1905 we find a particular relish for the effects of dusk, mist, vapour, 'pale & luminous waters' (*PA*, p. 284) and 'the pallor of the sandhills [making] the scene yet more ghostly' (*PA*, p. 290), and the essay 'A Walk by Night' (1905), for which Woolf quarried this journal, gives free rein to evoking a scene of dissolving contours and chiaroscuro effects, a habitat where 'only the phantoms and spirits of substantial things were now abroad' (*E* I. 82). It is inevitable that such effects should be associated with the past and its spectral presences, and the misty landscape of Cornwall prompts Woolf's expectation that, in the visit of 1905, in returning to it 'we should find our past preserved, as though through all this time it had been guarded & treasured for us to come back to one day' (*PA*, p. 281). If for Woolf historical continuity is expressed through the image of a river, where 'one sees through the surface to the depths', it is also suggested by the idea of a mist that softly 'links' tree to tree in Katharine's image from *Night and Day*, or in Mrs Dalloway's sense of being spread out 'like a mist between the people she knew best' (*MD*, p. 10). Opposed to these images of the continuous are the sentiments and categorisations that would separate past from present, or events like the First World War which effect a situation where 'we are sharply cut off from our predecessors' (*E* IV. 238), and which Woolf's writing, not only in *Night and Day*, seeks to redress.

In *The Voyage Out*, Rachel, caught between the experiences and scenery of England and 'abroad', and between the upbringing of the old aunts and the tutelage of the new, looks back on her past life to note, alongside its frustrations, that 'there's a sort of beauty in it' (*VO* p. 202). Her lack of 'definite outline' embodies her resistance to categorical choices. In this respect it is worth noting Hermione Lee's contrast between Vanessa's practice in moving into Gordon Square in 1904 and her sister's: where the former 'began a policy of cutting off from the Hyde Park Gate network ... Virginia would never be so ruthless about this'.[37] Lee in fact describes the continuities in Woolf's experience after the move to Bloomsbury: how 'the life she began to lead at Gordon Square was in some ways not so different from the life she had led at Hyde Park Gate'; indeed, how 'the "new odd Bloomsbury life" bore strong resemblances to the old Kensington life'. Thus she was followed from Kensington to Bloomsbury by many of the old routines, the old furniture and pictures, the old social callers and practices. Woolf's life in the early twentieth century was thus, in Lee's words, 'shaped by overlaps and gradual shifts, as well as by startling moments of change' (*Virginia Woolf*, pp. 206–8). One of the first things Woolf did after recovering from her illness of 1904 and moving into Bloomsbury was to set to work on the note she contributed to Maitland's biography of her father (*PA*, 219), so that, as Mitchell A. Leaska puts it, 'as she helped to preserve the memory of her father, her own life became revitalised' (*PA*, 214). Her later contribution to preserving the family memory, *Reminiscences* (discussed below, pp. 165–7), is an act of communicating across the generations, not only being expressly written for the latest family addition, Julian Bell, but following in the Stephen tradition of writing family accounts for the use of children, as with her father's *Mausoleum Book* and her grandfather's *Memoirs*. The stress on linking the generations – of a generational consciousness – with regard to both the family and the literary tradition, is a permanent feature of Woolf's writing.

In the early phase of that writing, that is, until after the appearance of *The Voyage Out* in 1915, we have then little awareness of any Post-Victorian position to be taken up, given that the Victorian period itself is not yet seen as significantly 'other'. The move to Bloomsbury in 1904, often regarded as Woolf's key 'break' with the past, only takes on any suggestion of this nature in pieces by Woolf that date from well after the event itself, and not in her early letters or journals. Thus the memoir on 'Old Bloomsbury', delivered to the Memoir Club around 1922, suggests a sharp contrast between different locations by dwelling at the outset on Woolf's pre-Bloomsbury experience: '46 Gordon Square could never have meant what it did had not 22 Hyde Park Gate preceded it', so that 'The light and the air after the rich red gloom of Hyde Park Gate were a revelation' (*MOB*, pp. 182, 184). It is tempting to draw on such remarks in suggesting ideas of a wholesale anti-Victorian polemic, as the editor of 'Old Bloomsbury' does in describing 'the throwing open of windows which flooded with fresh air and light the dark, cramped, heavily upholstered upper middle class Victorian world in which many of the "Bloomsberries" had spent their youth' (*MOB*, p. 179). This paraphrase of Woolf's position is bolstered here by a typical elision between Woolf and the rest of 'Bloomsbury', and misleadingly informs some readings of *Night and Day* such as Janis Paul's. But the debate between, in Woolf's words, 'light and air' and 'rich red gloom', and which continues the use of atmosphere and of light effects as period markers, is not in any case so one-sided: if 'gloom' seems unmistakeable in its meaning (the type of thing we saw Anne Ritchie 'always escaping from'), adjectives like 'rich' and 'red' are positive terms in Woolf's Victorian lexicon, as in her comments on the 'dusky rich red past' associated with her mother, and the atmosphere of 'greatness' with which Henry James made the Hyde Park Gate drawing room seem 'rich and dusky'. It is also important to note that 'Old Bloomsbury' was delivered to a Bloomsbury audience, an audience that Woolf was always mindful of tailoring some of her comments for.[38]

The memoir was also delivered in the early 1920s, by which time the exciting, forceful and disturbing character of the modern had become clearly apparent to Woolf, and with it a keener sense of difference and rivalry between Victorian and modern, requiring new strategies of linkage, beginning with what I call in the following chapter 'synchronicity'. The conciliations of *Night and Day* tend as we have seen to swallow up an emerging modernity in the novel's clinging somewhat defensively onto the past, but the sense of the new being only half-digested is indicated by a series of questions the novel leaves conspicuously unanswered: will the Alardyce biography continue to burden Mrs Hilbery (and her daughter) and will it ever be finished? Will Katharine pursue her mathematics as a married woman? Will Katharine and Ralph actively support Mary Datchet's political movement? One of these questions, that of the Alardyce biography, signals problems with the Victorian inheritance that Woolf was certainly not blind to even while she strove to reclaim it; that is, the problem of sheer output, what she calls in *Orlando* 'the undistinguished fecundity' of the Victorian age, whether this is measured in terms of the number of books or of children it produced (*O*, p. 159). The Victorian 'great men ... wrote twice as much as they ought to have written' (*E* II. 81), while the invention of the penny post facilitated the 'enormous daily volubility' by which 'the Victorian age killed the art of letter writing' (*E* IV. 379). The heap of Alardyce documents Katharine and her mother wade through signals this burdensome aspect of Victorian gianthood, a situation traced in Edward Garnett's contemporary short story 'The Dead Reformer', where the biographer's dejection at the endless pile of papers his Victorian subject has left behind eventually leads him to abandon the biography and bury them.[39]

Strachey began *Eminent Victorians* with the statement that 'our grandfathers ... accumulated so vast a quantity of information' that 'the history of the Victorian Age will never be written: we know too much about it' (p. 3). Woolf agreed, arguing that the attempt to encompass this information in the 'stout official biography' was in any case far less revealing than the method of Anne Ritchie's memoirs, for example, which brings her contemporaries vividly before us in 'some little hint or fact or fancy dropped lightly' (*E* III. 18). What is of value in biography, Woolf later observed in 'The Art of Biography', is not the accumulation of fact en masse but what she calls 'the creative fact; the fertile fact; the fact that suggests and engenders' (*DM*, p. 126). She was indeed thankful for the Stracheyan practice that 'compressed four stout Victorians into one slim volume' and through selection and synthesis rendered biography an art rather than a mere chronicle (*E* IV. 475). As she herself turned from a novel like *Night and Day* to much slimmer fictions like the short stories and *Jacob's Room*, a turn anticipating her call in *A Room of One's Own* for 'shorter, more concentrated' books, 'framed so that they do not need long hours of steady and uninterrupted work' (*RO*, p. 71), she deliberately enters the season of modernist 'note-books' with their brilliant 'shorthand' observations taken down 'under pressure' (*E* IV. 241, 238). Although the Victorian period for Woolf and others was characterised by an 'energy' and 'indefatigability' which were to be admired, the salute to the 'grandparents' in 'On Re-Reading Novels' and the approval of their relationship with their grandchildren does not preclude the difficulty of finding time and inclination to read these 'fat Victorian volumes', these 'gigantic, sprawling' books, properly (*E* III. 337, 344). Even as Woolf applauds 'the splendid opulence of the Victorian age' (*E* III. 385) and compares Strachey unfavourably with Lord Macaulay as essayists (*E* III. 435), she embraces the desire for modern forms, at the same time welcoming the reappearance of old novelists like Meredith in new editions. This reappearance is very much 'to the credit of the Victorians' (*E* III. 336), and Victorian and modern writers are seen here as not needing to exclude each other.

Hermione Lee has called *Night and Day* Woolf's 'long, melancholy comedy of the break with Victorianism' (*Virginia Woolf*, p. 375), but Woolf never breaks with Victorianism, in the sense that the Victorians always remain powerfully present to her, and are always asking, like the portrait of the grandfather in that novel, for some sort of perpetuation in the culture of the present which otherwise risks impoverishment. Such issues may be explored by Woolf in rather different ways in the works that followed *Night and Day*, but the argument Woolf is addressing remains remarkably constant. It was never her project simply to despatch the Victorian period to the escaped-from regions of the past and congratulate herself on her own modernity. In fact, *Night and Day*, the poor relation among Woolf's novels in terms of the critical attention it has received, sets an agenda that remains foundational to Woolf's writing throughout the 1920s, and I have some sympathy with Jane Marcus's championing of it as 'the key to [Woolf's] creative life', even if our interpretations of it have little in common (*Virginia Woolf and the Languages of Patriarchy*, p. 19). The novel that is of course Woolf's best-known search for reconciliation between the Victorian past and the modern period is *To the Lighthouse* (1927), and one might anticipate the discussion below in showing how its quest for such reconciliation continues in the track of the visual effects discussed in *Night and Day*, as in James's eventual approach to the lighthouse:

> 'It will rain', he remembered his father saying. 'You won't be able to go to the Lighthouse'.
>
> The Lighthouse was then a silvery, misty-looking tower with a yellow eye that opened suddenly and softly in the evening. Now –
>
> James looked at the Lighthouse. He could see the white-washed rocks; the tower, stark and straight; he could see that it was barred with black and white; he could see windows in it; he could even see washing spread on the rocks to dry. So that was the Lighthouse, was it?
>
> No, the other was also the Lighthouse. For nothing was simply one thing.
> (*TL*, pp. 201–2)

Here retrospect is expressed in terms of a misty lighting that contrasts with the harsh clarity of the present moment and its 'stark' rationality (which instances the 'postwar masculinization of culture' in Elizabeth Abel's phrase),[40] suggesting how one of the many symbolic functions of the lighthouse is its dual embodiment of period differences.[41]

CHAPTER 2

Synchronicity: Mrs Dalloway

As Woolf discovered her own modernity in the short stories collected in *Monday or Tuesday* (1921) — stories that, as she indicated in her diary, gave her the 'form' for the novel *Jacob's Room* (1922)[1] — and as the compelling novelty of contemporary writing like that by Joyce and Eliot pressed more on her attention, she was forced to recognise that the post-War present and the realm of the 'new' could not so easily be joined with the past as in the programme of *Night and Day* and the task facing its protagonist Katharine Hilbery. *Mrs Dalloway* (1925), together with the series of well-known essays such as 'Mr Bennett and Mrs Brown' written simultaneously, do indeed find new ways of promoting Victorian–modern communications, but *Jacob's Room*, which we shall look at briefly here, shows Woolf documenting an alarming contemporaneity which, in all its admitted vigour and vividness, seems devoid of any secure linkage with the past. In this, the novel stands in practically an antithetical though congruent relationship to *Night and Day* and its retrospective obsessions. The diary entry noted above indicates Woolf's excitement at the 'entirely different' approach to writing she had discovered for *Jacob's Room*, a 'new form for a new novel' (*D* II. 13), but such a form is used to express the pathology of the new in cultural terms as much as its exhilaration.

Although *Jacob's Room* like *Night and Day* is set before the First World War, the sense of a new era is much more apparent in the freedom and independence that mark the career of its protagonist, indicating, of course, its difference of gender focus. But it is also apparent in the unconstrained world of painters and their models that features throughout, and is emphasised by the consistent use of the present tense to communicate a predominant sensation of the here and now ('Sunlight strikes in upon shaving-glasses; and gleaming brass cans; upon all the jolly trappings of the day ...', *JR*, p. 143). The acute sense of the intensity of the 'moment' – 'drums and trumpets ... are liable at any moment to blow music into the air' (*JR*, p. 97) – anticipates the heady urban scene of *Mrs Dalloway* (see for example the pleasure of the Holborn bus-ride described in *Jacob's Room*, p. 54), yet at the same time the melancholy and inadequacy of such 'music', given its inevitably fugitive status, is unmistakeable. Thus Julia Eliot experiences 'the tumult of the present' as 'an elegy for past youth and past summers, and there rose in her mind a curious sadness, as if time and eternity showed through skirts and waistcoats, and she saw people passing tragically to destruction' (*JR*, pp. 147–8). The First World War had obviously enforced the recurrent mood of 'overpowering sorrow' in the novel (*JR*, p. 40), but as Woolf's essay 'How It Strikes a Contemporary' (1923) makes plain, the War was also crucial in emphasising the condition of contemporaneity itself, so to speak, in that we now feel 'sharply cut off from our predecessors' (*E* III. 357). In the same essay Woolf talks about readers turning from contemporary writing to past works of literature as if driven by 'some imperious need to anchor our instability upon their security' (p. 357), and it is precisely the lack of any secure anchorage in the past that *Jacob's Room* diagnoses, summarised, for example, in the explicit presentation of Florinda's rootless and 'unanchored life' (*JR*, p. 66).

The sense of the fragility and evanescence of the moment (a vital component however of its precarious beauty, a 'loveliness' that is 'infernally sad', *JR*, p. 40) is embodied at one point in the 'semi-transparent' Clara Durrant (*JR*, p. 51), who no less than the figures glimpsed in 'Kew Gardens' invites comparison with a butterfly, just as Jacob himself does with a moth in his passage from dark to light across the Durrants' drawing-room (*JR*, p. 50) – both here seen as creatures of a moment, as it were.[2] We remember in *A Sketch of the Past* how 'the present when backed by the past is a thousand times deeper than the present when it presses so close that you can feel nothing else, when the film on the camera reaches only the eye' (*MOB*, p. 98), and this alerts us to the curious sense of 'pastlessness' that pervades *Jacob's Room*, an immersion in the present that affords some intense experiences of pleasure and delight while emphasising the theme of transience integral to this elegiac work. The figure of Jacob, based on Woolf's brother Thoby, is carefully differentiated from his biographical source in the absence of any familial tradition or context to 'back' him, to deepen his present, thus emphasising his uncompromising determination to go it alone, 'which makes youth so intolerably disagreeable' – ' "I am what I am, and intend to be it", for which there will be no form in the world unless Jacob makes one for himself' – and which pits him against 'the world of the elderly' in throwing over the generational inheritance and continuity that Woolf's previous novel had asserted (*JR*, p. 28). 'We are curiously cut off from communication with the old', Woolf noted in a review of 1916, illustrating this with the incomprehension of the elderly towards the Post-Impressionist aesthetic that features so strongly in *Jacob's Room* (*E* II. 61–2). Jacob's own 'monolithic' quality (*JR*, p. 145) may be part of his splendour, and indeed of the splendour of youth generally that, in spite of its 'intolerably disagreeable' quality, the novel evokes, even while it acknowledges that the attempt to make the world anew is a naive one: 'We start transparent, and then the cloud thickens. All history backs our pane of glass. To escape is vain' (*JR*, p. 40). Here the 'backing' that history provides is merely a reminder of the engulfing cloud of mortality, and a past that is essentially the cumulative record of youth's perishability is able to offer no resource.

The vivid and present 'tumult' of *Jacob's Room*, plus the *carpe diem* mood that corresponds to it, are conveyed in descriptive passages of vibrant colour, which again contrast with the coloration and 'lighting' of *Night and Day* and its evocation of the shades of the past – we thus have the 'purple', 'emerald' and 'yellow' of the sea off the Cornish coast (*JR*, p. 39), or the faces on Parliament Hill 'which came out fresh and vivid as though painted in yellow and red' (*JR*, p. 62), or the bright clothing of artists' models like Florinda and Fanny Elmer (*JR*, p. 99). The novel's attention to contemporary painting and the Post-Impressionist style of the pre-First World War London Jacob moves in forms a striking divergence from *Night and*

Day, with attention on the painter's own concentration on the scene before him emphasising the immersion in the present 'moment', communicated also by a painterly lifestyle of casual liaisons and fleeting passion the novel depicts – 'But Nick perhaps, or Fanny Elmer, believing implicitly in the truth of the moment, fling off, sting the cheek, are gone like sharp hail' (*JR*, p. 105). This last comment indicates doubts about the lifestyle of 'the moment' which pervade *Jacob's Room*, imaged in the squalor of Florinda's 'dirty lodging-house wallpaper' (*JR*, p. 65). The colourful world of the painters can thus be crude and tawdry; we see Nick Bramham, with his 'rather bloodshot' eyes, 'as if from staring and staring', painting Fanny while she sits stiffly as 'an unshaded electric light hung above her head' (*JR*, p. 100). Of the way women 'paint' themselves, we are told 'The women in the streets have the faces of playing cards; the outlines accurately filled in with pink and yellow, and the line drawn tightly round them' (*JR*, p. 100), an attempt to 'fix' the 'glowing ruby' of beauty that is unavailing, or can at best capture this 'flying' quality only momentarily. Our first sight of Florinda, in the light of a bonfire, shows us hers as 'the most prominent' of 'the faces which came out fresh and vivid as though painted in yellow and red ... As if dazed by the glare, her green-blue eyes stared at the flames. Every muscle of her face was taut. There was something tragic in her thus staring ... (*JR*, p. 62). The emphasis on unshaded electric light as a symptom of the contemporary is already familiar from *Night and Day*, but the accompanying elements of staring eyes, bright colour, tautness, stiffness and linearity are forcibly echoed later in *Orlando*, where 'the present moment' of the eleventh of October 1928 is described as one of an extreme brightness that 'brought out the colour in everything and seemed to stiffen the muscles of the cheeks', and where thought is 'tightened' and the nerves 'stretched ... very taut' (*O*, p. 206).[3]

Jacob himself is both immersed in this gaudy world and its affairs and yet aloof from it, the latter stance reflected in his preferring to read Marlowe rather than his contemporaries and in his resolve to 'detest your own age' (*JR*, p. 92). His search for something beyond his 'moment' will lead him to the monuments of Ancient Greece, but this emphasises his own impermanence in the ironic identification the novel makes between him and the Parthenon, both seen as august and 'composed' (*JR*, pp. 127, 130). Jacob's sublime and 'statuesque' form and attitude (*JR*, p. 149) – 'He stood on the exact spot where the great statue of Athena used to stand' (*JR*, p. 130) – does afford a contrast between his 'classical' beauty and the hectic colouring of lovers such as Florinda, just as the brightness of the 'astonishingly clean-cut' Greek landscape (*JR*, p. 128) and the 'extreme definiteness' of its buildings where all is in 'sharp outline' (*JR*, pp. 130, 132), emphasise the travesty of a modern urban aesthetic described as we have seen in similar terms, so that the dazzling 'glare' of the Parthenon in the midday sun is to be distinguished from an ugly urban glare. But the identification of Jacob with Greek art is illusory, and adds to the pathos of his short existence – it is only the Parthenon that might 'outlast the entire world' (*JR*, p. 130). Jacob remains the creature of a summer's day, not of the ages, though of course in becoming the subject of Woolf's own work his transience is transmuted into permanence and 'solidity' (*JR*, p. 60).

'The mellow light which swims over the past', which dominates *Night and Day*, is therefore replaced in *Jacob's Room* by a mode of illumination that is frequently alienating and exposing, an index of an isolated modernity that can find no sustaining traditions to shelter in and that cannot commune with the past, so that the city of Athens itself can appear 'cadaverous from electric light' (*JR*, p. 140). Throughout the novel this attentiveness to the squalid effects of urban lighting is conspicuous – 'the lamps of Soho made large greasy spots of light upon the pavement' (*JR*, p. 68), lamps that are the venue for various sordid episodes, such as that where people are seen 'vociferating' around the 'drunken woman battering at the door' as Jacob reads the *Phaedrus* in his room (*JR*, p. 94). The likely influence of Eliot's poem 'Rhapsody on a Windy Night' in this attention to urban illumination and what it reveals has been rightly pointed out, and if Woolf can also give the Eliotic everyday a benign makeover, as in the passage quoted above – 'Sunlight strikes in upon shaving-glasses; and gleaming brass cans; upon all the jolly trappings of the day ...' – she also duplicates the effects of a poem like 'Preludes' – 'The street market in Soho is fierce with light. Raw meat, china mugs, and silk stockings blaze in it. Raw voices wrap themselves round the flaring gas-jets' (*JR*, p. 83).[4] 'Raw flesh' was a term Woolf would later disparagingly apply to a work which immersed itself in her eyes in the vulgarity of the present, Joyce's *Ulysses*: 'how egotistic, insistent, raw, striking, & ultimately nauseating. When one can have the cooked flesh, why have the raw?' (*D* II. 189). At a crisis point in the novel where Jacob sees Florinda 'upon another man's arm' we are told (twice) that 'The light from the arc lamp drenched him from head to toe' (*JR*, p. 81). In short, the city of *Jacob's Room*, 'fierce with light', is repeatedly that of a pathological visibility, bright and strident in its coloration, and oppressive to the 'staring' eyes that have to negotiate it; a place indeed where characteristically 'the present ... presses so close that you can feel nothing else, when the film on the camera reaches only the eye'.

Jacob's Room pitches into this culture of brash visuality, which is also manifest in cosmetics, as we have seen, which fail to capture the 'glowing ruby' of beauty more than momentarily.[5] 'Ruby' is conversely a key term in Woolf's Victorian palette, as in her reminiscence of the effect of Stella Duckworth's engagement to Jack Hills, a scene of some importance for *Mrs Dalloway*: 'it was through that engagement that I had my first vision ... of love between man and woman. It was to me like a ruby ... glowing, red, clear, intense ... I connect it with respectable engagements; unofficial love never gives me the same feeling'.[6] The effect on Stella herself was to make her 'incandescent', to become 'lit up' like moonlight (*A Sketch*, p. 105); in the earlier memoir *Reminiscences* Woolf speaks of Stella's 'phantom loveliness' (*MOB*, p. 42). 'Incandescent' is another term one might add to the list Woolf uses in lighting her past, alongside terms discussed in chapter 1, such as dusky, misty, iridescent (as in her description of the 'filter' provided by Lady Ritchie's writing) – all terms that contest the vivid light and coloration of modernity. Similar terms are in fact used to describe the plan of *Jacob's Room* itself, as in the diary entry already noted: 'Suppose one thing should open out of another ... no scaffolding; scarcely a brick to be seen; all crepuscular, but the heart, the passion, humour, everything as bright as fire in the mist' (*D* II. 13–14). Here 'crepuscular' seems to refer to

Woolf's desire to avoid strong demarcation in the novel, to achieve a state where 'one thing ... open[s] out of another', echoing her insistence in the essay 'Modern Novels' that, in opposition to the bricks and scaffolding of Edwardian materialism, 'if one were free and could set down what one chose, there would be ... a vague general confusion in which the clear-cut features of the tragic, the comic, the passionate, and the lyrical were dissolved beyond the possibility of separate recognition' (*E* III. 33). The rejection of the 'clear-cut' is one of widespread significance in Woolf, as previously noted, and the resort to the crepuscular is further explained in 'Modern Novels' in terms that echo Woolf's tribute to the Jamesian 'half light', this time in connection with Chekhov's short story 'Gusev':

The emphasis is laid upon such unexpected places that at first it seems as if there were no emphasis at all; and then, as the eyes accustom themselves to twilight and discern the shapes of things in a room, we see how complete the story is, how profound ... it is impossible to say that this is humorous or that tragic ... (*E* III. 35)

The Russian writers' probing of 'the soul and heart', their 'natural reverence for the human spirit' as countering the 'sick[ness] of our own materialism' (p. 35), is exemplified in the 1917 essay on Dostoevsky in his ability 'to read the most inscrutable writing at the depths of the darkest souls' (*E* II. 86). John Mepham has argued that Woolf's much-quoted talk of life as a 'luminous halo', which it is the novelist's task to 'convey' in 'Modern Novels', is a hypothesis that she advances to explain what Joyce and other contemporaries are seeking (not altogether successfully) to do, rather than the fundamental objective of her own fiction, as is often suggested (*E* III. 33–4). This necessary sensitivity to the 'myriad impressions' of life has to be combined with the profound probing of 'soul and heart' if it is to avoid becoming an aesthetic programme alone; the writer must enter the Russian 'twilight', or follow, in the wake of Dostoevsky, 'the whole train of thought in all its speed, now as it flashes into light, now as it lapses into darkness; for he is able to follow not only the vivid streak of achieved thought, but to suggest the dim and populous underworld of the mind's consciousness where desires and impulses are moving blindly beneath the sod' (*E* II. 85).⁷ Whatever the 'crepuscular' method of *Jacob's Room*, Woolf in fact declines probing the depths of the protagonist's consciousness therein, not only, as some critics have argued, because these may turn out to be rather shallow in his particular case, but because of the novel's insistence on exposing a world of 'surface', psychologically, temporally and, in its casual liaisons, emotionally. In attending to the bright colours, lighting and tight linearity that dominate the visual fashions presented in *Jacob's Room*, Woolf accosts what one could call the 'anti-crepuscularity' of contemporary style, particularly in relation to cosmetics and painting. And, as we shall argue, in that Woolf's work continues its frequent celebration of effects of mist, shadow and chiaroscuro, there are critical differences between it and the Post-Impressionist investment in colour and 'significant form' that need to be attended to.

The vivid, immediate world of the painters in *Jacob's Room* and a bohemian lifestyle that snatches the moment before it is 'gone like sharp hail' are things that Woolf consistently dissociated herself from in her pull towards the romance of 'respectable engagements'. In this her outlook differed markedly from that of her sister, to whom she wrote in 1922 in terms precisely evoking the 'flinging off' of the painter's life: 'What it comes to is this: you say "I do think you lead a dull respectable absurd life ... Look at me now – only sixpence a year – lovers – Paris – life – love – art – excitement – God! I must be off". This leaves me in tears' (*L* II. 506). Whatever the envy that might be disclosed here, Woolf kept a distance between herself and this painters' world, and with it that of an unbridled modern sexuality – thus in *A Room of One's Own* she rejects the typical 'indecency' of the modern novel in favour of the lyrical sublimations of Victorian courtship in the poetry of Tennyson and Christina Rossetti. Sexual explicitness, she notes, 'aware of the awful nature of the confession, seems somehow dull' (*RO*, p. 91); as in the letter to her sister just quoted, we see her playing somewhat ironically the role of old maid here.⁸ In spite of Woolf's involvement with and support for the two Post-Impressionist exhibitions of 1910 and 1912, she could write at the same time to Violet Dickinson, 'The Grafton, thank God, is over; artists are an abominable race. The furious excitement of these people all the winter over their pieces of canvas coloured green and blue, is odious' (*L* II. 15). Although there is an element of Woolf's playing to a conservative audience here, nowhere in her writing do we have anything to match the sense of ferment and exhilaration the exhibitions sparked in the lives of other members of Bloomsbury – an obvious instance of this being Vanessa's essay 'Memories of Roger Fry', where the exhilaration is inseparable from the beginnings of her affair with Fry.[9] Even what is commonly seen as the famous indirect tribute to the first exhibition in Woolf's essay 'Character in Fiction' – 'on or about December 1910 human character changed' (*E* III. 421) – is significantly qualified in the essay itself, as noted in my Introduction. When Woolf hypothesises the painterly treatment of a period of recent time in her diary – a stretch of eleven days of 'non-being' – she adds 'But painters lack sub[t]lety; there were points of light, shades beneath the surface, now, I suppose, undiscoverable' (*D* I. 239). It is precisely the chiaroscuro of experience, the sense of that which lies 'beneath the surface', that Woolf seems to doubt painters can capture, given the commitment to bright colour and 'form' that the Bloomsbury Post-Impressionists characteristically pursued and that is shown as an alienating condition in *Jacob's Room*. In our discussion of *To the Lighthouse*, where Woolf does treat a contemporary painter sympathetically in the person of Lily Briscoe, these important distinctions between Woolf's work and her sister's shall be pursued in opposition to some recent criticism which in my view does not acknowledge them adequately.

The exposing light of modernity, permitting no shadows, is always to hand as the object of critique in Woolf's writing, and also applicable to individuals, as in her report of an uncomfortable evening spent in May 1920 dining with the socialists George and Margaret Cole, whose manner – 'quick, hard, determined' – was like 'electric light full in the eyes – unbecoming at my age', and where 'one can see Mrs Cole rapidly becoming the cleverish elderly fox terrier type of intellectual woman – as it is not a shade or valley in her mind' (*D* II. 41).[10] Here electric light has links with the suggestion of new and distasteful social formations, just as Woolf's resort to the 'mellow light' of the past can be associated with the glamour of the aristocracy, a recurrent fascination for her. Shadow for Woolf not only has connotations of mystery, romance and imagination, but also individualises objects in giving them relief, as in the James review's discussion of 'the shadow in which the detail of so many things can be discerned which the glare of day flattens out'. Such 'flattening out' carries political as well as aesthetic overtones in reducing things to a level uniformity, whereas the nostalgia expressed in *Orlando* for 'women in aprons carrying wobbly lamps' significantly makes use of the image of a domestic servant.

If *Night and Day* is a heavily retrospective work, while *Jacob's Room* shows an acute but extremely qualified sense of the contemporary, Woolf's next novel, *Mrs Dalloway* (1925), aims precisely at combining the worlds of past experience and present receptivity to 'deepen' its sense of the present 'when backed by the past', to the advantage of both. The novel's insistent up-to-dateness is signalled by its being set in the heart of the present moment, a June day in 1923 (thus also gesturing towards its momentous contemporary, Joyce's *Ulysses*), but its demands on the past are indicated by a note in Woolf's diary of 15 October 1923 referring to the writing of the novel: 'It took me a year's groping to discover what I call my tunnelling process, by which I tell the past by instalments, as I have need of it. This is my prime discovery so far . . .' (*D* II. 272). Earlier in the diary Woolf had described how this tunnelling – 'how I dig out beautiful caves behind my characters' – gives 'exactly what I want; humanity, humour, depth' (*D* II. 263). One might say that the characters of *Jacob's Room*, by contrast, lack precisely this depth, these 'caves' behind them.

On this June day in 1923, therefore, we are told of the principal character, Clarissa, that 'all day she had been thinking of Bourton' (*MD*, p. 202), that is of her childhood home and of the romantic intrigues there involving Peter Walsh and Sally Seton that took place 'early in the 'nineties' (*MD*, p. 64) when she was a young woman. The sense of existing simultaneously in the present and the past is announced on the very first page, when Clarissa's sense of the 'freshness' of the present morning, into which she is about to embark outdoors, together with her thoughts on the removal of the interior doors from their hinges to accommodate her party, immediately take her to the Bourton days, and the 'squeak of the hinges' the French windows made there (*MD*, p. 3). Removing/opening doors gives both spatial and temporal access, a Woolfian metaphor of communing with the past we find elsewhere.[11] Peter Walsh too spends much of the day 'thinking of Bourton', and more particularly of a series of episodes that came to a head at 'three o'clock in the afternoon of a very hot day' when his youthful relationship with Clarissa ended, in a scene 'which he believed had mattered more than anything in the whole of his life' (*MD*, p. 69). It is clear that *The Hours*, an early title for the novel (*D* II. 248), refers not only to the conspicuously striking hours of the present June day but to those that continue to reverberate from over thirty years earlier. These hours come together in the novel's final, climactic words describing Clarissa's appearance to Peter:

What is this terror? what is this ecstasy? he thought to himself. What is it that fills me with extraordinary excitement?
    It is Clarissa, he said.
    For there she was. (*MD*, p. 213)

This final, simple, irreducible phrase had earlier been used twice in succession to describe the Clarissa of Peter's memory: 'it was Clarissa one remembered. Not that she was striking; not beautiful at all; there was nothing picturesque about her; she never said anything specially clever; there she was, however; there she was' (*MD*, p. 83).

In the re-enactment of Peter's numinous passion for Clarissa the hours of two hot days therefore link arms across a historical interval that would disjoin them, a potential breach enforced by the First World War, which the novel is highly conscious of. In *Orlando*, Woolf will suggest that to be fully alive is precisely the attainment of such 'synchronicity':

the most successful practitioners of the art of life ... synchronise the sixty or seventy different times which beat simultaneously in every normal human system so that when eleven strikes, all the rest chime in unison, and the present is neither a violent disruption nor completely forgotten in the past. (*O*, pp. 210–11)

If in *Jacob's Room* the present does seem something of a 'violent disruption', while in *Night and Day* it is on the way to being, if not forgotten, then subsumed within the past, here the image of striking hours that 'chime' with those from a different time forcibly echoes the theme in *Mrs Dalloway*. The novel's attention to the War, to historical change and the passage of time generally acknowledges the forces that can disrupt this synchronicity; thus Clarissa herself had 'grown very white since her illness' (*MD*, p. 4). Peter's years in India have rendered him particularly sensitive to such change, upon which he is the novel's main commentator; thus he is aware of (and approves) the greater freedom for women in particular with regard to fashion, sexual relations and cosmetics – 'the delicious and apparently universal habit of paint' – that has developed in England since the War, perceiving 'that shift in the whole pyramidal accumulation which in his youth had seemed immovable' (*MD*, pp. 78–9, 178). Here Peter anticipates the description of the 'hideous' and dismaying Victorian pyramid in *Orlando* (*O*, p. 160), which on the eve of modernity had 'vanished and left not a stain, not a puddle even, on the pavement' (*O*, p. 205). Even so, Peter's claim to feel 'as young as ever' (*MD*, p. 177), because of his progressive views (which are by no means entirely Woolf's own as her remarks on modern cosmetics have indicated) and his relationship with the twenty-four-year-old Daisy (*MD*, p. 172), is treated with some irony; his up-to-dateness and frequently declared belief that his present age offers the ideal combination of youthful feeling and mature wisdom (*MD*, pp. 86, 178, 212) is undone by the greater power invested in Clarissa that can sweep aside ideas of temporal development and land him right back among the passions of Bourton again, so that in the emphatic emotions of his final encounter with Clarissa – 'terror', 'ecstasy', 'extraordinary excitement' – he is genuinely rendered 'as young as ever'. This 'beatific vision', it has been suggested, is imbued with various kinds of eucharistic and transcendental imagery, so that the party's 'guests from the purgatorial past' can be seen as received into a 'heavenly communion' through the means of Clarissa's 'divine' presence.[12] Certainly in Peter's case his climactic experience strongly evokes Dante's reunion with Beatrice in the *paradiso terrestre* at the top of Mount Purgatory, where a sense of stupefaction and fear is inseparable from the 'antico amor' reborn in him: 'Men che dramma / di sangue m'è rimaso che non tremi: / conosco i segni dell'antica fiamma' ('Not a drop of blood is left in me that does not tremble; I know the marks of the ancient flame').[13] The repeated references in the novel to Clarissa 'stand[ing] at the top of her stairs' at the party (*MD*, p. 19) emphasise this Beatrice theme, while the very name 'Clarissa' takes us here not to Samuel Richardson's novel, but to the poetry of the *dolce stil nuovo* and the numinous *clarità* the lady's presence sheds.[14] Dante's reunion with the Beatrice of his youth after a self-confessed interval of straying from her to follow the 'falso ... piacer' of 'presenti cose' ('false pleasure of present things', 31. 34–5) is a return to his authentic past that underwrites Woolf's staging of the climax to this day in June 1923 as one incorporating her own powerful nostalgia for past passions.[15]

Thus in August 1922, when she was 'laboriously dredging my mind for Mrs Dalloway & bringing up light buckets', and was also two hundred pages into *Ulysses* (*D* II. 188–9), she was remembering the scene twenty-five years earlier when 'Jack [Hills] came to Hindhead & was accepted by Stella in the moonlit garden'. The diary entry of 22 August records the anniversary of this event – 'it still seems to me like a real thing, unsmothered by the succeeding years' (*D*, II. 190), a response that anticipates the paean to this episode of youthful love in *A Sketch of the Past*, where the moonlight comes to invest Stella's whole body (*MOB*, p. 105). Woolf tended to conflate the episode in the Hindhead garden with that in the garden at Talland House where Kitty Lushington became engaged, 'under the jackmanii in the Love Corner' – 'my first introduction to the passion of love' ('22 Hyde Park Gate', *MOB*, p. 165); in *A Sketch* it is Jack and Stella's engagement that provides 'my first vision ... of love between man and woman' (*MOB*, p. 105). The figure of Clarissa Dalloway not only derives in part from Kitty Maxse, as she became (*D* II. 5, n6), but the latter died at the point when 'Mrs Dalloway has branched into a book' after Woolf's earlier uncertainties about whether it would form a series of short stories (*D* II. 207). This diary entry and the previous one (of 8 October 1922) discuss side-by-side Woolf's plans for the novel and her memories of Kitty, centring again on the engagement 'by the greenhouse in the Love Corner' – 'I keep going over this very day in my mind' (*D* II. 206), just as Clarissa in the novel spends 'all day ... thinking of Bourton' (*MD*, p. 202). It is clear that the retrospective scenes in *Mrs Dalloway* have their source in just such days from Woolf's past, even if Peter was rejected rather than accepted by Clarissa; for him she can still 'make the moon ... rise at Bourton on the terrace in the summer sky' (*MD*, p. 52) in a manner that evokes the 'moonlit garden' of Hindhead.

In his study of Woolf and Pater, Perry Meisel argues that both writers prioritise 'timeless, passionate states of contemplation and communion, largely unattached to "before" and "after" ', and that the typical 'plunge' of Clarissa 'into the very heart of the moment' exemplifies this attachment.[16] The 'gemlike flame' that images such a state in Pater 'and the autogenesis with which it is linked represent ... the wishful priority of modernity itself, engaged as it always is, in all its renaissances, in an attempt to achieve "the advantage of having no past" ' (p. 69). Although there are instances later in her career that might lend weight to Meisel's argument, Woolf is far more insistent on modernity and its moments being anchored in and stabilised by the past, the absence of which leads precisely to the pathology of 'autogenesis' in *Jacob's Room* – 'there will be no form in the world unless Jacob makes one for himself'. *Mrs Dalloway* plays out its evocation and treasuring of the past even as it is set in the thick of an exciting modernity, so that Clarissa can both 'kindle' at her party 'that very night' (*MD*, p. 5) while she is 'kindling all over with pleasure at the thought of the past' (*MD*, p. 188 – compare Woolf's comment on the 'enkindling effect of the past' in her review of Smyth, above, p. 31). It is as if the novel needs to anchor its exciting sense of the contemporary, which is constantly stressed – 'the strange high singing of some aeroplane overhead was what she loved; life; London; this moment of June' (*MD*, p. 4) – to a previous era, as if the former is precarious and insufficient in spite of the exhilaration it provides.

A similar enterprise of relating past and present characterises some of Woolf's most celebrated essays from the period when she was writing *Mrs Dalloway*. Thus the first version of 'Mr Bennett and Mrs Brown', published in November 1923, talks about the 'fatal' Edwardian age when in literature 'character disappeared or was mysteriously engulfed', as shown by the work of Arnold Bennett *et al.*, following the 'procession' of characters, 'endless and alive', in Victorian writing (illustrated specifically by Thackeray's *Pendennis*): 'so it goes on from character to character all through the splendid opulence of the Victorian age ... The whole country, the whole society, is revealed to us ... through the astonishing vividness and reality of the characters' (*E* III. 385). The task facing modern novelists is 'to bring back character from the [Edwardian] shapelessness into which it has lapsed' (*E* III. 387), or, to anticipate the metaphor from the revised version of the essay, to get it on track again after the derailment occurring in the novels of Bennett's generation (*E* III. 430). Woolf is at the same time quite clear that this is not a matter of returning to Victorian conventions, which are 'discredited' in the light of a modern sense of the complexity of the individual pioneered by Dostoevsky and the Russians (*E* III. 386), and when a much-extended version of the essay was delivered as the lecture 'Character in Fiction' in May 1924 Woolf emphasised the necessary vandalism of the moderns, the 'smashing and crashing' ('Mr Joyce for example breaking up the old traditional form of the novel'), which was done (as with innovations in poetry and biography) 'from the most honourable motives' (*E* III. 515). She is still, however, using Victorian writing as a measure of the modern; though conventions change from age to age, this is the mark contemporary writing needs to aim at in securing the literary inheritance, even if in an age of transition 'we cannot expect the Georgians to give us a series of complete masterpieces coming out year after year in succession such as the Victorians enjoyed'. Thus Strachey's *Eminent Victorians* has not the 'depth or richness which it would have done' had it been written in 'an age like the Victorian age' (*E* III. 516). Ideas of a literary 'inheritance' pick up on the essay 'On Re-reading Novels' of July 1922, discussed in chapter 1, where the good relations between Victorian 'grandparents' and Georgian 'grandchildren' are applauded after the dereliction of the lost generation of the Edwardians (*E* III. 336).

Woolf repeats this last point in a letter to Janet Case of 1922: 'don't you agree with me that the Edwardians, from 1895 to 1914, made a pretty poor show. By the Edwardians, I mean Shaw, Wells, Galsworthy, the Webbs, Arnold Bennett' (*L* II. 529). The comment casts an interesting light on Woolf's attitude towards the *fin de siècle* and the writers who are conventionally associated with that period, Dowson, Wilde, Symons, the *Yellow Book* circle and so on, and on any claims it might make to muddy the waters of the Victorian–modern distinction. In spite of Woolf's commitment to the 'crepuscular', she never in her writing pays much attention to these 'moth-like spirits' abroad in the 'evening time' of the century, as she put it in a 1916 review (*E* II. 45), given her belief that the truly significant 'twilight' lies elsewhere, as in Russia. In the review referred to, of Elizabeth Robins Pennell's *Nights: Rome, Venice in the Aesthetic Eighties. London, Paris in the Fighting Nineties* ... (1916), Woolf is characteristically sceptical about claims for the 'revolutionary' glamour and importance of the 'Fighting Nineties', bridles at the 'artistic exclusiveness' of Pennell's associates and resists the lure of Parisian nights 'when the little tables in a café attract all the artists in a quarter' (*E* II. 45–6). Something of this resistance extends into the presentation of the bohemian world of the painters featured in *Jacob's Room*, as we have argued. In her review of Richard Le Gallienne's *The Romantic 90s* of 1926 she again describes the author's extravagant claims for the 'revolutionary energy' of his peers as 'a curious overstatement' (*E* IV. 359–60), while Hayim Fineman's over-estimation of the importance of John Davidson in a study of 1916 elicits Woolf's scepticism in its opening with a critique of earlier writers via 'a cannonade of sonorous general statements about Victorian life and literature which it is difficult to bring into relation with actual books and facts' (*E* II. 143). Woolf's respect for what she calls 'the robust lion, the Victorian age' and her response to Le Gallienne's circle as merely its 'tapering tail' (*E* IV. 360) leads, in the comment to Case above, to what is practically the effacing of the 90s generation and the subsuming of half that decade within the 'Edwardian', given that it is the contrast between the Victorian novelists and Galsworthy, Bennett and others that constitutes recent literary history for Woolf. Her ancestral position in the 'respectable' literary establishment is a totally other world to the late Victorian decadence, provincial in her eyes in spite of its cosmopolitanism – the review of Le Gallienne ends with a sly dig at his having been born in Liverpool (*E* IV. 360) – and the deepest responses 'the 90s' evoke in Woolf are always domestic, familial.[17] Its more exotic manifestations tend to provoke her scorn.[18]

Woolf notes in the lecture 'Character in Fiction' how 'the sound of breaking and falling and destruction ... is the prevailing sound of the Georgian age', and is 'rather a melancholy one, if you think what melodious days there have been in the past – if you think of Shakespeare and Milton, or even of Dickens and Thackeray' (*E* III. 515). At the same time she ends with the idea that this destruction is the necessary preface to a major renewal – 'We are on the threshold of a very great age in English literature' (*E* III. 517). The attitude to her contemporaries here seems a curious mixture of regret and assertion, and this ambiguity becomes further apparent after the lecture was revised for publication, in July 1924, under the same title, 'Character in Fiction'. Here again we have the description of an exhilarating, yet disturbing, literary vandalism committed by the moderns, the 'smashing and crashing', the Joycean breaking of windows in the house of fiction, even talk of how 'the strong are led to destroy the very foundations and rules of literary society' (*E* III. 433–4).[19] Thus discussing T. S. Eliot, she notes:

> I think that Mr Eliot has written some of the loveliest lines in modern poetry. But how intolerant he is of the old usages and politenesses of society – respect for the weak, consideration for the dull! As I sun myself upon the intense and ravishing beauty of one of his lines, and reflect that I must make a dizzy and dangerous leap to the next ... I cry out, I confess, for the old decorums, and envy the indolence of my ancestors who, instead of spinning madly through mid-air, dreamt quietly in the shade with a book. (*E* III. 434–5)

Regret for 'the old usages and politenesses of society' (imaged characteristically as a resort to the 'shade' out of the sun) echoes a comment Woolf had made earlier in the essay that 'At the present moment we are suffering ... from having no code of manners which writers and readers accept as a prelude to the more exciting intercourse of friendship' (*E* III. 434). In *A Sketch of the Past* Woolf would note the element of 'politeness' in her own writing, its 'Victorian manner', linking it there with the social politenesses of the tea-table in which she had been brought up, and pondering how far it had been of value to her especially in her critical work (*MOB*, p. 150). Her desire for 'the old decorums' in reading regrets the demands of Joyce's indecency and Eliot's intolerance in harking back to a model of leisured ease – dreaming quietly in the shade with a book – which also features at the opening of an essay of 1919 entitled 'Reading' (which seems to be the germ of *The Common Reader* (1925), itself originally to be called *Reading* (*D* II. 172)). Here we have the well-stocked library of a country house as the appropriate venue for comfortably retracing the English literary tradition: 'I liked to read there. One drew the pale armchair to the window, and so the light fell over the shoulder upon the page. The shadow of the gardener mowing the lawn sometimes crossed it ...' (*E* III. 141). The essay is a reminder of how Woolf's own reading is grounded in a world of privilege – the time and library resources afforded her as the daughter of Leslie Stephen – and also how backward-looking, to a degree, the project Woolf unfolds in *The Common Reader* is, in its tracing a literary tradition beginning with Chaucer and ending with the contemporary under the aegis of Dr Johnson's 'common reader' (*E* IV. 19). Although the book is innovatory and even iconoclastic in extending the tradition beyond canonical names to include neglected genres and writers, the stabilising framework it provides in which to integrate the contemporary helps to smooth over the shock of the new, imaged as a class of unruly pupils under the eyes of 'Time ... a good schoolmaster', or as a turbulent passage at sea, as in the final essay 'How It Strikes a Contemporary':

Literature ... has lasted long, has undergone many changes, and it is only a short sight and a parochial mind that will exaggerate the importance of these squalls, however they may agitate the little boats now tossing out at sea. The storm and the drenching are on the surface; continuity and calm are in the depths. (*E* IV. 241)

The common reader, in a shady armchair with the gardener mowing outside, can yet absorb these threats to her peace. In our discussion of *Three Guineas* and associated works we shall return to the paradoxical spectacle of this leisured common reader in a rather more combative guise.

And yet, in 'Character in Fiction', where the moderns' determination to rescue Mrs Brown from discredited conventions even results in the 'sound of their axes' reaching the reader's ear, Woolf asserts that such a sound is 'vigorous and stimulating ... unless of course you wish to sleep' (*E* III. 435) – or dream quietly in the shade one might add. Woolf's ambivalence towards the contemporary pervades her writing in the early 1920s, prompting both applause and anxiety, and Joyce, as the major axe-bearer, was a particular source of tension. *Mrs Dalloway* is a clear riposte to *Ulysses* in also being set on a single June day while parting company with Joyce's 'indecency' and lack of breeding; the diary entry noted above – 'I am laboriously dredging my mind for Mrs Dalloway' – follows immediately on from the previously quoted passage where Woolf reports on reading Joyce's work:

An illiterate, underbred book it seems to me: the book of a self taught working man, & we all know how distressing they are, how egotistic, insistent, raw, striking, & ultimately nauseating. When one can have the cooked flesh, why have the raw? (*D* II. 189)

Woolf noted in *A Sketch* how the civilised 'Victorian manner' is 'helpful in making something seemly out of raw odds and ends' (*MOB*, p. 150), and we saw how 'raw meat' in *Jacob's Room* is part of a complex of signs instancing a modernity that touches a nerve in Woolf (the contrast might be with the leisurely cooking of the ancestral *boeuf en daube*). Another key term in the string of adjectives decrying Joyce here is again one of the less vociferous, 'striking'. The striking hours that punctuate the day on which *Mrs Dalloway* is set are an emphatic reminder of present time, anticipating Orlando's rude awakening to the 'present moment':

the clock ticked louder and louder until there was a terrific explosion right in her ear. Orlando leapt as if she had been violently struck on the head. Ten times she was struck. In fact it was ten o'clock in the morning. It was the eleventh of October. It was 1928. It was the present moment. (*O*, p. 206)

The choice of verb in the essay title 'How It Strikes a Contemporary' (deriving from a poem of that name by Browning) is thus no accident – 'striking' signals both the vivid freshness and the aggressive intrusion of the new.[20]

The above comment on Joyce and *Ulysses* was made when Woolf was two hundred pages into his novel, and completing it did not make her change her mind: 'It is underbred, not only in the obvious sense, but in the literary sense ... I'm reminded all the time of some callow board school boy ...' (*D* II. 199). The repeated charge of *Ulysses* being 'underbred', that both Joyce and his work lack a proper pedigree, is telling; in another diary entry from this period Woolf remarks on various interruptions to her progress in writing *Mrs Dalloway*, and reports that one way 'to rock oneself back into writing' is 'the reading of good literature', adding 'It is a mistake to think that literature can be produced from the raw. One must get out of life ... By the way, Thackeray is good reading, very vivacious, with "touches" ... of astonishing insight' (*D* II. 193). Although Woolf's comments on *Ulysses* in the series of essays contemporary with the writing of *Mrs Dalloway* are not as outspoken as her diary entries, it is clear that she felt a kind of sublime distaste for a work in the forefront of the 'smashing and crashing' that characterises the Georgian intervention. Thus in the first version of 'How it Strikes' *Ulysses* is summed up as 'a memorable catastrophe – immense in daring, terrific in disaster' – one wonders if the fate of Dante's Ulysses is at the back of her mind here (*E* III. 356 – see *Inferno* 26. 112–42). Woolf had felt something like this as early as 1919, when she began reading instalments of the novel serialised in the *Little Review*, and, in spite of Joyce's impact, concluded by complaining 'how much of life is excluded and ignored'; by comparison, it came 'with a shock to open *Tristram Shandy* and even *Pendennis*, and be by them convinced that there are other aspects of life, and larger ones into the bargain ...' ('Modern Novels', *E* III. 34). In the same essay this narrowness of Joyce is compared with 'being in a bright and yet somehow strictly confined apartment' (*E* III. 34 – 'being in a bright yet narrow room, confined and shut in' in the revised essay, *E* IV. 162), an image of Joyce's residency in the house of fiction which returns us to Woolf's way of describing modernity as exposing illumination.

On 26 September 1922, she noted in her diary a discussion with Eliot about *Ulysses;* the latter, always a fervent admirer, hailed Joyce's novel as a radical 'landmark' that 'destroyed the whole of the 19th Century', while admitting that there was nothing new or particularly effective in the psychology of Bloom; Woolf agreed with this last remark, telling Eliot she 'had found Pendennis more illuminating in this way' (*D* II. 203). It is significant how often Woolf brings *Pendennis* forward as a kind of antidote to the excesses of Joyce, or, as in the first version of 'Mr Bennett and Mrs Brown', as a reminder of the great 'procession' of Victorian literature compared with the 'flimsy' achievements of the Edwardians. Reading Thackeray as a way back into the writing of *Mrs Dalloway*, and lamenting the underbred quality in Joyce, indicate Woolf's own contrasting sense of a pedigree that is both literary and familial, traced back through her aunt Anne Ritchie, Thackeray's daughter. Eliot's enthusiasm for Joyce is resisted by Woolf, for whom the '19th Century' was not to be so easily destroyed, though the very talk of destruction must have confirmed her in the language of violence and vandalism she uses to characterise the moderns.[21]

At the same time Woolf was writing *Mrs Dalloway* she was also at work on *The Common Reader*, observing a 'plan of the two books running side by side' in their composition (*D* II. 205), resulting in both being published in 1925. 'How It Strikes a Contemporary' was lightly revised for publication in the volume after its first appearance in 1923 – Woolf noted in her diary that it was one of the things that must be written while *Mrs Dalloway* gets 'shelved' (*D* II. 240) – and it acts as an effective summary of Woolf's excitement in the face of the contemporary even as she diagnoses its dangers and shortcomings, its 'dizzy and dangerous leap[s]'. The merit of contemporary literature lies in its ability to depict 'the sense of personality vibrating with perceptions' which has been previously unexplored, the concentration on 'some particular person at some precise moment' serving 'to make that person and that moment vivid to the utmost extreme' (*E* III. 358), a self-reflecting commentary on both the strengths and the limitations of *Jacob's Room*, perhaps. 'There is something about the present with all its trivialities which we would not exchange for the past, however august ...', Woolf states, and modern literature in its determination to convey the contemporary shows 'courage', 'sincerity' and 'widespread originality'. Yet the accolade acts as a preface to a note of protest:

> But our exhilaration is strangely curtailed. Book after book leaves us with the same sense of promise unachieved, of intellectual poverty, of brilliance which has been snatched from life but not transmuted into literature. Much of what is best in contemporary work has the appearance of being noted under pressure, taken down in a bleak shorthand which preserves with astonishing brilliance the movements and expressions of the figures as they pass across the screen. But the flash is soon over, and there remains with us a profound dissatisfaction. The irritation is as acute as the pleasure was intense. (*E* III. 356–7)

Woolf then turns from this cinematic quality in contemporary writing to the masterpieces of the past, driven 'by some imperious need to anchor our instability on their security', finding in them indeed 'that sense of security which gradually, delightfully, and completely overcomes us', and tracing this to the 'conviction' with which such writers can present generalised truths rather than modern solipsism (*E* III. 357–8).[22] The essay ends, however, by rejecting this note of pessimism when surveying the contemporary. We may have to put up with a season of 'notebooks', but notebooks are 'the stuff from which the masterpieces of the future are made'. If we have no great contemporary writers, and as a consequence, Woolf argues, no great contemporary critic, we can be confident that in seeing 'the present in relation to the future' such figures will arise; the essay concludes, indeed, with a messianic flourish (*E* III. 359).

The need to 'anchor' a modern instability to the securities of the past is emphasised by having the revised essay conclude *The Common Reader*, so that the contemporary takes its place within an extended literary continuity, a heritage that is itself the guarantor of the greatness to come, despite the present season of storm agitating 'the little boats now tossing out at sea' – as quoted above, 'The storm and the drenching are on the surface; continuity and calm are in the depths' (*E* IV. 241). This nautical metaphor, which is not in the first version of the essay, and which emphasises the 'anchoring' theme, is found elsewhere in Woolf to signal the condition of a turbulent modernity in its relation to tradition. Thus in *A Room of One's Own* reading a representative modern novel, Mary Carmichael's *Life's Adventure*, 'was like being out at sea in an open boat. Up one went, down one sank' (*RO*, p. 73), and the post-War voyage of the Ramsays, in *To the Lighthouse*, is part of a network of symbolism characterising the modern in relation to the land-based Victorian securities of the novel's first part. In the last sentence of the revised 'How It Strikes' the need to see 'the present in relation to the future' in the first version is changed to 'see[ing] the past in relation to the future'(*E* IV. 241), as the place of the contemporary within a lengthy historical tradition is emphasised. The word 'drenching' in the above quotation is also carefully chosen – it evokes not only the unsheltered exposure to modernity discussed in *Jacob's Room* – 'The light from the arc lamp drenched him from head to toe' – but also the famous 'incessant shower of innumerable atoms' from the 'Modern Novels' essay, a receptivity to which, as to the sense of life as a 'luminous halo' (*E* III. 33), is not enough to guarantee the success of modern fiction without its continuing to probe the depths of the heart.

A passage common to both versions of the essay expresses the radical features of the contemporary as a response to the historical situation:

Nor has any generation more need than ours to cherish its contemporaries. We are sharply cut off from our predecessors. A shift in the scale – the war, the sudden slip of masses held in position for ages – has shaken the fabric from top to bottom, alienated us from the past and made us perhaps too vividly conscious of the present. Every day we find ourselves doing, saying, or thinking things that would have been impossible to our fathers ... No age can have been more rich than ours in writers determined to give expression to the differences which separate them from the past and not to the resemblances which connect them with it. (*E* III. 357, IV. 238)

However much *Mrs Dalloway* itself shows a keen consciousness of the present, and however conspicuous the technical and formal differences are of Woolf's own writing from traditional modes, her novels and essays work to restore 'cut off' communications with the past and to appease that sense of modern alienation. This had been the case ever since a Post-Victorian consciousness began to declare itself in her writing around 1916. In an essay of 1917 she again notes the novel pleasures of contemporary writing (remarking 'No age of literature is so little submissive to authority as ours, so free from the dominion of the great'), but once more as a preface to turning back to the classics with reading skills sharpened by this sojourn among the moderns, in which case we shall find 'New books may be more stimulating and in some ways more suggestive than the old, but they do not give us that absolute certainty of delight' afforded by masterpieces of the past (*E* II. 59–60). This essay seeking to accommodate tastes for both new and old is significantly entitled 'Hours in a Library', the title of Leslie Stephen's essay collections of 1874 and 1876, and again evokes throughout the leisurely reading practices of a past age.

Allen McLaurin has discussed the frequency of Woolf's use of the verb 'cut' in *Mrs Dalloway*, but distinguishes the eponymous protagonist from the classifying and categorising the word can imply: 'she . . . hesitates to have any clear-cut opinion of her "character" or that of her friends: "she would not say of anyone in the world now that they were this or were that. She felt very young; at the same time unspeakably aged"'.[23] Clarissa's sense of herself as a 'mist' embodies a far-reaching and gendered position of continuity and integration in Woolf that is the antithesis to male activities of 'cutting', represented in this novel by Peter Walsh and his pocket-knife, desirous though incapable through his relationship with Daisy of sundering himself from the past. The First World War is a gigantic act of 'cutting off' to be countered, while other strategies, such as Woolf's aesthetic of 'crepuscularity', with its desire to 'dissolve' the 'clear-cut features of the tragic, the comic' and so forth (*E* III. 33), indicate how pervasive her resistance to categorisation and 'the line drawn tightly round' (*JR*, p. 100) is. At the start of *To the Lighthouse* James proves his modernist and masculine potential in a telling manner: 'his mother, watching him guide his scissors neatly round the refrigerator, imagined him all red and ermine on the Bench or directing a stern and momentous enterprise in some crisis of public affairs' (*TL*, p. 7); one of Woolf's early memories of her father (who in the guise of Mr Ramsay also comes to be associated with modernity in the novel) is that he 'cut [animals] out of paper with a pair of scissors' to amuse his children (*E* I. 127). At the end of the novel James 'finds' his womanly affiliation (and thus androgyne status) in looking back at and acknowledging the 'misty-looking' lighthouse of memory as an integral part of its identity. The form of *Mrs Dalloway* itself, the first of Woolf's novels not to be divided into chapters, embodies the resistance to segmentation underlined by her quoting approvingly a passage from Augustine Birrell in a review of 1920: 'Life . . . is not a series of episodes . . . but consists in the *passage of Time; of perpetually stepping towards the westering sun*' (italics in original). It is the 'duty of the biographer' (in Woolf's words) to try 'to record the changes wrought by the chiming hours' (in Birrell's), an obligation to the continuous and to continuity again suggestive for *Mrs Dalloway*.[24]

The War in 'How It Strikes' is a major factor in the contemporary sense of feeling cut off from the past, though by no means the only one. If it brought the Victorian period into focus because of the definitive ending to the old order of things it might seem to represent, Woolf was unwilling to grant what she called 'this preposterous masculine fiction' such significance as a historical landmark (*L* II. 76). Woolf's 1916 review of John Harris's study of Samuel Butler (see p. 12) suggests that it is writers and artists like Butler himself who create periods and instigate historical change, a change already evident in both social and aesthetic terms in the later years of the pre-War period, instanced in the celebrated statement that 'on or about December 1910 human character changed' ('Character in Fiction', *E* III. 421). In this latter essay Woolf again sees Butler as one of the key instigators of such change – in his books 'the first signs of it are recorded' – and she illustrates it by comparing the subterranean life of the Victorian cook with her counterpart in the Georgian era, 'a creature of sunshine and fresh air' (*E* III. 422). In *Mrs Dalloway*

Peter Walsh's sense of a 'shift' in things since his youth is similarly illustrated by 'a housemaid's laughter', together with other 'intangible things you couldn't lay your hands on' (*MD*, p. 178). If there is a sense of a new, post-War order in social terms which Woolf can welcome (though it would be naïve to see the reference to a liberalisation in master–servant relations as evidence of Woolf's democratic aspirations, as some critics have), it is important that this is subsumed within a deeper affirmation of continuity that is itself both social and aesthetic. If human character did change in December 1910, the same essay later tells us that Mrs Brown 'is eternal, Mrs Brown is human nature, Mrs Brown changes only on the surface...' (*E* III. 430), just as 'How It Strikes' relates 'surface' change to the 'continuity and calm [that] are in the depths'. *Mrs Dalloway*, we have suggested, embraces the new not in isolation from the old (as the protagonists seem tragically forced to do in *Jacob's Room*), but in a manner that affirms continuity through the synchronic 'chiming in unison' of different times, rather than the 'striking' of the present moment alone.

But we should now consider the novel's examination of the social and political order in greater detail, and explore how far in this respect Woolf viewed the War as an opportunity for a break with the past, as some critics maintain. An important question here is to what extent *Mrs Dalloway* embodies a radical or future-oriented politics in its approach to questions of social class: discussing the novel in her diary, Woolf noted 'I want to criticise the social system, & to show it at work, at its most intense', but then added 'But here I may be posing' (*D* II. 248). Alex Zwerdling has influentially argued that in *Mrs Dalloway* 'Woolf gives us a picture of a class impervious to change in a society that desperately needs or demands it, a class that worships tradition and settled order but cannot accommodate the new and disturbing' (*Virginia Woolf and the Real World*, p. 124).[25] The importance of a cultural tradition, together with the difficulties of accommodating 'the new and disturbing', are, however, key elements in Woolf's own outlook at this time, as we have argued; similarly, Elaine Showalter's claim in her Introduction to *Mrs Dalloway* that the relative absence of the impact of the War on the principal characters in the novel is Woolf's way of signalling 'the emotional repression of English polite society' leaves out of consideration Woolf's own desire to subordinate the impact of the War, referred to above (*MD*, p. xliii). Zwerdling suggests that the novel offers a positive recuperation of war in social terms: 'If the war had any justification, it could be only as a liberating force likely to transform society and human relations. Perhaps the brave new world it might help to bring to birth could make one believe in its necessity' (p. 123). However creditworthy Zwerdling's desire is that the novel should say such things, *Mrs Dalloway* nowhere suggests that the War does or can have any such 'justification', just as it refuses to deal in any vision of a 'brave new world'; to understand Woolf's true radicalism, Lyndall Gordon has suggested, 'it is essential to see in her resistance to war an outrage so complete that, taking a line more extreme than anti-war poets, she refused to treat war at all'.[26] This comment is perhaps most applicable to the position of 'indifference' outlined in *Three Guineas*, given that *Mrs Dalloway* certainly does treat the War, or at least its effects, even within a narrative that refuses the War's power to alienate characters from their pasts. But even the major 'symptom' of war, Septimus Smith, has a broader function in the novel for Woolf that draws on the experience of her own youthful illnesses and lessens his historical specificity: 'I adumbrate here a study of insanity & suicide: the world seen by the sane & the insane side by side' (*D* II. 207), a comment that makes no reference to shell shock and suggests that Septimus's prime polemical function in the novel is to voice Woolf's own hatred and distrust of the male medical establishment, and the controls it employs, rather than to upbraid a society bent on the repression of war-memory (which Richard Dalloway in any case is not, *MD*, p. 126).[27] There are also problems in using Septimus as evidence of Woolf's supposed desire to 'transform' society in picturing him as a representative 'tragic figure of the class system', in Showalter's words (*MD*, p. xxxix).[28] Using Septimus as a key to Woolf's focus on the War as a pretext for transformation in *Mrs Dalloway* sits oddly alongside her later and somewhat dismissive pondering 'whether the book would have been better' without 'the mad chapters' (*D* II. 321), as well as her sense that her next novel, *To the Lighthouse*, was 'easily the best' of her books, 'occupied with more interesting things than Mrs D. & not complicated with all that desperate accompaniment of madness' (*D* III. 117).

If the housemaid's laughter, or the sunny nature of the Georgian cook, are welcomed by Woolf as signs of a more benign social order, such comments continue to recognise the hierarchical master–servant system within which this liberalisation occurs. Showalter's and Zwerdling's desire to cast Woolf as a democrat looking to the future rather than the past can certainly find some support, especially in her later writing, but the case of *Mrs Dalloway*, heavily weighted towards retrospect, is hardly the best place to go searching for it. There is no need to dwell here on Woolf's lifelong susceptibility to the 'charm' of the aristocracy (*D* I. 309), which long predated her encountering the 'perfect lady, with all the dash & courage of the aristocracy' in the person of Vita Sackville-West (*D* II. 313), especially as this has been thoroughly treated in Sonya Rudikoff's study of Woolf's 'conflicting identifications',[29] but comments in the memoir 'Am I a Snob?' of 1936 – 'the aristocrat is freer, more natural, more eccentric than we are'; 'I want coronets; but they must be old coronets; coronets that carry land with them and country houses; coronets that breed simplicity, eccentricity, ease ...' – enforce precisely the sense of the importance of 'breeding' for Woolf which has already been evident in her comments on Joyce (*MOB*, p. 208).[30] Woolf's attraction towards the aristocratic nature is inseparable from her 'lifelong enchantment with ancestral houses', as Rudikoff puts it (p. 118), and is clearly seen in her conflating the glamour of Vita Sackville-West with that of Knole. A comment in a review of 1917, 'The House of Lyme', turns to such houses, just as Woolf turned to the literary tradition, in the search for continuity in time of war: 'In a world which seems bent on ruin and oblivion we cannot refuse a feeling of affectionate respect for the courage with which such old houses still confront life, cherish its traditions, and are a sanctuary for the lovely wreckage of the past' (*E* II. 100).

While the Dalloways are not themselves aristocrats, Clarissa's party is attended by several, just as Woolf's own diary from the period of *Mrs Dalloway* is full of engagements with Lady Colefax, the 'free & easy' Lady Horner and the rest (II. 275). This is the type of circle Woolf's novel is, according to Zwerdling, 'sharply critical' of, and which is seen as 'living on borrowed time' (*Virginia Woolf and the Real World*, pp. 120–1), a view Showalter endorses (*MD*, p. xv). According to the latter, upon Clarissa's party 'all that is snobbish and artificial about London society converges ... Here are gathered the pompous, the frivolous, the narrow-minded and the moribund' (*MD*, p. xliv), a sweeping condemnation and categorisation that contradicts Woolf's own sense within the pairings she planned the novel around (past/present, sanity/insanity, life/death) that the party 'expresses life, in every variety' to offset (though pay heed to) Septimus's death.[31] Woolf is in fact critical of prejudices that would condemn the upper echelons of society so categorically – 'which is worse – Mayfair snobbery, or Bloomsbury?' she asks, in response to a member of the latter circle who denied that aristocrats can be intelligent (*L* III. 241). One of the short story spin-offs from *Mrs Dalloway*, 'The Man Who Loved His Kind', is a withering examination of the hatred experienced for the 'fine ladies and gentlemen' at the party by the self-proclaimed 'man of the people' Prickett Ellis, consumed, rather like Doris Kilman in the novel, by a sense of his own insecurity (*CSF*, p. 196).

'The doubtful point', Woolf noted in her diary, 'is I think the character of Mrs Dalloway. It may be too stiff, too glittering & tinsely' (15 October 1923, II. 272).[32] If this reflection seems to offer support to Showalter's accusation of artificiality above, we should be hesitant to accept that reservations or uncertainties about individual characters are symptomatic, with Woolf, of wholesale class judgements. As always in her fiction, she crucially attends to the individual case; indeed, in 'Character in Fiction' she famously takes Wells and Galsworthy to task for taking their eyes off individuals and making them representatives of a social class and pretexts for the discussion of class issues (*E* III. 428). In a letter to Philip Morrell following the novel's publication, she says of two members of the establishment she depicts, 'I meant Richard Dalloway to be liked. Hugh Whitbread to be hated' (*L* III. 195), and the attitudes of figures like Lady Bruton and old Miss Parry can be satirised by Woolf without our subscribing to Zwerdling's claim in *Virginia Woolf and the Real World* that in the novel we see depicted an entire 'class ... living on borrowed time' (p. 121). It is ironic, to put it mildly, that insensitivity to the individual case is precisely a feature of Zwerdling's critique of Clarissa's circle – 'The ability to translate individual human beings into manageable social categories is one of the marks of the governing-class mentality Woolf examines in the novel' (p. 128) – when Zwerdling himself can think only in terms of 'manageable social categories': in this case, that of the 'governing class'.[33] Thus Richard Dalloway, while a Conservative MP, is the most socially troubled and conscientious figure in the novel, his climactic moment coming when he is seized with the desire to go home and tell Clarissa he loves her, the fullness of his present happiness again 'chiming' with his sense of the past:

> he liked continuity; and the sense of handing on the traditions of the past. It was a great age in which to have lived. Indeed, his own life was a miracle; let him make no mistake about it; here he was, in the prime of life, walking to his house in Westminster to tell Clarissa that he loved her. Happiness is this, he thought. (*MD*, p. 128)

The tribute to tradition is prompted by his passing Buckingham Palace with its statue of Queen Victoria on his walk home, triggering his memory of seeing the Queen 'in her horn spectacles driving through Kensington' (*MD*, p. 128). Dalloway is no political reactionary, however; his radical activities include collecting evidence about police malpractices, 'champion[ing] the down-trodden and follow[ing] his instincts in the House of Commons', showing a concern with refugees and having views on the injustices of our 'detestable social system' (*MD*, pp. 126–7), though there is no warrant to think that he aspires to any reform of the latter that interferes with rank and property. The use of interior monologue does indeed permit the exposé of the complacencies of the private mind (as indeed does access to Woolf's own diaries), and perhaps we can agree that there is some 'emotional repression' (or insufficient survivor guilt) in his thinking 'it was a great age in which to have lived' when 'thousands of poor chaps' had been 'shovelled together' (*MD*, p. 126). Even so, Richard Dalloway seems to embody an awareness of the political needs of the moment that is yet mindful of continuity and the claims of the past, and as such might be said to justify Woolf's own liking of him and to embody her own Post-Victorianism.[34]

Mrs Dalloway can indeed be called 'a consciously "modern" novel',[35] but in what ways it is socially forward-looking is open to doubt – that mix of 'the experimental and the nostalgic', which Hermione Lee finds in *To the Lighthouse*, seems similarly apparent in it (Introduction, *TL*, p. xxxviii). Showalter argues that the menopausal theme underlines how Clarissa, 'by the novel's end ... has come, if only fleetingly, to accept the loss of the "triumphs of youth" and to face the next stage of her life' (*MD*, p. xiv). But at 'the novel's end' we are precisely left with a restaging of the triumph of Clarissa's youth, as we have seen, in a carefully chosen climax, and the idea of a project of reconstruction – 'the next stage of her life' – seems as problematic as the idea of political reconstruction which some critics, including Showalter, have seen working in it. The future Clarissa anticipates is rather the solitary stoicism represented by the old woman glimpsed through the window during her party (*MD*, pp. 203–4), or even the apocalyptic vision sounded several times through the novel 'when London is a grass-grown path and all those hurrying along the pavement this Wednesday morning are but bones with a few wedding rings mixed up in their dust and the gold stoppings of innumerable decayed teeth' (*MD*, pp. 17–18). Clarissa's mending of her dress, drawing the green folds together with her needle, is compared with the motion of the sea, 'which sighs collectively for all sorrows, and renews, begins, collects, lets fall', a sigh that echoes the dirge from Shakespeare's *Cymbeline* that itself recurs like a wave throughout the novel, 'Fear no more the heat o' the sun' (*MD*, p. 43). *Mrs Dalloway*, as is frequently the case in Woolf, is much more animated by ideas of the past than of the future, and it would be wrong to call it a 'post-War' novel with any implication that it seizes on the period as the opportunity for a radical new beginning that would reject the old. To call it Post-Victorian, however, does bring out the way it embraces a sense of the contemporary that yet needs to retain ties with the past.[36] The greater welcome to, and enjoyment of, the contemporary in *Mrs Dalloway* is only possible, indeed, where we have a past that can 'back' the present and prevent it from splintering, so that it becomes 'a thousand times deeper than the present when it presses so close that you can feel nothing else' (*A Sketch*, p. 98).

Among the most prominent critics who, in maintaining an exclusively progressive Woolf, deny her retrospective affiliations are Sandra Gilbert and Susan Gubar, who consistently seek out 'annunciations' or other epiphanic tropes in her writing that herald 'the birth of the new'.[37] Thus Clarissa's final appearance to Peter in *Mrs Dalloway* is a channel for what is 'a virtually divine grace' which goes much beyond its effect on Peter alone and 'regenerates the postwar world' (II. 318). Although such a description endorses the Beatrice theme in the novel discussed above, the complete silence in Gilbert and Gubar's lengthier discussion of *Mrs Dalloway* (III. 21–8) about the Bourton episodes and the two temporalities which run side by side throughout and here fuse climatically, indicates the effacing of the Woolfian retrospect that seems a necessary casualty in the establishing of a future-oriented, 'regenerative' Woolf. In passing from the discussion of *Mrs Dalloway* between volumes two and three of *No Man's Land* the baton of regeneration seems to pass in fact from Clarissa to her daughter Elizabeth ('the fated icon of the new', III. 27), as if the latter's youth is a necessary element in this iconic status. But Elizabeth's commitment to her father, her dogs and the country, stressed at the end of the novel (*MD*, pp. 206, 213), underlines a patrician identity that makes her only doubtfully serviceable as such an icon, and as Elizabeth Abel argues, Woolf's offering 'little access' to Clarissa's daughter's consciousness points the difference between a past that is surrounded with an 'aureole' and a future largely gestured towards in silence.[38] The difficulty of making Woolf reveal more of this future is repeatedly felt in Gilbert and Gubar's frustration that 'annunciations and epiphanies', or 'oblique glimpses' of it, are all she can give us, thus endorsing their claim that Woolf 'could barely begin to imagine the details of the revolution she desired' (11. 46–7). Alex Zwerdling's criticism is quoted to back their own: 'What eluded [Woolf] was any understanding of how the present could conceivably lead to the future she imagined' (*Virginia Woolf and the Real World*, p. 327), a critical alliance that does not acknowledge Zwerdling's recognition of the deep strain of conservatism in Woolf which is, however, unaccountably in abeyance in his discussion of *Mrs Dalloway*. The eager anticipation of a Woolfian 'revolutionary' future inevitably creates its own sense of betrayal, and this is occasioned by not attending sufficiently to the manifest constraints on such a future arising from Woolf's commitment to continuity and various forms of inheritance. Even where change is desirable it is often approached with caution, while the more utopian imaginings of others are treated with some scepticism, as we shall see. Woolf's desire for change, in fact, often smacks of the gradualism of George Eliot, a point to be pursued.

On the other hand it would also be mistaken, if more justifiably, to see Woolf purveying no more than retrospect in *Mrs Dalloway*, and in Abel's welcome emphasis on the prelapsarian importance of Bourton, contrasted with the fall into a post-War modernity, there is the converse danger that the novel's nostalgia might stifle any sense of the importance of the contemporary and *Mrs Dalloway*'s insistence on 'synchronising' past and present, with the Post-Victorian becoming merely the neo-Victorian. Thus whereas Abel sees Bourton as a lost pastoral world presided over by the mother, or the mother-substitute Sally Seton, a 'female-centered world anterior to heterosexual bonds' (*Virginia Woolf and the Fictions of Psychoanalysis*, p. 34), the War marks the 'turn from feminine to masculine dispensations', the novel thus charting its protagonist's progression 'from a pastoral female world to an urban culture governed by men' (pp. 41–2). Although this does pick up pertinently on Woolf's worries about a masculine modernity inimical to romance and sentiment, it ignores Clarissa's sense of the exhilaration of the contemporary city – 'I love walking in London ... it's better than walking in the country' (*MD*, p. 6) – and forces too severe a distinction between the natural and the urban where the latter scene is in any case characterised by city parks and flower-shops. While there are serious doubts about seeing Clarissa (as with Katharine Hilbery) as urban flâneuse, it is significant that over the evolution of the novel Woolf did make her feel more at home in the modern city, and thus more even-handed in her sympathies with the two eras the novel brings together. Thus in 'Mrs Dalloway in Bond Street', a short story published in July 1923 that represents some first thoughts for the novel, Woolf gave the memory of Queen Victoria in her horn spectacles to Clarissa rather than, as above, to Richard, and made her far more anti-modern in her criticisms of contemporary painting and fashion – 'For all the great things one must go to the past, she thought' (*CSF*, pp. 153–5). In the novel this attitude of denigrating the contemporary, which echoes rather strongly that of Mrs Hilbery in *Night and Day*, is absent from Clarissa in her enthusiasm for the scene before her eyes – 'what she loved was this, here, now, in front of her' (*MD*, p. 9).

In making the modern world a scene solely of loss and restriction in Clarissa's life, with the War 'as a vast historical counterpart' to the male intervention of marriage that prevents any return to the Edenic (p. 41), Abel at once demonises the contemporary and grants the disjunctive power of the War to determine not only historical change but to disable the imagination's power to access the past, a power Woolf insists on again and again in her writing. As Abel says, Bourton may have been 'inherited, significantly, by a male relative' and thus be out of Clarissa's actual reach (p. 31), but just as Jack Hills and Stella's engagement scene in 1896 'still seems to me like a real thing, unsmothered by the succeeding years', so Bourton remains accessible to the mind in a manner more powerful than its physical accessibility alone would permit, in the same way that Clarissa repeatedly 'comes to' Peter at critical times in the spirit if not the body (*MD*, p. 168). Moreover, there is a danger in reading *Mrs Dalloway* in an overly Clarissa-centric manner, as it were: to adopt a famous moment in George Eliot, why always Clarissa? As noted, Richard Dalloway achieves his own sense of past/present integration, and Peter Walsh, to whom the last, climactic experience in the novel belongs, achieves a more ecstatic communion with his past self.

Nevertheless, we do have the suggestion in *Mrs Dalloway*, and certainly elsewhere in Woolf, of the gendering of historical period which Abel discusses, whereby a 'pervasively masculine present' is contrasted with 'a mythically feminine past' (p. 42). The main casualty of this split is arguably not Clarissa, but Peter, who seems to represent to a conspicuous degree both modern manliness (with his penknife and ongoing predatory sexuality) and Victorian feeling (with his tears and swoons). For the most part an unsuccessful androgyne, we might feel, one who is sundered by rather than able to integrate his two sides, and in his 'unfitness' for the modern world – with no job and little stability, literally a 'hanger-on' – a warning of the redundancy of passion and individuality in a world of efficiency and conformism.[39] As will become plainer in *To the Lighthouse*, Woolf in the 1920s does tend to equate the productive element of the Victorian with the mother, and the mother with the idyllic garden; as Abel notes, 'a casual party guest's brief comparison of Clarissa to her mother "walking in a garden" brings sudden tears to Clarissa's eyes' (p. 34, *MD*, p. 193), and right at the end of her life Woolf will create the memorable tableau of a summer's afternoon 'dream' of her mother in the garden of Little Holland House (*MOB*, pp. 86–7). Even while Woolf insists on synchronising the garden of the past with the city of the present in *Mrs Dalloway*, there remains the sense of antithesis between the two; an antithesis that is overcome, if not permanently, in her next novel *To the Lighthouse*, where the idea of synchronicity is replaced with a more consolidated project of integration.

CHAPTER 3

Integration: To the Lighthouse

In May 1924, Woolf's Post-Victorianism was given iconic expression in the famous photograph of her wearing her mother's dress that appeared in *Vogue* magazine.¹ As Jane Garrity observes, given *Vogue*'s 'couture mission' to register 'every radical shift in fashion in the 1920s – from short skirts and dropped waists to geometric futurist fabrics and shingled hair', such an image seems odd in the extreme.² While Garrity recognises that the illustration shows 'a modernist who is haunted by her Victorian past' (p. 202), she prefers to explain it at the level of *Vogue*'s own blend of the chic and the conservative, its desire to reconstitute 'the modern woman as an object of sanctified domesticity' (p. 204), though this fails to account for the exceptional nature of the image which Garrity herself calls attention to. This also denies Woolf's own agency in the matter, a Victorian splash in the heart of a modern style which, as we have seen, Woolf was notably resistant to.³ As a publisher as well as writer, Woolf works to keep the Victorian image alive in the 1920s, bringing out works like *Victorian Photographs of Famous Men and Fair Women* (Hogarth, 1926), and constantly soliciting books from friends and acquaintances that memorialise the past. One of these, Jane Ellen Harrison's *Reminiscences of a Student's Life* published by Hogarth in 1925, resembles Woolf's own position in its author's being 'advanced in my views [and] eager to be in touch with all modern movements' (p. 12), while at the same time admitting to a 'conservative' fondness for Victorian literature, deportment and a 'miscellaneous' system of education where 'I might choose what poetry I wished ... Nowadays it seems you learn only what is reasonable and relevant' (pp. 22–4). Like Woolf, Harrison has a grudging admiration for *Ulysses* (pp. 25–6), but is 'proud to have known' Tennyson, whom, together with Anne Ritchie, she particularly commemorates (pp. 46–9). Her belief that the best education is to 'let children ... browse freely in a good library' (pp. 37–8) continues a laissez-faire pedagogy that Woolf will also espouse in her later writing.

Of all Woolf's novels *To the Lighthouse* (1927) works out her vision of the Post-Victorian – which is also Lily Briscoe's at the end of the novel (*TL*, p. 226) – most fully. While it is to date Woolf's most explicit critique and rejection of Victorian patriarchy and the toll it takes on the women and children of the Victorian family, and thus sits alongside the intensifying feminist concerns of Woolf's writing at the end of the 1920s, particularly *A Room of One's Own* (1929), it is also keenly nostalgic for a set of values associated with Victorian culture. The Ramsays' marriage, deeply unequal yet deeply affecting, assumes not only an archetypal status, with its partners becoming 'the symbols of marriage, husband and wife' (*TL*, p. 80), but, in the mystical rite of remarriage that Lily's painting performs at the end of the novel, a symbol of partnership and union that reconciles a range of oppositions, including that between key values of the Victorian and the modern. A similar symbolism of marriage is presented in Woolf's two succeeding works, *Orlando* (1928) and *A Room*. Lily's complicated and conflicted response to the Ramsays, where she is 'made to feel violently two opposite things at the same time' (*TL*, p. 111), is composed in the completion of her painting, a creating of wholeness out of division that Woolf indeed specifies as a prime function of the artwork. This does not mean that *To the Lighthouse* ignores the marital, social and economic injustices that Victorian women laboured under, and from henceforth attention to these becomes more marked in Woolf's work. Lily is determined to cast off the shackles of Victorian marriage at the same time as she acknowledges in her habit of retrospection qualities which the modern world will be impoverished by rejecting.[4]

The claim that *To the Lighthouse* should be read in terms of a 'conquering feminism', in the words of Jane Goldman,[5] ignores this project of reconciliation in reading the novel from a position resembling that modern state of 'sex-consciousness' which Woolf criticises in *A Room* (p. 103). Woolf deplores this even as she continues to insist on the disadvantages women writers and artists labour under, and while her analysis of women's subordination has quite reasonably occupied the minds of many modern readers, it is important to stress, once again, how one-sided readings are that pay no attention to the Woolfian retrospect except to see it as an act of negation. Surveying some responses to the novel, Goldman disputes the proposition that 'the old order values of Mrs Ramsay are preserved rather than challenged by Lily Briscoe's art in the post-war part of the novel' (*Feminist Aesthetics*, p. 169), but this prolonging of an either/or understanding of *To the Lighthouse* seems inappropriate to Woolf, given that complex of desire and rejection, preservation and challenge her writing constantly shows towards 'the old order', and that Lily's painting here strives to negotiate. In developing her position, Goldman tends to misrepresent Peter Knox-Shaw's elegiac reading of the novel, which far from seeing in it Woolf's simple 'reinstatement ... of the past' in Goldman's phrase (p. 169), talks of the novel's upholding ideas of progress and 'cultural growth' which do not, however, repudiate the claims of the past and the importance of a sense of historical continuity: 'of all modernist texts [*To the Lighthouse*] is perhaps the one that most lucidly illustrates the need for a *critical retrieval* of the past' (my emphasis).[6]

The ambivalent response of new to old permeates the novel, announced at the outset in the younger generation's questioning of their mother's code of 'deference and chivalry' at the same time as their sensing that 'there was something in this of the essence of beauty, which called out the manliness in their girlish hearts, and made them ... honour her strange severity, her extreme courtesy' (*TL*, pp. 10–11). Likewise, towards the end of the novel Cam and James are tormented by a 'division of feeling' towards their father (*TL*, p. 184) composed of love, respect, hatred and resentment, a brew that mirrors Woolf's own conflicted state with regard to Leslie Stephen described in *A Sketch of the Past* (*MOB*, p. 108). Qualities like chivalry and courtesy – 'the old usages and politenesses of society' that Eliot's writing was so intolerant of – are in Woolf's eyes alien to the modern temper, and as we have seen she was worried that *To the Lighthouse*, like her previous works, would be accused of 'sentimentality', even 'Victorian' sentimentality, and not simply in its parts: 'Is the whole theme open to that charge?' she asked herself (*D* III. 106, 110, 134). By the 'whole theme' Woolf may be worrying, as Clarissa Dalloway had done, that the very act of 'thinking of the past' in the vibrant immediacy of the modern world, as memorably described in the final section of *Orlando* (pp. 211–2), is 'sentimental' (*MD*, p. 39). One passage that Woolf may have seen as particularly open to the charge is the ending of Part 1, where the picture in *Reminiscences* of her parents' marriage as 'triumphant', as embodying 'the highest and most perfect harmony', with its mutual exchange of worship and honour (*MOB*, pp. 33–4, 37), underlies the male provision of veneration and the female provision of beauty in the Ramsays' match ('You are more beautiful than ever. And she felt herself very beautiful'). This leads to a climactic fulfilment – 'Nothing on earth can equal this happiness' – which is Mrs Ramsay's 'triumph', offsetting Lily's triumph with her painting at the end of Part 3 (*TL*, p. 134). One way, Woolf tartly notes in *A Room*, in which the moderns avoid any charge of sentimentality is demonstrated in Mary Carmichael's novel, where the fear 'of being called "sentimental"' results in a 'terseness' ('she remembers that women's writing has been called flowery and so provides a superfluity of thorns', *RO*, p. 73) that characterises contemporary writing generally, and that Woolf's romancing plainly parts company with. It is not difficult to find critics who are unwilling to grant the romance of the Ramsays' marriage, or who are silent on any possibilities of 'happiness' it might provide – even if Woolf's own words suggest otherwise, it presumably smacks of a continuing sentimentality to take them at face-value. Thus Jane Goldman, whom I return to at greater length below in outlining my differences with her stimulating account of Woolf's 'feminist aesthetics' (particularly in relation to Woolf's use of light and shade), sees the finale of Part 1 of *To the Lighthouse* as essentially recapitulating the presence of the patriarchal shadow in which Mrs Ramsay 'languishes' throughout (*Feminist Aesthetics*, p. 176).

As noted previously, whatever the deficiencies of the Victorian period for Woolf, it provided a hospitable climate for 'the beautiful, the noble, the poetic', compared with 'our conscious and much more critical day' (*E* II. 171–2), features which were particularly apposite to Victorian romance. At the outset of *A Room of One's Own* Woolf contrasts the post-War luncheon party she is attending with its pre-War equivalent, noting that although 'people would have said precisely the same things . . . they would have sounded different, because in those days they were accompanied by a sort of humming noise, not articulate, but musical, exciting, which changed the value of the words themselves'. Woolf identifies that 'humming' with a verse from Tennyson's *Maud* on the one hand ('There has fallen a splendid tear / From the passion-flower at the gate . . .'), and one from Christina Rossetti's 'A Birthday' on the other:

> My heart is like a singing bird
>   Whose nest is in a water'd shoot;
> My heart is like an apple tree
>   Whose boughs are bent with thick-set fruit;
> My heart is like a rainbow shell
>   That paddles in a halcyon sea;
> My heart is gladder than all these
>   Because my love is come to me.   (*RO*, p. 11)

The contrast, prompted by the sight of a Manx cat without a tail ('It is strange what a difference a tail makes', *RO*, p. 12), parallels other occasions where Woolf presents the Victorian period as that of a lost lyricism and passion. The words of Christina Rossetti prompt a little later in *A Room* a visionary experience of a burgeoning springtime garden at Fernham at dusk, when the 'excitable heart' responds to 'the beauty of the world which is so soon to perish' and which thereby has 'two edges, one of laughter, one of anguish, cutting the heart asunder'. The romantic vision indeed perishes, abruptly routed by the arrival of a 'plain gravy soup' which signals the spartan conditions of the women's college and the reality of a present time where economic antagonisms and rivalry between men and women — a component of the strident sex-consciousness of the age

(RO, p. 89) – vanquish the possibility of any romantic 'illusion' in their relations persisting (RO, p. 15). Woolf returns to the lines from Tennyson and Rossetti at the end of *A Room*, in discussing the relationship between the protagonists of 'a new novel by Mr A', Alan and Phoebe:

> As he no longer hums under his breath, 'There has fallen a splendid tear from the passion-flower at the gate', when Phoebe crosses the beach, and she no longer replies, 'My heart is like a singing bird whose nest is in a water'd shoot', when Alan approaches what can he do? Being honest as the day and logical as the sun, there is only one thing he can do. And that he does, to do him justice, over and over (I said, turning the pages) and over again. And that, I added, aware of the awful nature of the confession, seems somehow dull. (RO, p. 91)[7]

This dullness thus contrasts with the 'exciting' quality of the pre-War 'music'. Woolf's protest here reminds us of her dislike of the 'indecency' in Joyce (E III. 34, 434), while she goes on to argue that Alan's display of 'virility', expressed in an image that is entirely symptomatic for her of modernity – 'logical as the sun' – is an extension of the author's own in the face of the growth of the women's movement, an assertion of threatened superiority. In this climate, 'men ... are now writing only with the male side of their brains' (RO, p. 91), in contrast with a Tennysonian lyricism that harmonises with Christina Rossetti's and that illustrates what she will posit towards the end of *A Room* as the androgynous nature. Conversely, the protest of women against men, inevitable and necessary in the economic sphere, results in a state of sex-consciousness fatal to the artwork and which Lily's painting, with its own 'androgynous' reconciliation, rejects, while the Ramsays' marriage provides Lily with the stimulus towards such reconciliation even if its injustices remain apparent. *A Room of One's Own*, as an explicit investigation of gender injustice, does however show some willingness to question, or at least puzzle over, its own nostalgia, as we shall see.[8]

Woolf's identification of the Victorian past with a romance lacking in modernity is illustrated in *To the Lighthouse* by the love between Minta and Paul that is staged in the first part of the novel, investing the two of them with a 'golden haze' and a 'glow' (*TL*, pp. 107, 110), a restaging once more of the romance between Stella and Jack Hills (and between Clarissa and Peter Walsh). Though none of these relationships survives, for different reasons, and although Lily is sardonic about the banal married outcome of that of the Rayleys, her memory of the 'splendour' of their youthful love, embodied in Paul, survives unabated:

> for a sight, for a glory it surpassed everything in her experience, and burnt year after year like a signal fire on a desert island at the edge of the sea, and one had only to say 'in love' and instantly, as happened now, up rose Paul's fire again. (*TL*, p. 191)

The memory of Paul's ravening 'fire' both repels and intoxicates Lily, as it does in her original experience and analysis of it during the dinner-table scene in Part 1: 'It is so beautiful, so exciting, this love, that I tremble on the verge of it ... also it is the stupidest, the most barbaric of human passions ...' (*TL*, p. 111). The dinner becomes an ambiguous celebration of love's 'festival': 'what could be more serious than the love of man for woman, what more commanding, more impressive ... at the same time these lovers, these people entering into illusion glittering-eyed, must be danced round with mockery, decorated with garlands' (*TL*, p. 109). This ambivalence about 'love' comprises an immemorial literary tradition, Lily's battling with her responses evoking the so-called 'battaglia dei pensieri' ('battle of conflicting thoughts') in the poetry of the *dolce stil nuovo*, as in chapter 13 of Dante's *Vita nuova*, where Dante tries to reconcile his response to love as both virtue and folly.[9] It is not the first time that Woolf's presentation of love's triumph has evoked this school of poetry, as we saw with the ending of *Mrs Dalloway*, and indeed Christina Rossetti's lyric 'My heart is like a singing bird' is indebted to the opening of one of the most famous canzoni of the school, Guido Guinizelli's 'Al cor gentil', where love takes its station in the noble heart like a bird nesting among the leaves.[10] Woolf's picking up on the significant neo-Dantesque strain in Victorian versions of love links with the memory of her mother in *A Sketch of the Past* seated 'at the head of the table underneath the engraving of Beatrice' (*MOB*, p. 84); certainly Mrs Ramsay's code of 'chivalry' and 'extreme courtesy' and the honour it inspires invests her with a medievalising aura that suggests Woolf is recalling her mother via the Pre-Raphaelite filter of Burne-Jones, for whom she sat as a model.[11] In *To the Lighthouse*, however, Woolf is at pains to stress that Mrs Ramsay is no mere courtly ideal, not even of the Angel in the House variety that represents in part the Victorian secularisation of Dante's Beatrice (Ellis, *Dante and English Poetry*, p. 106). We are therefore invited to criticise her 'highhandness', her manipulation of others to marry (*TL*, pp. 55–6), and to speculate upon her vanity (*TL*, pp. 47–8); she also broods over thoughts that would be unworthy of the 'Angel', such as a conviction of the 'sterility of men' (*TL*, p. 91) and of the 'inadequacy of human relationships' (*TL*, p. 45), displaying a pessimistic sense of 'all the poverty, all the suffering' in the world (*TL*, p. 75; cf. pp. 71, 133). In this latter mood she might be seen in relation to another medievalising discourse, the *Madonna dolorosa*, an identity that informs Lily's first painting of her with James on her knee, over whose inevitable loss of childhood happiness she broods (*TL*, p. 65). Mrs Ramsay is thus a far more complex figure than the Angel Woolf famously describes herself killing in her 1931 talk 'Professions for Women' (*DM*, 151), for the quest of Woolf's novel is not simply to kill Mrs Ramsay off but to salvage and uphold the importance of various qualities that she and the era she lived in signify in Woolf's eyes, including beauty, romance and a code of courtliness in man–woman relations that the twentieth century, as *A Room* confirms, is foolishly bent on rejecting.

Lily's sensitivity to this significance in the first part of the novel anticipates her incorporation of it into her painting at the end, though the fact that her painting will look nothing like a Burne-Jones indicates the passage of the Victorian into the Post-Victorian:

Directly one looked up and saw [the Ramsays], what [Lily] called 'being in love' flooded them. They became part of that unreal but penetrating and exciting universe which is the world seen through the eyes of love. The sky stuck to them; the birds sang through them. And, what was even more exciting, she felt, too, as she saw Mr Ramsay bearing down and retreating, and Mrs Ramsay sitting with James in the window and the cloud moving and the tree bending, how life, from being made up of little separate incidents which one lived one by one, became curled and whole like a wave which bore one up with it and threw one down with it, there, with a dash on the beach. (*TL*, p. 53)

That this world is described as 'unreal' should not encourage us to dismiss it in *To the Lighthouse*; we have seen in *Night and Day*, for example, Woolf's questioning of positivist notions of 'truth' that do not allow for inner worlds of vision, imagination and romantic 'illusion'. James's climactic encounter with the lighthouse itself represents this dichotomy and the claims of both its components, as we have argued; acknowledging that the lighthouse is in actuality a 'tower, stark and straight . . . barred with black and white', he is yet insistent that the romanticised lighthouse of memory, of the past, associated with his mother, is 'also the Lighthouse', the 'silvery, misty-looking tower with a yellow eye that opened suddenly and softly in the evening', and that it is retrievable across the years (*TL*, p. 202). The antithetical terms here, one series associated with the clear, the rational, the phallic, the day-lit and with present time, the other with the hazy, the romantic, the maternal, the evening and the past, are largely consistent with how we have seen Woolf presenting the modern–Victorian contrast hitherto. Lily, pursuing her painting of Mrs Ramsay after her death seated outside the window, a subject synonymous with 'tunnelling her way . . . into the past' (*TL*, p. 188), also incorporates into it Mr Ramsay's present-time voyage to the lighthouse, with all its associated symbolism above; her acute consciousness of and communion with the latter enterprise is encapsulated in the final line she adds to the painting, consequent on and triggered by his reaching the 'stark and straight' tower (here I dissent from exclusively matricentric readings of Lily's painting like that by Abel in *Fictions of Psychoanalysis*, pp. 82–3). The very last section of the novel opens with Lily unifying the duality of the distant, hazy view with that of the arrival – 'the Lighthouse had become almost invisible, had melted away into a blue haze, and the effort of looking at it and the effort of thinking of him landing there, which both seemed to be one and the same effort, had stretched her body and mind to the utmost' – just as the section closes with her making this unity manifest in the painting, with its consequence to her of 'extreme fatigue' (*TL*, pp. 225–6), a unity that is also, as this quotation suggests, a coming together of body and mind.

Lily's painting, and the responses to Mr and Mrs Ramsay that inform it represent the realisation of the androgynous vision Woolf later puts forward in *A Room*, based on her 'profound, if irrational, instinct in favour of the theory that the union of man and woman makes for the greatest satisfaction, the most complete happiness' (*RO*, p. 88). While, as Lisa Rado says, discussion of *To the Lighthouse* in terms of Woolfian androgyny is now considered rather passé, the subject still bears examination as Rado's own book shows, together with Ann Banfield's recent study, and what is of particular interest to me here is how Woolf uses historical periodisation to embrace the series of oppositions noted above, together with the imperative of their reconciliation.[12] Mr Ramsay is very different in some respects from the actual Leslie Stephen, as John Bicknell has pointed out,[13] but perhaps the crucial departure from biographical fact lies in his very survival into the modern era – to become indeed in the final part of the novel a personification of modernity's 'conscious and much more critical day', while Mrs Ramsay represents the series of past values noted above, so that Lily's painting ultimately figures an androgyny of historical period, a Victorian–modern unification. While working on *To the Lighthouse*, Woolf noted in her diary a meeting with Francis Birrell, who told her her father 'dominates the 20th Century' by virtue of his rationalism and agnosticism – '"He made it possible for me to have a decent life" he said. "He pulled down the whole edifice . . . [though] He never realised that if God went, morality must follow"' (*D* III. 61). Mr Ramsay, standing straight and tall in the boat as it reaches the Lighthouse, 'as if he were saying, "There is no God" . . .' (*TL*, p. 224), represents here this dominant modern position, though the stark black and white tower that is his counterpart clearly indicates the limitations of such an outlook in its precluding the imaginative and even mystical apprehension associated with Mrs Ramsay, the Madonna figure who finds herself saying (though later recanting the statement) 'We are in the hands of the Lord' in the first part of the novel (*TL*, p. 70) – just as Alan's honesty and logical mind, above, preclude him from quoting

Tennyson ('"imagination" – the quality I most admired & missed most in my father & his agnostic friends', *D* III. 246). Here the 'irrational Xtian in me', which Woolf confessed in 1926 provoked the dislike of her own husband, seems to be given voice (*D* III. 80–1).[14] Woolf describes Leslie Stephen's 'simply constructed ... black and white world' in *A Sketch of the Past*, and compares the 'type' her father represented to 'a steel engraving ... with an infinity of precise clear lines. There are no crannies or corners to catch my imagination ...' (*MOB*, pp. 115, 109); she also comments on the type's plentiful modern succession, 'like Charlie Sanger, like Goldie Dickinson – whom I knew later' (*MOB*, pp. 108–9). In contrast to how she presents her father here we remember the nostalgia for a world of 'odd corners' recorded in *Orlando* (p. 205).

Alongside Lily's marked rejection of Victorian codes of wifely subjection to a husband's labours (*TL*, p. 15), of the patriarchal tyrannising over children (*TL*, pp. 162–3) and of the Angel in the House and her rapture of self-surrender (*TL*, p. 164), there are thus critical elements to be retrieved from the Victorian era to offset the rationality and categorisation of the modern attitude, the novel thereby underlining that development of the 'heart' rather than the 'brain' in which the Victorians excelled the moderns (*L* II. 391). This is a difficult attitude to the past for Lily (and indeed the reader) to negotiate, with all its contradictions, though Woolf felt that the ability to harbour such oppositions, rather than adopt the security of categorisation, was precisely a feature of the womanly mind; thus in the essay 'On Being Ill' (1926) she talks about women 'in whom the obsolete exists so strangely side by side with anarchy and newness' (*E* IV. 320). The womanly mind had a 'subtlety', 'unconventionality' and 'suggestive power' missing from that of men (*RO*, pp. 100, 92), and the suggestion of the womanly as the particular site of antithesis helps ensure the choice of a woman artist in *To the Lighthouse* to embody in her painting both the 'masculine intelligence ... like iron girders spanning the swaying fabric' (*TL*, p. 115) and feminine subtlety: 'Beautiful and bright it should be on the surface, feathery and evanescent, one colour melting into another like the colours on a butterfly's wing; but beneath the fabric must be clamped together with bolts of iron' (*TL*, p. 186). Lily's sensitivity to colour and texture is also part of that precious 'creative power' handed down through generations of women as they have, in the words of *A Room*, 'sat indoors all these millions of years' attending to the look of the rooms they have been confined to (*RO*, pp. 78–9), and this is part of the specifically aesthetic component of Mrs Ramsay's 'legacy' to Lily. This power, however, needs to be structured, indeed 'curbed' (though 'not castrated: no, the opposite') if it is not to become 'too fluent', to quote Woolf's criticism of Vita Sackville-West's writing in a comment dating from the year of *To the Lighthouse*'s publication (*D* III. 126). Right at the end of her life Woolf will talk about reading her father's writing in order to 'stiffen my fluid vision' (*A Sketch*, *MOB* p. 115), and *To the Lighthouse* she estimated as a 'hard muscular book, which ... has not run out & gone flabby' (*D* III. 123); certainly its conspicuous tripartite structure represents a departure from her previous novels in foregrounding the work's emphatic design, with the two outer parts balanced round the short middle section of 'Time Passes'. Leslie Hankins notes how Woolf's theory and practice here raise issues of collusion with a 'male theoretical discourse of form' that stigmatises 'female excess',[15] but we could say that Woolf appropriates both form and fluidity as elements that women artists alone might succeed in combining, just as allowing the Victorian past to come through into the present along the narrow corridor of 'Time Passes' is an act of communication requiring the particular Post-Victorian 'permeability' of a woman's mind (as opposed to male fixations with the 'precision' of the Poundian 'clean line', above, p. 11).[16]

We shall return to Woolf's novel after discussing a similar response to the relation between Victorian and modern – that is, the need to work with the legacy of the past rather than throw it over – evident in the work Woolf published between *To the Lighthouse* and *A Room*, *Orlando* (1928). Here Woolf has some wittily caustic things to say about the nineteenth century, an era metaphorically covered by 'a turbulent welter of cloud' (an image deriving from the famous denunciation of Ruskin)[17] that bred a damp climate conducive to the riot of ivy and evergreen outside the home and the 'undistinguished fecundity' of multiple childbearing and multi-volume literary production within (*O*, pp. 156–9). The twentieth century, however, is presented in terms of an equally alarming reaction to such gloom, based, as we might have anticipated, on the provision of electric light:

> At a touch, a whole room was lit; hundreds of rooms were lit; and one was precisely the same as the other. One could see everything in the little square-shaped boxes; there was no privacy; none of those lingering shadows and odd corners that there used to be; none of those women in aprons carrying wobbly lamps which they put down carefully on this table and on that. At a touch, the whole room was bright. And the sky was bright all night long; and the pavements were bright; everything was bright. (*O*, p. 205)

This extreme of light is accompanied by a 'dryness' in the modern atmosphere in contrast to the previous damp; if everything in the nineteenth century was muffled and somnolent we now have a culture that is exposed and tense, where the dryness 'brought out the colour in everything and seemed to stiffen the muscles of the cheeks', and where Orlando's thoughts

> became mysteriously tightened and strung up as if a piano tuner had put his key in her back and stretched the nerves very taut; at the same time ... she could hear every whisper and crackle in the room so that the clock ticking on the mantelpiece beat like a hammer. (*O*, p. 206)

The narrative thread that links this migraine-inducing modernity[18] and the dark nineteenth century is Orlando's marriage to Marmaduke Bonthrop Shelmerdine. Although the 'spirit of the age' in the nineteenth century is 'antipathetic to [Orlando] in the extreme', and to yield to it means to 'submissively ... take a husband' after her previous lives of amorous freedom (*O*, pp. 167–8) (anticipating the fate of Victorian domestification that overtakes a later hero of Woolf's, Flush, in Wimpole Street) Orlando manages to effect a compromise with that spirit by finding a husband who is emphatically a figure of romance and who, in his absences voyaging round the Cape, leaves her a good deal of freedom. Thus her formal 'obeisance' to the spirit of the age contrasts with her illicit practice, prompting Woolf's comparison with smuggling goods through the customs:

> Orlando had so ordered it that she was in an extremely happy position; she need neither fight her age, nor submit to it; she was of it, yet remained herself. Now, therefore, she could write, and write she did. She wrote. She wrote. She wrote. (*O*, pp. 183–4)

To be 'of' the age yet not defined by it is the major emphasis towards which the conclusion of *Orlando* moves, and a major requirement for the writer in Woolf's eyes, involving the synchronisation in consciousness of past and present which we have examined in *Mrs Dalloway*; *A Room* also insists on how the novelist's effectiveness is impeded by the distractions of either fighting against or submitting to the age's version of the sex-war. In fact Woolf retrieves the Victorian institution of marriage in *Orlando* to a remarkable degree by enabling her heroine to flourish within it: 'she had never felt better in her life' (*O*, p. 183). This is facilitated by drawing upon the heavily romanticised version of marriage presented in *Jane Eyre*, though Woolf stages a gender reversal whereby Orlando has the accident on the moor and Marmaduke rescues her from it (*O*, pp. 170–4), a pointer to the 'androgynous' nature of both parties (' "You're a woman, Shel!" she cried. "You're a man, Orlando!" he cried', *O*, pp. 174–5). This capacity, as we saw in *A Room*, was noted as a feature of the Victorian temperament, in so far as a lyrical 'passion' can be expressed unashamedly by both sexes. Their surprise 'at the quickness of the other's sympathy', their ability to communicate states of mind either by using the scantiest of language or by bypassing it altogether, also causes them to marvel that they do not share the same sex (*O*, pp. 178–9), and is reminiscent of the moments of wordless communion built into the happiness of the Ramsays' relationship, as it also evokes in its more ecstatic episodes Jane Eyre's mystical apprehensions of the fate of Rochester (*O*, pp. 199, 226–7). As a final bonus in this lyricised Victorian scenario Orlando experiences 'all fulfilment of natural desire' in being 'safely delivered of a son' (*O*, p. 204).

Orlando ends with the return of the husband (now in an aeroplane) as *deus ex machina*:

'Here! Shel, here!' she cried, baring her breast to the moon (which now showed bright) so that her pearls glowed like the eggs of some vast moon-spider. The aeroplane rushed out of the clouds and stood over her head. It hovered above her. Her pearls burnt like a phosphorescent flare in the darkness.

And as Shelmerdine, now grown a fine sea-captain, hale, fresh-coloured, and alert, leapt to the ground, there sprang up over his head a single wild bird.

'It is the goose!' Orlando cried. 'The wild goose ...'

And the twelfth stroke of midnight sounded; the twelfth stroke of midnight, Thursday, the eleventh of October, Nineteen hundred and Twenty Eight. (*O*, pp. 227–8)

Although the entire husband–wife relationship is treated with the mock-exaggeration typical of *Orlando* as a whole, it is significant that the work ends on this note of updated Victorianism, showing the present moment working within the marital legacy of the past, and the Victorian adventurer subsumed within the modern aeroplane pilot. The wild goose that springs out of this midnight rite of union seems to represent the writer's creative power itself, or the realised artwork, as suggested by a passage in the manuscript of *A Room* which celebrates consummation within the mind thus: 'The right state of mind then is peace; The marriage night comes at last, when experience has been won ... Communication must be done at dead of night, without a mouse stirring. The writer must lie back in perfect peace & let ... ideas marry each other', the fruit of this process here being symbolised as a swan 'sailing past one down the river' rather than a wild goose (*Women & Fiction*, p. 164). The figure of the 'marriage night' also represents that need for writerly privacy which Woolf insists on more and more as the media-hungry twentieth century progresses.

Vita Sackville-West herself seems to have been completely baffled by the ending of *Orlando*, suggesting in a letter to her husband that the inclusion of Shelmerdine 'was a mistake' and that he 'does not really contribute anything either to Orlando's character or to the problems of the story, (except as a good joke at the expense of the

Victorian passion for marriage)'. She pondered the question in a further letter: 'The more I think about it, the weaker I think the end is! I simply cannot make out what was in her mind'.[19] The 'Victorian passion for marriage' operates as far more than a 'joke' in this text and in others, however, showing Woolf's characteristic reliance, in Elena Gualtieri's words, 'on marriage and heterosexual union as a prototype for the resolution of conflicts and splits'.[20] Gualtieri challenges at some length what she sees as Sackville-West's 'misreading' of the Orlando–Shelmerdine theme, arguing rather for 'the seriousness of the function' it fulfils in Woolf's text (p. 112). In establishing Orlando's security and productivity as a writer, it contrasts with the earlier elopement with Rosina Pepita that inaugurated the phase of romantic adventure in Orlando's life, thus representing Woolf's establishing her own 'respectable' identity in distinction to the bohemian and exotic, a distinction we explored in connection with *Jacob's Room*. For Gualtieri, the last section of *Orlando* 'abandons' the focus on Sackville-West as biographical subject and can be seen 'to appropriate for Woolf's own literary activities the claims to legitimacy and rightful inheritance that are embodied in Sackville-West's aristocratic lineage' (p. 113).

We can thus see how the marriage with Shelmerdine is a device that effects Woolf's typical concerns: a representation of union and fertilisation within the writer's mind, a celebration of androgyny, and, at a precisely realised modern moment ('the twelfth stroke of midnight, Thursday, the eleventh of October, Nineteen hundred and Twenty Eight') a culminating Post-Victorianism. More generally, the final tableau epitomises the insistence in *Orlando*'s concluding pages on redressing the 'terror' of a present that is cut off from, or 'unsheltered' by, the past (*O*, pp. 206, 223), and on the need (to repeat a phrase from *Night and Day*) to 'join the present on to this past' (*O*, p. 223). The unmitigated present that keeps striking Orlando on the head is bold, bright, frenetic, 'a great shock to the nervous system', that speeds the heroine in her car along the Old Kent Road so that 'after twenty minutes the body and mind were like scraps of torn paper tumbling from a sack' (*O*, pp. 211–12). It is presented as a culture of fierce visibility (echoing the situation in

Jacob's Room) – 'in this ... light everything near her showed with extreme distinctness' – and is summed up in Orlando's sight of the carpenter's hand:

> She saw with disgusting vividness that the thumb on Joe's right hand was without a finger nail and there was a raised saucer of pink flesh where the nail should have been. The sight was so repulsive that she felt faint for a moment, but in that moment's darkness, when her eyelids flickered, she was relieved of the pressure of the present. (*O*, pp. 220, 223)

The 'disgusting vividness' of the carpenter's nail-less thumb as an index of the unsheltered present is puzzling perhaps until we remember the 'raw meat' of *Ulysses* as a literary symptom of the same situation, and of the effect of contemporary writing's concentration on 'some particular person at some precise moment ... serv[ing] to make that person and that moment vivid to the utmost extreme' (*E* III. 358). *Orlando* then goes on to stress the importance of the shadow that will redress the 'pressure of the present' and its 'disgusting vividness':

> There was something strange in the shadow that the flicker of her eyes cast, something which (as anyone can test for himself by looking now at the sky) is always absent from the present – whence its terror, its nondescript character – something one trembles to pin through the body with a name and call beauty, for it has no body, is as a shadow without substance or quality of its own, yet has the power to change whatever it adds itself to. This shadow now, while she flickered her eye in her faintness in the carpenter's shop, stole out, and attaching itself to the innumerable sights she had been receiving, composed them into something tolerable, comprehensible. (*O*, p. 223)

The present's being shaded from Orlando's eyes in this way is then given metaphorical development, with the past imaged as 'a pool where things dwell in darkness so deep' situated at 'the back of [the] brain'. The country scene before Orlando's eyes now becomes simultaneously a scene of previous experience – 'the hawthorn bushes were partly ladies and gentlemen sitting with card-cases and gold-mounted canes' – summed up in a phrase that evokes James's final understanding of past–present relations in *To the Lighthouse*: 'everything was partly something else' (*O*, p. 224).[21]

Integration: To the Lighthouse

By the end of the work, Orlando herself has reached that state of multi-temporal consciousness whereby

> the most successful practitioners of the art of life ... somehow contrive to synchronise the sixty or seventy different times which beat simultaneously in every normal human system so that ... the present is neither a violent disruption nor completely forgotten in the past. (*O*, pp. 210–11)

This state of synchronicity is further imaged in Orlando's mind becoming 'a forest with glades branching here and there; things came nearer, and further, and mingled and separated and made the strangest alliances and combinations in an incessant chequer of light and shade' (*O*, p. 224). This use of the figure of a forest chiaroscuro to represent the interplay of past and present in the mind, of memory and actuality, is anticipated in *To the Lighthouse* where James's attempt to retrieve his childhood experience is akin to 'turning back among the many leaves which the past had folded in him, peering into the heart of that forest where light and shade so chequer each other that all shape is distorted' (*TL*, p. 200). Woolf's questioning of an all-illuminating modernity and presentism that would banish the shadows of the past is further emphasised by the very ending of *Orlando*, where the return of that past in the person of Shel employs dramatic chiaroscuro effects: a concluding night piece presided over by the moon, which Woolf invokes as a constant in Victorian romance, be it at Clarissa's Bourton or in the 'moonlight' that invested Stella following her engagement. Thus we see Orlando 'baring her breast to the moon (which now showed bright)', and using her moonlit pearls to guide Shel's landing. Mr and Mrs Ramsay's marriage, of course, is conducted within a pervasive context of dark and light presided over by the lighthouse, whereas in the modern portion of the novel the lighthouse becomes a stark tower, exposed by and to the daylight. Thus the lighting scheme of *Night and Day* remains emphatically in play.

I have returned at some length to the significance of Woolfian chiaroscuro because a contrary view of her aesthetics of lighting has been argued by Jane Goldman, who rightly notes how such an aesthetic relates to key political, historical and philosophical issues in Woolf's work, though Goldman's interpretation is in my opinion vulnerable on several counts. She argues that Woolf's work critiques and rejects chiaroscuro in favour of a 'predilection for the luminous', and that this links Woolf with contemporary painting, above all with the 'luminously colourful and shadowless art' of Vanessa Bell, seen as a prime exponent of 'Post-Impressionism's colourist displacement of chiaroscuro' (*Feminist Aesthetics*, pp. 14, 155).[22] Woolf rejects chiaroscuro, Goldman argues, because the interplay of dark and light is always gendered in her work; shadow is that within which women have dwelt 'these million years' (*RO*, p. 88), a shadow cast by what Goldman calls 'oppressive solar masculinity' (*Feminist Aesthetics*, p. 17). The foundation of Goldman's argument is her reading of Woolf's 1928 essay 'The Sun and the Fish', in which Woolf describes the total eclipse of the sun of 29 June 1927, which she and a group of friends made an excursion to Yorkshire to get the best sight of.

While the masculine sun slowly disappears and reappears in the eclipse Goldman argues that Woolf traces in her essay colouristic changes that take place in the Yorkshire landscape; a predominance of purple, white and green appears during 'the defeat of the sun', colours which have a special place in the suffrage movement, appearing on banners, posters and so forth (*Feminist Aesthetics*, pp. 68ff). The reappearance of the sun is not simply a return to the status quo, but signals in various ways Woolf's feminist appropriation of luminosity, her belief in and support for a politics that 'creates the world anew' (p. 88). Goldman then reads *To the Lighthouse* and *The Waves* in terms of the aesthetic symbolism she has proposed in discussing the essay. The argument is vigorous and stimulating, but it raises a good many problems. On occasion, Woolf certainly does present the light/shadow antithesis in this way – female endeavour is obscured by male authority, Cam feels 'overcast' in her father's presence (*TL*, p. 183), woman is 'this organism that has been under the shadow of the rock these million years' (*RO*, p. 77), Mrs Ramsay could feel her husband's 'mind like a raised hand shadowing her mind' (*TL*, p. 133) – though in this last instance, as the context suggests, Mr Ramsay's act is one of sheltering his wife from her mind's brooding pessimism, a contribution to that state of 'crepuscular' intimacy between them at the end of Part 1 of the novel discussed above. But shade and shadow are frequently a necessary relief from (modern) 'reality' in Woolf, and not reducible to any univocal significance of oppression, while the evocation of chiaroscuro, omnipresent in her work, is by no means sacrificed in favour of colouristic values. Nor, however much she admired Vanessa Bell's art, can Woolf's writing be equated unproblematically with the project of Post-Impressionism 'on or about' 1910. All these issues have a bearing on the subject of Woolf's Post-Victorian positioning.

Thus the 'incessant chequer of light and shade' in *Orlando* represents a mind that can hold (temporal) multiplicity together, while many instances have been traced of Woolf's fondness for 'those lingering shadows and odd corners that there used to be' as a stimulus to the imagination and the importance of romance. *Orlando* as it happens features its own 'eclipse' scene (not discussed by Goldman) where the blazing Turkish hillside on which the heroine is sitting during her gipsy period is suddenly covered by a shadow in which she has a nostalgic vision of her English country-house (akin somewhat to Rachel Vinrace's longing in Santa Marina for cloudy English meadows in *The Voyage Out*): 'She could see the deer stepping delicately from shade to shade, and could even hear the hum of insects and the gentle sighs and shivers of a summer's day in England'. Here the 'violet shades' and the 'violet shadows' show colour and shade working in unison to evoke what is, of course, the Knole of the Sackville-Wests (*O*, p. 106).[23] *Orlando*, however, is hardly mentioned in Goldman's study, as if its celebration of the aristocratic tradition casts too deep a shadow over the radicalism with which she invests Woolf, a problem we shall return to. Another telling and entirely consistent suggestion of the value of chiaroscuro occurs in the account of the carriage ride Orlando takes with Alexander Pope, a ride moving repeatedly through an alternation of bright light and deep darkness as the oil lamps that light London's streets are passed and then left behind. 'The less we see the more we believe', the narrator notes, as Orlando remarks on Pope, 'When one sees you plain, how ignoble, how despicable you are! Deformed and weakly, there is nothing to venerate in you ...', whereas in the intervals of darkness Orlando is able to lapse back into the most exaggerated tribute to Pope's genius, having mistaken a hump on the cushion for the majestic swelling of his noble brow (*O*, pp. 142–3). As one of the lamps 'blazed in her eyes' Orlando reflects how 'The light of truth beats upon us without shadow, and the light of truth is damnably unbecoming to us both', but by the time the dawn has risen and the two part in the 'equable but confused light of a summer's morning in which everything is seen but nothing is seen distinctly', proper relations between them, and an 'equable' response to Pope that avoids such stark contrasts, have been established (*O*, p. 144).

The violent opposition of light and darkness, rejected here in favour of an integration and balance between the extreme claims of 'truth' and 'falsehood' they represent, carries with it, as we have seen, a whole range of associations; chiaroscuro for Woolf, that is, light *coexisting* with shade, signifies the union of reason and imagination, the present and the past, man and woman, reality and romance, efficiency and beauty, and, in a modernity that threatens to reject all that shadow stands for as oppression, obscurantism and outmoded sentiment – a stance imaged as an inundation of electric light – the 'Victorian' functions for Woolf as a necessary counterpart, and its claims are upheld.[24] This does not mean, of course, the simple 'exoneration' of the Victorian period in Woolf's work – some pretty awful things are to be found in the shadows that need routing by a modern enlightenment – but the quest to dispel the shadow completely shows a skewed grasp of the Woolfian retrospect and of what it signifies. Woolf's habit of estimating people in terms of their personal chiaroscuro has been noted with regard to Margaret Cole in the previous chapter, and a similar early impression of Vita herself ('a little unshaded', *D* II. 307) is later revised in a series of images which invest her with a 'candle lit radiance' (*D* III. 52; compare *D* III. 204 and *L* III. 224, 226 – 'if ever a woman was a lighted candlestick, a glow, an illumination ... it was Vita'). What Woolf consistently applauds is glow rather than (modern) glare, summed up in the description of Orlando as 'a million-candled Christmas tree ... incandescent; enough to light a whole street by ... he looked as if he were burning with his own radiance, from a lamp lit within' (*O*, p. 39). The term 'incandescent' is precisely that used in *A Room of One's Own* in relation to the androgynous, 'undivided' mind (*RO*, p. 89), as it is to describe the bodily state of Stella Duckworth in love (*MOB*, p. 105). But candles, unlike a uniform electric lighting, 'light' darkness rather than 'annihilate' it, to borrow a distinction from Lynda Nead's discussion of the development of urban lighting in the nineteenth century, leaving the shadows intact and even enhancing them.[25] Such discretion extends to literary criticism itself in Woolf's eyes: 'if we want to hold a candle to some dark face in the long portrait gallery of literature there is no better illuminant than Edmund Gosse' (*M*, p. 78).

Such discretion tends not to characterise the modern spirit, with its iconoclasm (the 'smashing and crashing' of the Georgians) and intrusiveness (the 'searchlight' of Strachey's *Eminent Victorians*, or the phallic 'shaft of white light' turned on Woolf's mother), together with the modern media intrusion to be discussed in the following chapter. Moreover, the vocal equivalent to this visual exposure, a modern outspokenness famously inaugurated for Woolf by Strachey's question 'Semen?' ('Can one really say it? I thought ... With that one word all barriers of reticence and reserve went down ... Sex permeated our conversation', 'Old Bloomsbury', *MOB*, pp. 195–6), though initially exciting as the memoir reveals, is by no means embraced unreservedly in Woolf's fiction. The all-revealing, all-unveiling climate of modernity prompted both doubt and affirmation in Woolf, and led to a frequent weighing of the relative merits of speech and silence. We have seen her noting in her diary how her parents' circle 'would sit talking till 2am – but what about? So many things could never be said, & the remaining ones coloured by the abstinence' (*D* II. 89). The moderns, on the other hand, both in literature and in life, had a candour that Woolf could applaud, as in her review of Hemingway's *Men Without Women* of 1927, where she notes the 'admirable frankness [and] an equal bareness of style' of the stories, their 'outspoken' approach to describing life 'openly, frankly, without prudery', and argues precisely that 'it is here that we steal a march upon the Victorians ... Such candour is modern and it is admirable' (*E* IV. 451). Even so, Woolf then complains about the 'sex consciousness' of Hemingway, and his 'disagreeable' emphasis on sexual characteristics, his 'display of self-conscious virility' (*E* IV. 454), which she also regrets in Joyce and Lawrence and returns to discuss in *A Room*; thus in the manuscript of the latter Alan's coupling with Phoebe on the beach is described as 'horribly perfectly frank. Everything ... was done ... openly that used to be done privately. Everything was said plainly ... Nothing could have been more indecent' (*Women & Fiction*, p. 153). Hemingway himself turns out to be, perhaps, a little too 'outspoken' – his 'excessive use of dialogue' leads Woolf to sympathise with the little girl's pleading in one of his stories, 'Would you please please please please please please stop talking' (*E* IV. 455). The reserve of the Victorians by contrast – 'so many things could never be said' – is apparent in *To the Lighthouse*, where the Ramsays' relationship is inhibited by much that cannot be expressed in dialogue – 'No, they could not share that; they could not say that' (*TL*, p. 75), seen above all in Mrs Ramsay's inability to say 'I love you' to her husband at the end of Part 1. On the other hand, communication takes place between them telepathically, or is coded in the language of lyric poetry (here Charles Elton rather than Christina Rossetti) – 'Come out and climb the garden path, / Luriana Lurilee. / The China rose is all abloom and buzzing with the yellow bee'; words which 'say[ ] quite easily and naturally what had been in [Mrs Ramsay's] mind the whole evening ...' (*TL*, p. 120).[26] Reserve is also enabling of Mrs Ramsay's acts of 'extreme courtesy' – 'had she not, at that very moment, given him of her own free will what she knew he would never ask' (*TL*, p. 72). In *Mrs Dalloway* Woolf had already debated the difficulties of choosing between a relationship characterised by such reserve (as in the Dalloways' marriage) and that offered by Peter Walsh, where 'everything had to be shared; everything gone into'; the latter, whatever the anguish of foregoing it, would have been 'intolerable' in Clarissa's eyes (*MD*, p. 10). Part of what was noted above as the migraine-like environment of modernity in *Orlando*, alongside the unshaded light and bright colours, is the acoustic exposure of hearing 'every whisper and crackle in the room' (*O*, p. 206), and the comment quoted earlier on Vita herself is prompted precisely by her frankness: 'no inhibitions, no false reserves; anything can be said; but as usual, that fatal simplicity or rigidity of mind which makes it all seem a little unshaded, & empty' (*D* II. 306–7). Here again is an equation between shadow and reserve that offers some relief from the outspokenness of modernity.

Let us not then shy completely from the shadows in Woolf and what they represent, and recognise her fidelity to that 'which the glare of day flattens out'. A key moment for Goldman comes in *To the Lighthouse* when Mrs Ramsay covers the skull in the children's bedroom with her green shawl, in order to enable Cam, who is frightened by it and the shadows it casts, to get to sleep. Goldman reads the episode thus:

> Mrs Ramsay's solution bears the seeds of social and artistic progressiveness. Her green shawl imposes a Post-Impressionist colourist solution to the play of light and dark of skeletal structure. This may also be a proto-feminist act: the chiaroscuro which keeps women in the shadow of masculine light has perhaps been obliterated by a green cover potentially suggestive of a suffrage banner. (*Feminist Aesthetics*, p. 174)

Even though the reading is self-confessedly speculative, 'may', 'perhaps', 'potentially', it is difficult to see how chiaroscuro *per se* has been obliterated here by the act of covering the skull – the shadow the skull casts in the room, which is what frightens Cam, will remain, even if its shape is now changed, while Mrs Ramsay immediately goes on to reassure James that 'the skull was still there under the shawl' (*TL*, p. 125). After discussing the skull episode Goldman continues the 'demotion' of shadow, arguing that Lily's description of the lighting of her painting – 'A light here required a shadow there' – is an insincere language she uses only in talking to a man, when 'a colourist explanation' is really the key to what she is about. Any communication relating to the painting with the man in question, William Bankes, is interpreted as necessarily 'ironic', though no support is offered for this reading and it ignores Lily's thoughts in the final part of the novel of how 'One could talk of painting then seriously to a man. Indeed, his friendship had been one of the pleasures of her life. She loved William Bankes' (*TL*, p. 192). Lily herself does not separate colour from light/shade considerations in approaching her painting, and her 'androgynous' function is emphasised by her not setting up a divide between men and women in the way that Goldman suggests.

Critics have in fact regularly ignored Woolf's obsession with shade, shadow, writerly effects of 'half light', twilight and what they signify. In much of the discussion of Woolf's relation to Post-Impressionism there is a silence on this subject in the desire to affirm Woolf's identification with the practice of Fry and Bell. Thus McLaurin's *Virginia Woolf: the Echoes Enslaved* treats in detail the Woolf–Fry relationship in terms of their common treatment of properties like colour and space but has nothing on this other critical pictorial component, light and shade, and a similar objection can be made to Diane Gillespie's discussion of Woolf and Bell and to Banfield's discussion of Woolf's aesthetic exclusively in terms of colour and form.[27] In fact, Fry's attack on a use of light and shade that is inimical to the 'fundamental divisions of design' and to the 'language of form' led to his 'hazard[ing] the speculation that European art has hardly yet recovered from the shock which Leonardo's passion for psychological illustration delivered': 'illustration' here meaning the subtle chiaroscuro that brought out 'psychologically significant movements of facial expression'.[28] The first Post-Impressionist exhibition was seen by Vanessa Bell as a departure from a situation in which 'English painters were on the whole still under the Victorian cloud, either conscientiously painting effects of light, or trying to be poets or neo-Pre-Raphaelites'.[29] But the cost of removing the play of light and shade in the interests of foregrounding colour and form led Woolf to regret the type of suggestiveness and 'depth' that she felt was thus sacrificed: 'painters lack sub[t]lety; there were points of light, shades beneath the surface, now, I suppose, undiscoverable' (quoted above, p. 51).

In the third of the 'Portraits', 'probably part of a collaborative work' between Woolf and Bell from 1937, according to Susan Dick

(*CSF*, p. 307), the narrator gives us a figure seen through Post-Impressionist eyes together with her animus against her:

> And it seemed to me sitting in the courtyard of the French Inn, that the secret of existence was nothing but a bat's skeleton in a cupboard ... so very solid she looked. She was sitting in the sun. She had no hat. The light fixed her. There was no shadow. Her face was yellow and red; round too; a fruit on a body; another apple, only not on a plate. Breasts had formed apple-hard under the blouse on her body.
>
> I watched her. She flicked her skin as if a fly had walked over it ... her coarseness, her cruelty, was like bark rough with lichen and she was everlasting and entirely solved the problem of life. (*CSF*, p. 243)

Woolf's satire here on a woman 'in the sun' lacking in grace, mystery, discretion or any sense of the profundities glimpsed, say, in the Russian twilight, echoes her suggestions elsewhere that a visual 'fixing' (as in developing a photograph) is at the opposite pole to the writer's imaginative portrayal. Thus the short piece 'The Lady in the Looking-Glass: A Reflection' (1929) contrasts the imaginative 'reflection' on its subject in the observer's mind with the final and reductive reflection in the looking-glass itself: 'the looking-glass began to pour over her a light that seemed to fix her ... Here was the woman herself. She stood naked in that pitiless light. And there was nothing' (*CSF*, p. 225). Throughout Woolf's short stories, notably in 'The Mark on the Wall' and 'An Unwritten Novel', we have the visual sign as cue and starting-point for a fictional journey that often returns to where it begins in the banal world of shadowless 'truth', as also at the end of 'The Shooting Party': 'in the full blaze of the station lamps it was plain – she was quite an ordinary rather elderly woman, travelling to London on some quite ordinary piece of business' (*CSF*, p. 260). Conversely, Vanessa Bell turned the tables on her sister in a lecture she gave in 1925, where she took one of Woolf's most famous imaginative creations – Mrs Brown from the recently published 'Mr Bennett and Mrs Brown' – and suggested that her sister, no less than Wells and Bennett themselves, never really looks at Mrs Brown in spite of the tale she tells of her – 'did any of them really *see* her? Not in a way that I should call seeing'.[30] And what this 'seeing' amounts to is expanded on in the remainder of the lecture: 'It is indeed so exciting and so absorbing, this painters' world of form and colour, that once you are at its mercy you are in grave danger of forgetting all other aspects of the material world' (p. 157). Earlier in the lecture Bell had reminisced about the liberation of this world of 'colour and form' from the Victorian household where everything had been 'veiled in shade', arguing however that such a liberation was not very significant for writers – 'I know the species well' – to whom 'the world ... is not very interesting in form and colour' (pp. 153–5).

Much more is at stake here than a debate about Post-Impressionism alone. Thus in declining to accept the value, indeed the necessity, of shadow in Woolf, Goldman's reading in *Feminist Aesthetics* goes beyond claiming Woolf's support for the luminous creation of 'the world anew' through feminism (p. 88) and wishes to see a more general 'social and artistic progressiveness' and political modernity in her work. She thus quotes the passage discussing social change in 'Character in Fiction', referred to previously, where the 'Victorian cook', previously kept 'like a leviathan in the lower depths', is now 'a creature of sunshine and fresh air' (*E* III. 422), and suggests that this observation shows Woolf's participation in the 'radical political climate of the period' (pp. 111–12, 120). Woolf's interest in the painting of Sickert, and its portrayal 'of ordinary, working people', is later linked with her 'interest in the rise of the lower classes from darkness into light' (p. 142), even though the only instance brought forward to support this 'interest' is the passage on the cook, which might be read, as we have suggested, as approving some amelioration in the state of the hierarchy but hardly its radical alteration. Goldman's suggestion of a link between Woolf's feminism and her attack on the 'aristocratic way of life' (p. 79) is rooted in her reading of the presence of the 'Yorkshire Squire' at the eclipse scene in Woolf's essay, together with his 'four large lean, red dogs' (*E* IV. 521), figures representing a feudal hierarchy whose own eclipse is presaged by that of the sun (pp. 57–8).

Among the problems that ideas of a radical project in Woolf relating to social class have to take on board are the manifold instances in her writing where she applauds and upholds an aristocratic tradition, this problem of omission being evident in Goldman's study where the cost of reading a small sample of Woolf's work in such brilliant chromatic detail is necessarily some critical myopia. Thus, although Woolf's diary entry of 30 June 1927 describing the eclipse is analysed at length (*D* III. 142–4), there is no mention at all of the very next (and almost equally long) entry in her diary, which describes a visit to the Nicolsons at Long Barn – 'Vita very opulent, in her brown velvet coat with the baggy pockets, pearl necklace . . . Of its kind this is the best, most representative human life I know: I mean, certain gifts & qualities & good fortunes are here miraculously combined . . .' (*D* III. 144). Admittedly, unlike the Yorkshire squire Vita was not on this occasion attended by her dogs, as she often was when Woolf saw her at Knole ('a sort of covey of noble English life', *D* III. 125), and as she tends to be throughout *Orlando*. Discounting the shadows in Woolf, in the far-reaching symbolism of chiaroscuro we have traced, not only can result in misjudging Woolf's attitude towards the past, particularly the Victorian past, and disregarding its complexity, its mixed nature of rejection and recuperation; it also betrays an exaggerated belief in Woolf's consistent and thoroughgoing radicalism, in her hopes for a new sociopolitical order, for a 'luminously colourful and shadowless' world, so to speak. No-one will deny Woolf's radical feminism, nor the presence of 'Post-Impressionist' colour in her work, but these coexist with conservative elements which, while weakening in the 1930s, as we shall see, by no means disappear entirely. In her essay 'Women and Fiction' (1929), Woolf describes the requirement on the woman novelist at the present time to 'observe how [women's] lives are ceasing to run underground . . . to discover what new colours and shadows are showing in them now that they are exposed to the outer world' (*W & W*, p. 50). Here Woolf no more highlights colour than the new 'shadows' which will also need observing,[31] and this indicates not only, I think, the ongoing struggles of women's experience, and the fact that the appearance of Judith Shakespeare is still a good way off (*RO*, p. 117), but Woolf's belief more generally that shadow is ineluctable, as in the scene with the skull in *To the Lighthouse* – 'Wherever they put the light . . . there was always a shadow somewhere' (*TL*, p. 124). This qualifies any 'prismatic' optimism in Woolf's writing and also emphasises what she herself saw as its elegiac function: the *memento mori* can be covered up, but, as Mrs Ramsay assures James, the 'skull was still there' (*TL*, p. 125).[32] Woolf is no utopian, and is unwilling to embrace naively a shadow-less future, a point to be pursued.

Mrs Ramsay's attempt in this episode to meet James's hard-headed empiricism and its philosophical implications half-way – the 'skull was still there' – is repaid in the final part of the novel when he insists on the rights of the 'silvery, misty-looking' tower alongside the 'stark and straight' one (*TL*, p. 202), in the quest to integrate the man/womanly difference, the partnership of light and shade and all it signifies, and the communication between eras. The stress on reconciliation of difference climaxes in the very last section of the novel, primarily in Lily's completion of the painting, but also in the reference to body–mind integration and in her (wordless) communication with Carmichael, this last a tableau of the sexes, as well as of youth and age, coming together. Moreover, if we cast the 'shaggy' Carmichael as a Tennyson redivivus, with his wisdom imaged in a reference to the 'Morte d'Arthur' as a hand flashing a sword from 'the surface of the pool' (*TL*, p. 194), we have further emphasis on the Victorian past needfully surviving into present time.[33] Indeed, ideas of reconciliation, integration and a continuity that overcomes the threat of time passing are strikingly and even obtrusively insistent in *To the Lighthouse*, its emphatic sense of 'finish' conspicuously at odds with the more familiar Woolfian position that 'if honestly examined life presents question after question which must be left to sound on and on after the story is over' (*E* III. 36). And what of course the completion of this novel means is that, after delivering her Post-Victorian 'vision', Woolf is now free to move on. She famously noted in *A Sketch of the Past* that until she wrote *To the Lighthouse* 'the presence of my mother obsessed me', but that when the novel was finished this obsession ceased: 'I expressed some very long felt and deeply felt emotion. And in expressing it I explained it and then laid it to rest' (*MOB*, pp. 80ff). What this emotion involved was no less than a totalising mother/father ideal of union in which the parental terms signify a programme for historical and cultural integration which has indeed been 'long felt', as we have seen, anticipated in Woolf's earlier writings though there less explicitly formulated. That the present should be mindful of the past; that scepticism, logic and rationality need to be complemented by imagination, passion and feeling; that structure and order can be compatible with lyricism and individuality; that novelty pay its dues to tradition; this represents a modern–Victorian conciliation – an androgyny of historical period – figured by the union of light and shadow. Yet Lily's central line which completes her vision at the end of the novel is also Woolf's line drawn under the past, and, like all 'ends', *To the Lighthouse* is also a beginning, and its moment of stasis around that central line a point of departure. The romance of the Victorian is retrieved in *To the Lighthouse* but at the same time practically laid to rest, along with the mother; thereafter, we shall see a more critical examination of the period emerge in Woolf's work.

Significantly, one of Woolf's first pieces of writing after publication of the novel in May 1927 was an essay whose title alone indicates a departure from retrospect, 'Poetry, Fiction and the Future', which appeared in August. Here Woolf envisages traditional literary practice giving way under the stress of modern life, using a series of images with which we are by now familiar. Thus while Keats could effect the harmony of chiaroscuro – 'the emotion which Keats felt when he heard the song of a nightingale is one and entire, though it passes from joy in beauty to sorrow at the unhappiness of human fate. He makes no contrast. In his poem sorrow is the shadow which accompanies beauty' – the moderns, who are 'extremely alive to everything – to ugliness, sordidity, beauty, amusement', and discuss everything openly, find themselves having to encompass a much greater range of impressions and experience all seen and felt with an equal vividness, where nothing is in shadow. And so

In the modern mind beauty is accompanied not by its shadow but by its opposite ... There trips along by the side of our modern beauty some mocking spirit which sneers at beauty for being beautiful; which turns the looking glass and shows us that the other side of her cheek is pitted and deformed. (*E* IV. 433)

Woolf admires the 'honesty in modern writing' (*E* IV. 434) that is determined to give voice to these 'monstrous, hybrid, unmanageable emotions' (*E* IV. 429) that 'bite and kick at each other' (*E* IV. 433), but a literary form has yet to be found that will be flexible enough to 'take the mould of that queer conglomeration of incongruous things – the modern mind' (*E* IV. 436). Such a form can only lie in the development of the novel, for only prose has the suppleness required to range the heights and depths of the modern's omnivorous experience, and will not forget 'our emotions toward such things as roses and nightingales, the dawn, the sunset, life, death and fate' (*E* IV. 435), at the same time as it acknowledges 'the emotions bred in us by crowds, the obscure terrors and hatreds which come so irrationally in certain places or from certain people' (*E* IV. 439).

If the heritage of nineteenth-century romance is still necessarily present in such things as roses and nightingales, the figure of chiaroscuro is hardly appropriate for the titanic mastering of 'monstrous' oppositions that will require all the future novelist's courage. The contrast between the modern mind as a beauty in a looking-glass whose other cheek 'is pitted and deformed', and a pre-modern beauty who is 'shadowed' by sorrow, harbours a recollection of the mother as an embodiment of the latter, as the passage from *Reminiscences* (1907–8) discussing Julia Stephen reveals:

> You may see the two things in her face. 'Let us make the most of what we have, since we know nothing of the future' was the motive that urged her to toil so incessantly on behalf of happiness, right doing, love; and the melancholy echoes answered 'What does it matter? Perhaps there is no future'. (*MOB*, p. 36)

The mother with 'no future' is implicitly laid to rest in Woolf's essay, just as she had been in the novel of the same year. And in the following year, 1928, Woolf said farewell to another imposing Victorian matriarch in her obituary on Lady Strachey:

> Last summer, though too weak to walk any more, she sat on her balcony and showered down upon the faces that she could not see a vast maternal benediction. It was as if the Victorian age in its ripeness, its width, with all its memories and achievements behind it were bestowing its blessing. And we

should be blind indeed if we did not wave back to her a salute full of homage and affection. (*E* IV. 576)

These final lines of the obituary could stand as a motto for *To the Lighthouse*, and a warning to a 'blind' modernity that refuses such retrospective homage. They confirm the novel's identification of the Victorian (or the valuable parts of the Victorian legacy) with the maternal and are perhaps as near as Woolf comes to identifying the period with the great Queen-matriarch herself, on whom Woolf is generally silent, though Mrs Ramsay, a 'queen' in her children's eyes (*TL*, p. 11), is seen 'against a picture of Queen Victoria' in one moment of epiphany (*TL*, p. 18).[34] These valedictions to the mother contrast with the ongoing life, via his writings, of the father, who continues to 'come back', Woolf noted in 1928, even as 'a contemporary' (*D* III. 208). Henceforth the switch of focus from mother to father represents a change of emphasis in Woolf's relation with the Victorian, a much less glamorised response that, however, sees him and his age as remaining a key resource, especially in *Three Guineas*, but also as representing the repressive patriarchal legacy that Woolf's writing of the 1930s attends to much more overtly.[35]

CHAPTER 4

Disillusion: The Years

Woolf's fiction and literary criticism, as in *The Common Reader* volume, insist on the continuity of the cultural and literary record 'from Chaucer even to Mr Conrad' in the face of a 'time passing' that, in the First World War, passed in a particularly disruptive and destructive way. However, when Woolf concentrates on economic issues, especially the position of modern women and the professional opportunities available to them or still denied, she is able to embrace the War more positively as a means of historical change. In *A Room* she offers thanks to both the Crimean and 'the European' war for the opportunities they provided for women's employment outside the home, the latter having 'opened the doors to the average woman' (*RO*, p. 97), and in *Three Guineas* she stresses the importance of 'the sacred year 1919' (*TG*, p. 141) when the opening of these doors was formally recognised in the passing of the Sex Disqualification (Removal) Act. This sense of progress, however, runs up against Woolf's romantic and retrospective longings in a deeply conflicting way, as we see in *A Room* itself in its flight from modern sexual relations towards Christina Rossetti and Tennyson, even though Woolf is prepared to ponder whether the War offered the further service of abolishing outmoded 'illusion':

When the guns fired in August 1914, did the faces of men and women show so plain in each other's eyes that romance was killed? Certainly it was a shock (to women in particular with their illusions about education, and so on) to see the faces of our rulers in the light of the shell-fire. So ugly they looked ... so stupid. But lay the blame where one will, on whom one will, the illusion which inspired Tennyson and Christina Rossetti to sing so passionately about the coming of their loves is far rarer now than then. (*RO*, pp. 13–14)

As the argument continues, however, it is clear that the narrator is unwilling to sacrifice such 'illusion', remarking that the contrary states of 'romance' and modern 'truth' are not so easily defined – 'which was truth and which was illusion, I asked myself?', and she illustrates the problem with the sight of some houses she passes: 'What was the truth about these houses, for example, dim and festive now with their red windows in the dusk, but raw and red and squalid, with their sweets and their bootlaces, at nine o'clock in the morning?' (*RO* 14). 'No conclusion was found' to the problem, she concludes, replaying here in the dusky evening/raw morning dichotomy a variation on the characteristic Woolfian manner of representing the Victorian/modern contrast. No more than James in *To the Lighthouse* is she willing to sacrifice the 'dusky' view of things for a modern disillusion that is only a half-truth, and Rossetti and Tennyson will resurface emphatically in *A Room*'s final chapter.

Zwerdling has suggested that Woolf's explicit attention to the destructive effects of war in 'Time Passes', as opposed to its more indirect presence in the earlier fiction, is of a piece with the occurrence in the later 1920s of a spate of celebrated war memoirs which their authors were only now able to produce in revisiting their combat experience.[1] In 'Time Passes', however, Woolf continues to downplay the historical potency and significance of the War in various ways, and is clearly conducting a critical dialogue with the cultural recollection now starting to take place. It would be a mistake to describe the structure of *To the Lighthouse* as consisting of a 'Pre-War' and 'Post-War' scene divided by the central section, as is commonly assumed, even though the War is obviously a major issue and its effects felt in Andrew's death in particular (*TL*, p. 145). The manuscript outline for 'Time Passes' includes the War as just one item in a list that comprises the ten-year interval presented here and 'the gradual dissolution of everything' that takes place therein, and the truly cataclysmic event, the death of Mrs Ramsay (and the disappearance of the era she embodies) precedes the War.[2] In the manuscript, James, as he approaches the lighthouse, reflects on how 'There was a gulf of some sort between the world before the catastrophe & the world after it: It was impossible to make the two things into one' (p. 311); the manuscript also describes how James sees his boyhood as set in a 'miraculous garden ... before the fall of the world (& he did really divide time into the space before catastrophe, & the space after)' (p. 309). The 'catastrophe' that Woolf is presenting here is the exile from the garden presided over by the Victorian mother, as anticipated in *Mrs Dalloway*, together with the death of childhood and of the mother herself. In the draft stage the lighthouse does not present itself to James as a means of symbolically fusing the gulf between before and after, maternal and paternal, but by the final version he too like Lily has won through to his vision of reconciliation and integration. In 'Time Passes' the War is thus seen as the dramatic enforcement of the catastrophe rather than its cause, a strategy of 'subordinating' the War that not only anticipates Woolf's attack on the 'masculine' valuation of war as a primary subject for fiction in *A Room* (*RO*, p. 67), but that refuses to allow its status as a determining historical marker; a perspective again anticipated in *Mrs Dalloway* and continued in *Orlando*, *The Waves* and *The Years*, where the War is either effaced in the historical record or treated as one event among many, examples practically of a fictional 'indifference' that anticipates the argument of *Three Guineas*. Woolf is not denying that the moderns have experienced 'a shift in the scale' that has 'shaken the fabric from top to bottom' and 'alienated us from the past', as she puts it in 'How It Strikes a Contemporary' (*E* IV. 238), where the War is referred to as one element in that shift. By the 1929 edition of *The Common Reader*, however, this reference to 'the war' has been significantly edited from the essay, and the 'shift in the scale' is now described solely in the more general terms of a 'sudden slip of masses held in position for ages'.[3]

 The feminist rewriting of history in *To the Lighthouse* replaces a 'great events' narrative with a domestic one, a strategy for women writers *A Room* will endorse, but this is no retreat into microcosm, given the far-reaching cultural implications of the 'fall' into modernity that the novel traces. The paradox of this fortunate fall lies in its being a journey towards independence, freedom and new values that must, however, guard against the 'death of the (Victorian) heart' and the sacrifice of other qualities associated with the past; indeed, in elaborating the reconciliation of difference in the figure of Lily, Woolf affords her the status of a Christ figure with her final words 'It is finished' (*TL*, p. 225). In focussing in detail on the domestic, moreover, that is, in allowing the two scenes of Parts 1 and 3 so many more pages than the ten years of the central section, Woolf continues to insist on the primacy of the novelist's task to capture 'life'; Mrs Ramsay and others may die famously in parentheses in 'Time Passes', showing how precarious and insignificant that life is, but Woolf then refocusses the domestic subject in the final part, minimising the short 'Time Passes' section and making it, together with the War itself, parenthetical – reasserting the importance of the individual human life and of the mind's ability to enable the past to live on.

However, the Post-Victorian consummation of *To the Lighthouse*, which 'laid to rest' Woolf's long and deeply felt emotion, starts to unravel in the 1930s into its component parts of critique and fidelity, which no longer make up a 'whole'; and this conflicted state is announced in the lecture Woolf gave to the London National Society for Women's Service in January 1931, which was the seed of the novel-essay *The Pargiters*. The lecture is a much fuller attack on the ideal of the 'angel in the house' than the essay 'Professions for Women', which derived from it, and in it Woolf completely contradicts her position in *A Room* in reprimanding the very same poets, Tennyson and Christina Rossetti, for helping promote such an ideal. 'A real relationship between men and women' was 'unattainable' in Victorian culture, she argues, protesting at the poetic compliments that passed between the sexes in 'a style which to me is really disgusting'. This forceful observation is cancelled in the typescript of the lecture and replaced by the milder suggestion that Victorian poetry contributed to 'a relationship between men and women that was both false and disagreeable' (*P*, pp. xxx–xxxi). Two years later, however, Woolf is still celebrating a Victorian poetic relationship in *Flush* (1933), where the iconic wedding-ring of *Orlando* now 'flashed ... in the sun' of Italy on Mrs Browning's hand (*F*, p. 108). Here the ring, no less than Italy itself, is the means whereby 'freedom and life and the joy that the sun breeds' are achieved (*F*, p. 109). If the telling of Flush's story enables Woolf to continue the theme of Victorian marital love in her work, at the same time it typifies her more explicit attack on Victorian patriarchy in the 1930s, with the significantly motherless figure of Elizabeth Barrett under the tyrannical captivity of the father; England as a land of fathers and dog-stealers is contrasted with an Italy where 'fear was unknown' (*F*, p. 113). *Flush* might be seen, indeed, as a resolution of the ambivalence of *The Voyage Out*, and the completion of the 'Italian project' which that novel refuses, in its forcible handling of the home and abroad theme; Elizabeth Barrett sounds very like Helen Ambrose in that 'she was never tired of praising Italy at the expense of England: " . . . our poor English", she exclaimed, "want educating into gladness. They want refining not in the fire but in the sunshine"' (*F*, p. 109). In the later work there is no Rachel Vinrace figure to counter this by expressing nostalgic 'home thoughts from abroad'; ironically enough, given that Robert Browning himself is to hand in the story Woolf is telling. The Brownings take up their Italian abode in 'a vast bare room flooded with sunshine . . . so hard, so bright, so big, so empty', where the light 'dazzled' Flush's eyes (*F*, p. 103); Casa Guidi itself is sunny and 'bare', allowing everything to be seen with clarity: 'The bed was a bed; the wash-stand was a wash-stand. Everything was itself and not another thing' (*F*, p. 115), and in this it contrasts with the somnolent dimness of Wimpole Street where the furnishings are 'vague amorphous shapes' and where in the invalid's bedroom 'nothing . . . was itself; everything was something else' (*F*, p. 21). But that this simple antithesis and rejection of England is by no means Woolf's last word on the Victorian scene is suggested by the contradiction of celebrating the hard, bright atmosphere of Italy in terms which hitherto we have seen Woolf employ as the condition of an exposing modernity; moreover, the state in which 'everything was itself and not another thing' is by no means a permanent refuge for a writer whose fiction insists, as in *To the Lighthouse*, that 'nothing was simply one thing'. If *The Years* will largely continue the unsympathetic portrayal of Victorian England, the mix of rejection of and nostalgia for it remains evident in other Woolfian texts of the 1930s in an undimmed complexity that was not perhaps appropriate in the biography of Elizabeth Barrett's dog.

The trajectory of Woolf's Post-Victorianism in the 1930s is therefore more challenging to discern compared with its presence in the writing of the previous decade. The indictment of such institutions as the 'angel in the house' and of Victorian paternal authority becomes more urgent; at the same time we shall see how the Victorian legacy can still be upheld when it counters aspects of modernity that Woolf remains alarmed by and resistant to. It may be worth summarising here how my sense of this trajectory differs from that in Alex Zwerdling's *Virginia Woolf and the Real World*, which, in tracing Woolf's 'complex and often contradictory sensibility' (p. 33), makes welcome allowance for that 'part of her that mourned the passing of the old order and identified the new freedom with the trivialisation of our deepest feelings' (p. 174). For Zwerdling the 'radical tendencies in Woolf's thinking are always in conflict with a persistent traditionalism' (p. 241), an observation I entirely support in the challenge it offers to 'ahistoricist thinking', in Zwerdling's term, that insists on seeing in Woolf a 'consistent socialist, pacifist, and feminist' package (p. 33). Zwerdling argues, however, that such traditionalism only comes to the fore with *To the Lighthouse*, which should not be seen as any kind of 'liberation fable' centring on Lily Briscoe (p. 200) but as heavily unbalanced by the sheer weight of Woolfian nostalgia; by 1927, when the novel was published,

> the revolutionary impulse of 1910 had largely spent itself, and more and more of the [Bloomsbury] rebels were looking back with a sense of loss to the way of life that had disappeared. In part this was the product of World War I, the horror of which heightened, retrospectively, the positive qualities of what came before. (pp. 201–2)

It will be clear by now that, on the contrary, I see *To the Lighthouse* as the culmination of Woolf's earlier writing in its reclamation of the Victorian heritage, whereas Zwerdling sees it in terms of a much more oppositional relationship to Woolf's prior 'rebelliousness'. But by paying little attention to *Night and Day* ('an early experiment ... rather than a mature vision', p. 222), and by insisting on singling out *Mrs Dalloway* as a wholesale critique of conservative thinking, as I discussed in chapter 2, Zwerdling neglects the foundations for several positions in *To the Lighthouse* that Woolf was laying down during the 1920s, arguing that the unheralded act of revisionism in this novel is so powerfully felt that even its commitment, in Part 3, to Lily's 'liberation' is questionable. I stress alternatively Woolf's attempt in the novel, as in much of her previous writing, to mediate between the old and the new, and to promote the qualities of both periods in a so-called 'androgynous' unification.

Nor does Zwerdling explain convincingly why we have such a violent oscillation between the post-War hopes he sees Woolf espousing in *Mrs Dalloway* and the pre-War refuge she succumbs to in a novel published just two years later, when in fact kindred narratives that evaluate and balance past and present and that resist the War's threat to continuity and to its creating precisely such a gulf between pre- and post-War partisanship structure both work. I would, however, agree with Zwerdling that Woolf's work 'in the 1930s seems significantly more fragmented, more divided against itself, than the work of the previous decade' (p. 270), certainly as far as her estimation of the Victorian is concerned, and that Woolf's retrospect, now no longer under the aegis of the mother, becomes increasingly, though not exclusively, critical and deromanticised (we might note in relation to this how short-lived the device of androgyny is in her work). In this passage from a 1920s piety and fidelity to a harsher critique Woolf tends to go against the prevailing response identified by John Gardiner:

> as the 1930s wore on, the Victorian past increasingly took on a burnished glow. It was not only that the trauma of war and the subsequent efflorescence of anti-Victorianism had died down; it was also that the nineteenth century now seemed rather far away, especially under the dark storm clouds that scuttled across from Europe.[4]

The idea of a departed 'golden age' is evident in several of the 1930s memoirs on the Victorian period known to Woolf, though she had had ample exposure to this 'burnished glow' in the previous decade as well, as it proceeded from the pages of James, Anne Ritchie, Laura Troubridge, Ethel Smyth and others, including Julian Hawthorne, whose rhapsodic *Shapes that Pass* she reviewed in 1928 (*E.* IV 565–7).

While she can embrace and take pleasure in such retrospect, even excusing what she calls Hawthorne's 'peroration' on the 1870s ('the British Lion was purring, and nothing could stop him .... Our foundations were firm; radium was no more anticipated than was the war or Bolshevism; if there were murmurs of approaching earthquake they were inaudible in the music of our purring. It was a golden age ...')[5] in *The Years* she plainly satirises such 'burnishing', especially when indulged in at second-hand, as well as the whole idea of 'perorations'. Thus, one way that Peggy copes with her sense of the evils of the present is by accessing her aunt Eleanor's memories, wishing 'to get her back to her past. It was so interesting; so safe; so unreal – that past of the 'eighties; and to her, so beautiful in its unreality' (*TY*, p. 244). For Woolf herself the 'realities' of the Victorian past bear on her more closely in the 1930s and tend to displace any dream-like quality: not only in the extraordinary powers of recall displayed in *A Sketch of the Past*, where past experiences 'can still be more real than the present moment' (*MOB*, p. 67) but in the extensive reading and documenting of Victorian social history and memoir that went into *Three Guineas*. And in reading this material Woolf is no longer looking for the glow of retrospect but for hard economic fact.[6]

Thus *The Years* (1937) represents to a large degree the end of Woolf's romancing of the Victorian as far as the novels are concerned, while what can be positively retrieved of the period passes somewhat unexpectedly perhaps into the non-fictional *Three Guineas*. As a telling instance of the end of such romancing, Stella Duckworth, 'beautiful, romantic and admired' in Hermione Lee's words, is transformed with her charity work into the character of Eleanor in *The Years*, who in her youth is none of these things (*Virginia Woolf*, pp. 121–4). Although as a 'novel of fact' *The Years* signified to Woolf a resumption of the genre of *Night and Day* (*D* IV. 129), it has little in common with the earlier novel's fidelities to the past in the face of the challenge of modernity, and with its quest to perpetuate the Victorian legacy. As I have argued, *Night and Day* illustrates Woolf's desire for a 'helpful relationship between the generations', but although *The Years* is centrally concerned with the issue of 'generations', the relationship between them is not presented as an easy or helpful one. In a critical episode from *Night and Day* Katharine, as we saw, communes with her grandfather's portrait and feels his identification with her in her present troubles; in an equivalent scene from *The Years*, Peggy, puzzling over her own discomfort, 'looked at the picture of her grandmother as if to ask her opinion. But she had assumed the immunity of a work of art; she seemed as she sat there, smiling at her roses, to be indifferent to our right and wrong' (*TY*, p. 239). The fact that Peggy's grandmother is near to death as the novel opens, and that neither her children nor her husband show any great sense of impending loss (the relief at her death both Delia and the Colonel anticipate is manifest), point up the fact that here we are to have no glamorised matriarch as in the case of Mrs Ramsay. This is symptomatic of the unsympathetic portrayal of Victorian family life which the Abercorn Terrace scenes record, summed up by Martin:

It was an abominable system, he thought; family life; Abercorn Terrace. No wonder the house would not let. It had one bathroom, and a basement; and there all those different people had lived, boxed up together, telling lies. (*TY*, p. 163)

In Delia's succinct phrase, 'It was Hell! . . . It was Hell!' (*TY*, p. 305). The sense of overcrowding and concealment is of course much closer to Woolf's own experience of Hyde Park Gate than is the uncrowded comfort and ease of the family house in *Night and Day*. Indeed, whereas the earlier novel mitigated Woolf's own domestic discomforts as we saw, she seems in the later determined to make the Victorian scene more oppressive in some ways than that of her own youth, so that whereas her father's profession and his encouragement of her reading helped compensate other aggravations, Abercorn Terrace is ruled by a military, adulterous patriarch in the person of Abel Pargiter.

The Victorian experience is presented in a disillusioned manner in the novel therefore, and as a consequence the Victorian retrospect here can offer little resource. Peggy's inability to communicate with her grandmother's portrait is an instance of a wider sense in the novel of generational difficulties, represented above all, perhaps, in the contrast in personality and outlook between Peggy herself and Eleanor, which comes to the fore in the novel's final section. Eleanor's optimism, happiness and vision of the 'wholeness' of the present moment (*TY*, p. 313), the radiance occasioned by her dream at the party and the sense of her life as a 'miracle' (*TY*, pp. 279–80), are contrasted with Peggy's frustration, fatigue and pessimism, summarised in her incapacity to understand her aunt's excitement (*TY*, p. 282). Eleanor's belief in progress, that things 'have changed for the better' since her girlhood, and that today 'We're happier – we're freer ...' (*TY*, p. 283), is silently contested in Peggy's brooding sense of 'a world bursting with misery':

On every placard at every street corner was Death; or worse – tyranny; brutality; torture; the fall of civilization; the end of freedom ... And then Eleanor says the world is better, because two people out of all those millions are 'happy'. (*TY*, p. 284)

Eleanor's enjoyment of the party is met with by Peggy's dampening 'Don't you think it's time to be going? ... you'll be so tired tomorrow', advice that calls down North's 'twitting' remark 'How like a doctor!' (*TY*, p. 281). Eleanor and Peggy embody a contrast between idealism and realism in the 'Present Day' chapter, with Peggy's analytical habits and personality, which is in her own eyes 'hard' and 'cold' (*TY*, p. 259), representing Woolf's characteristic evocation of a modern scepticism and rationalism,[7] though *The Years* no longer contrasts this outlook with the culture of a nostalgically realised Victorianism, nor indeed do distinctions and contrasts between the Victorian and the modern animate or structure it as they do the earlier novels. In a sense Peggy herself tries and fails to structure history in this way, a modern professional who wishes to pigeon-hole Eleanor as the 'portrait of a Victorian spinster' (*TY*, p. 244). But the Victorian period is one that those fostered by it are largely pleased to have escaped from, above all Eleanor herself, who thinks consistently 'I do not want to go back into my past ... I want the present' (*TY*, p. 246), whereas Peggy, as we have seen, wants the vicarious enjoyment of 'that past of the 'eighties ... so beautiful in its unreality' (*TY*, p. 244). With the modern woman wanting a 'safe' Victorian fiction and the Victorian woman naively embracing a 'happy' modernity – the Post-Victorian here sundered into the polarities of escapism on the one hand and dismissal on the other – it is small wonder that the opportunities for generational misunderstanding are rife, a situation that suggests the very terms 'Victorian' and 'modern' are increasingly unstable and unproductive in the novel. And perhaps the inadequacy of periodisation is shown in the way the temporal is eluded and defied by Eleanor in particular: '"Young?" said Peggy. "I shall never be as young as you are!"' (*TY*, p. 245; compare 'you look like a girl of eighteen!', *TY*, p. 283).

The sense of generational difficulty is emphasised by the relative absence of parent–child relationships in the novel: of the Abercorn Terrace siblings the majority have no children themselves, and of those who do only Morris has his children present in the large family gathering staged in the final chapter (the parent–child relationship in this particular case being hardly featured, and largely as an occasion for Peggy to practise her analytical training on greeting her father: 'Part sex; part pity, she thought. Can one call it "love"?', *TY*, p. 257). Kitty is never seen with her children and Maggie and Sara are orphaned. The lines of generational communication largely proceed between aunts/uncles and nieces/nephews, though not, as suggested above, with any great success (perhaps Woolf's own status as aunt rather than parent is underlined here – 'Most of all I hate the hush & mystery of motherhood. How unreal it all is!', *D* IV. 264). The final tableau of the 'old brothers and sisters' – '"Look, Maggie", [Sara] whispered, turning to her sister, "Look!" She pointed at the Pargiters, standing in the window' (*TY*, p. 316) – summarises how the generations largely consort among themselves, be they siblings or cousins, and how attempts to reach across the generations are fraught with too ready an acceptance of cultural commonplace, be this approving (as in Peggy's picture of the Victorian spinster: 'A wonderful generation, she thought . . .', *TY*, p. 243) or critical (thus Martin on Peggy – 'The younger generation were so serious', and so forth, *TY*, pp. 260–1). Moreover, the idea of the generations displacing each other, as in Kitty's regret for the eventual loss of her home to her son and his wife who 'would walk here after her' (*TY*, p. 203) indicates a recurrent mood of generational envy or resentment, further shown in North's response to Edward and Eleanor's 'taking their ease when the day's work is over': 'For them it's all right, he thought; they've had their day: but not for him, not for his generation' (*TY*, p. 300), a sentiment reciprocated in Kitty's declaration 'How nice it is ... not to be young!' (*TY*, p. 308).[8] Only Eleanor shows much success in mixing with and linking the different generations, though her relationship with Peggy is hardly one of mutual ease – 'Give up brooding, thinking, analysing, Eleanor meant [Peggy] knew. Enjoy the moment – but could one? she asked ...' (*TY*, p. 281).

Woolf's critique of the Victorian is of course much more explicit in her initial draft of the 1880 section, when the work was to be in the format of a 'novel-essay' and was provisionally entitled *The Pargiters*. In Woolf's writing on the Victorian period thus far we have seen, alongside its injustices and repressions, the affirming of a series of 'poetic' elements – romance, beauty, lyricism, individuality, imagination – to offset a more critical and less susceptible modernity. In *The Pargiters*, however, the 'poetry' of the Victorian period is vigorously exposed as fraudulent (an exposure already performed in the 1931 lecture referred to earlier) as Woolf accosts the conspiracy of concealment that refused to acknowledge the sexual feelings of her Victorian protagonists, in accordance with her statement in the lecture that it is vital for the future development of fiction that a woman writer is able to speak 'the truth about her body' (*P*, p. xl). We see how in *The Pargiters* 'the thought or the presence of someone of the other sex' has the power to stimulate in each of the adolescent sisters 'the consciousness of her own body' (*P*, p. 35), and how Edward's battle to overcome the sexual arousal the idea of Kitty causes results in his writing the type of bad poetry occasioned by sublimated feelings 'of reverence, of ecstasy, of romance' as these shy away from the 'genuine' physical emotion (*P*, pp. 67, 82–3). The ousting of 'romance' by sexuality in Woolf's treatment of the year 1880 is emphatic in the key scene of Rose's encounter with the man who exposes himself to her, illustrating how 'Abercorn Terrace was besieged on all sides by what may be called street love', or 'common love' (*P*, p. 38), leading to the siege situation of Victorian girls not being able to leave their houses unchaperoned. It is significant that Rose's experience takes place in a gaslit street, a setting described at greater length in the novel's final version: 'The trees were trembling their shadows over the pavement. The lamps stood at great distances apart, and there were pools of darkness between' (*TY*, p. 21). We have seen previously how such lamplit scenes prompt Woolf's sense of the mystery and beauty of the past (and indeed of the present: 'How beautiful a London street is [at evening], with its islands of light, and its long groves of darkness ...': 'Street Haunting: a London Adventure', *E* IV. 482);[9] but in *The Years* the street shadows no less than other Victorian settings harbour ugliness rather than beauty. Woolf consistently refuses in *The Years* to invest the Victorian setting with anything of the picturesque; the 'lingering shadows and odd corners' produced by 'women in aprons carrying wobbly lamps' in *Orlando* are conspicuously not evoked when Crosby comes into the front drawing-room at Abercorn Terrace 'carrying two silk-shaded lamps' and puts them down (*P*, p. 15; see also *TY*, p. 19). Woolf indeed explicitly resists the pull of any picturesque differentiation of the past – in terms of lighting as of other features – as a distraction from her presentation of the restrictions Victorian women laboured under: 'it may be advisable to dwell for a moment – not too much upon the jingling of hansom bells, and the shaded lamps which were as familiar in 1880, as the hoot of cars and the clarity of electric light are to us, but upon the more important differences' (*P*, p. 33).

The original project of the novel-essay was abandoned as *The Years* developed, and the emphasis on sexuality became less explicit, not only with the removal of the essay-commentary sections but in the fictional scenes themselves, a fact contributing to one critic's complaint that 'we as readers are thrown perhaps too much upon the fertility of our own imaginations to deduce some meaning from the book's seemingly endless ambiguities'.[10] Although Woolf believed in the value for fiction of being able to tell the 'truth' about the body, she argued that present-day 'conventions' are too strong to be challenged without doing harm to the novelist's imagination, and resigned herself to 'wait another fifty years' for this freedom

(P, p. xxxix); this position parallels that in *A Room* where (gender) polemic is too distracting an activity not to damage fictional form. Even so, the refusal to glamorise the Victorian, or to remove it into some safe hinterland of the modern imagination (as Peggy wishes to do), remains perfectly apparent in *The Years*, and in this Woolf's ongoing argument with the so-called 'historical novel' and other picturesque modes of writing history is emphasised. In a review of 1908, for example, she had challenged any portrayal of our ancestors as 'charming', with their 'simple' manners and quaint expressions, insisting that they were 'as ugly, as complex, and as emotional as we are', however much 'their simplicity is more amusing to believe in' (E I. 318). Although *The Years* is keen to address 'the more important differences' (particularly in the treatment of women) between 1880 and the present day, it also wishes to insist on underlying identity, an insistence particularly apparent in *The Pargiters* in the idea of humans being driven by the same sexual instincts, however culturally disguised. Mrs Brown, we remember, 'is human nature, Mrs Brown changes only on the surface', though Woolf does argue that codes and conventions, if enforced long and hard enough, can 'modify' sexual passion, 'even in a girl of perfect physique like Kitty' (P, p. 109). Nevertheless, both novel-essay and final novel wish to present scenes from the past as a vividly lived present (a discarded title for *The Pargiters* was *Here and Now*, D IV. 176), and with this in mind to offer a minimum of historical 'colour' in the form of visual details of, for example, fashion or external settings. Typically, Eleanor's excitement at the bustle of London is as apparent in 1891 as in the 'Present Day' section, and is described without period features such as 'the jingling of hansom bells':

They had left the residential quarter; the houses were changing; they were turning into shops. This was her world; here she was in her element. The streets were crowded; women were swarming in and out of shops with their shopping baskets. There was something customary, rhythmical about it, she thought, like rooks swooping in a field, rising and falling. (TY, p. 69)

The transference of 'history' into elemental, natural rhythms ('like rooks swooping in a field, rising and falling') is recurrent in *The*

Years, and enforces the suggestion above that the novel shows a desire to escape the context of historical periodisation altogether.

In *To the Lighthouse* Woolf gave the central section a title which could act as a simple epigraph or alternative title for *The Years*, 'Time Passes'. In the earlier novel, however, time can be said to pass more productively, suggesting not only an element of historical progress but also the sense of a structure and order to temporality. The novel suggests at one and the same time both the value of Lily's 'escape' from the past and its practices and the need for the present to be open to what *is* of value in the past (or to what the past is made to stand for) in order to allay modern deficiencies. Thus 'Time Passes' in *To the Lighthouse* between two clearly demarcated periods, which communicate with each other in a meaningful relationship, giving time a purposefulness emphasised by the symmetrical climaxes staged at the endings of the novel's two outer sections. But it is difficult to retrieve any such sense of the purposeful or the structured from *The Years*, a difficulty apparent in what seems the random choice of years featured there, where we have succession without obvious purpose, as indicated in the very first paragraph: 'Slowly wheeling, like the rays of a searchlight, the days, the weeks, the years passed one after another across the sky' (*TY*, p. 4). Woolf might be said here to be subjecting the Victorian period (and indeed the modern) to her own 'searchlight', in the far more detailed and dispassionate examination the novel provides.

There is also a powerful sense of simple transience, a lamenting of that which cannot be retrieved, as expressed by Kitty: 'I wish I hadn't quarrelled so much with my mother, she thought, overcome with a sudden sense of the passage of time and its tragedy' (*TY*, p. 135). Unlike Mrs Ramsay, the dead in *The Years* do not return – the party in the concluding section contrasts in this regard with the All Souls' motif of Clarissa Dalloway's party – nor is homage done to them or to the culture in which they figured. For Kitty 'The years changed things; destroyed things; heaped things up – worries and bothers...' (*TY*, p. 198). Her sense of being emotionally hounded by time – 'All passes, all changes, she thought...' – comes to a head when, as noted above, she broods over her home passing to her son and his wife, a scene followed by a reflex emotion of ecstasy experienced within a landscape invested appropriately (for Woolf) with chiaroscuro:

> Then, as she watched, light moved and dark moved; light and shadow went travelling over the hills and over the valleys. A deep murmur sang in her ears – the land itself, singing to itself, a chorus, alone. She lay there listening. She was happy, completely. Time had ceased. (*TY*, p. 203)

But this happiness is not, significantly, the experience of the present moment enriched by the past, as traced in previous chapters, but an experience beyond time altogether, a recurring desire throughout the novel to 'escape' from the years as if in despair at the possibilities of historicity. That this escape is however problematic is signalled rather blatantly by the above passage coming at the very end of the '1914' section, when history is about to crash down on Kitty's sense of ecstasy.

Although, therefore, *The Years* is of all Woolf's novels that which most closely attends to the historical record, it is also that which most finds history wanting. We can approve Eleanor's belief 'that things have changed for the better' over the course of her lifetime in the 'freedom', particularly for women, the years have brought (*TY*, p. 283), while realising that the 'new world' she hoped to see (*TY*, pp. 213–17) is as far off as ever. This reflects Woolf's own strain of political scepticism, again evident in a diary reaction of 1933 after attending the Women's Co-operative Guild Jubilee – 'they say things that arent true: they say we are on the brink of a new world ... Thats why I hate ceremonies – not a word that fits – all wind blown, gaseous, with elementary emotions' (*D* IV. 165). Ironically, Peggy, the main beneficiary of the new freedom, is fatigued and disillusioned, a victim of the stresses of professional practice which make the professions as deadening in her own eyes as the medieval cell or monastery (*TY*, p. 260), and which anticipate Woolf's concerns in *Three Guineas*.[11] Eleanor herself poignantly remembers her naïve enthusing over the prospective 'new world'[12] when she draws up a balance-sheet for modernity with hot water and electric light in the plus column and motor cars and the 'nuisance' of wireless on the debit side (*TY*, p. 241).[13] In fact Woolf conspicuously negates many possibilities for achievement and progress in *The Years* – Rose's suffragette activities are given no prominence, Delia's youthful rebellion rebounds on her – 'Thinking to marry a wild rebel, she had married the most King-respecting, Empire-admiring of country gentlemen' (*TY*, p. 292) – Kitty marries into the aristocracy rather than achieving her dream of becoming a farmer (which is made so much of in *The Pargiters*, providing, indeed, the finale of the novel-part of that text, *P*, pp. 148–9), and the career of Robson's daughter peters out tragically in the recesses of Kitty's memory:

'How one forgets things!' she went on. 'Of course – Robson. That was his name. And the girl I used to like – Nelly? The girl who was going to be a doctor?'
 'Died, I think', said Edward.
 'Died, did she – died – ' said Lady Lasswade. She paused for a moment.
(*TY*, p. 310)

'The skull', as noted in *To the Lighthouse*, and as always in Woolf, is still there.

History therefore seems to be going nowhere in the novel so to speak with the years dribbling away like a tap left running. One of the major elements of affirmation is by contrast the beauty of the natural world and the seasons, a conspicuous running theme from the moonlit setting of '1907', where the roads seem 'plated with silver', to the description of the 'incandescent' summer evening that opens the 'Present Day' chapter. The novel's ending, of course, is reminiscent of *The Waves*, reminding us that Woolf did regard it as a combination of the 'vision' of *The Waves* with the 'facts' of *Night and Day* (*D* IV. 151–2): 'The sun had risen, and the sky above the houses wore an air of extraordinary beauty, simplicity and peace' (*TY*, p. 318). A little earlier we are told that in the dawn 'everything looked clean swept, fresh and virginal' (*TY*, p. 316). The idea that nature can provide a 'new world' emphasises by contrast the absence of any assurance of this in the historical sphere, just as the continuity and sameness of the natural cycle – Eleanor listens to the pigeons cooing (a repeated motif) at dawn in preference to 'God save the King' (*TY*, p. 317) – again offers nature as a refuge (of constancy, of pattern) from the inconclusiveness of history. At the same time it suggests that Eleanor's momentary perception of a 'pattern' in human dealings – 'Does everything then come over again a little differently? she thought' – occasioned by Nicholas's repetitive behaviour and expressions (*TY*, pp. 270–1) – is based on assertions that are little more than the cooing of pigeons, a suggestion enforced by Sara's mocking observation (amply supported throughout the novel) that 'people always say the same thing' (*TY*, p. 217). Humans seem to be governed by a cycle that inspires a 'feeling of desolation' in Peggy: 'Directly something got together, it broke ... And then you have to pick up the pieces, and make something new, something different, she thought ...' (*TY*, p. 287).

There are, however, momentary perceptions of a more fruitful human and political enterprise in the novel; North's dismissal of 'joining societies' and 'signing manifestoes' (*TY*, p. 296) reflects of course Woolf's own position in *Three Guineas*, which stresses the value of remaining an outsider in an age of groupings and mass movements that can be easily and dangerously manipulated ('No idols, no idols, no idols, [Maggie's] laughter seemed to chime' (*TY*, p. 311 – see also p. 278)). Peggy too is alarmed by people 'who had not even the courage to be themselves, but must dress up, imitate, pretend' (*TY*, pp. 284–5). North is aware of the potential dangers of solitude and self-absorption in this attitude, a condition that both attracts and distresses him throughout; it is no accident that the 'only poem he knew by heart' is Marvell's 'The Garden', which at one point he quotes from: 'Society is all but rude – / To this delicious solitude ...' (*TY*, p. 248). On the other hand, he sees solitude as 'the worst torture ... that human beings can inflict' (*TY*, p. 310 – see also p. 295). The ambivalence is briefly resolved by the sight of bubbles rising in his glass, which leads him to a vision of individuality properly merged with the collective – 'the bubble and the stream, the stream and the bubble – myself and the world together – he raised his glass' (*TY*, p. 300), a blueprint Woolf endorses in the final endnote to *Three Guineas*, where she quotes Coleridge, Rousseau, Whitman and George Sand to the same effect: 'To find a form of society according to which each one uniting with the whole shall yet obey himself only and remain as free as before' (*TG*, p. 323, n. 49).[14]

A little later, however, 'the bubbles had ceased to rise' in his glass (*TY*, p. 310). The quest for and promotion of the values of individuality, joined with an active social awareness and sympathy, is perhaps the nearest we have to a programme in *The Years*, and is most fully embodied in Eleanor, whose life has been 'other people's lives', though 'perhaps there's "I" at the middle of it, she thought' (*TY*, p. 269), though certainly not the egotistical 'I, I, I' of the young poet (*TY*, pp. 264–5 – nor that of the male writer diagnosed in *A Room*, p. 90).

But North's brief 'vision', like Peggy's – 'she saw, not a place, but a state of being, in which there was real laughter, real happiness, and this fractured world was whole; whole, and free. But how could she say it?' (*TY*, p. 285) – is too private and fragile to instil conviction, nor is there any indication of the intention or course of action that could realise it. If we seek a more reassuring model of belief and behaviour we are forced back upon Eleanor, who, as noted above, has a centrality, linking the generations, in the novel. If the 'new world' is merely a fantasy, Eleanor's own ability to remain 'new' at every period of her life, and particularly in old age – optimistic, thirsting for fresh experience, keenly responsive to the present moment – is a key emphasis in *The Years*:

Her feeling of happiness returned to her, her unreasonable exaltation. It seemed to her that they were all young, with the future before them. Nothing was fixed; nothing was known; life was open and free before them. (*TY*, p. 280)

The way she outlives the objects of her past – 'she was suffused with a feeling of happiness. Was it because this had survived – this keen sensation (she was waking up) and the other thing, the solid object – she saw an ink-corroded walrus – had vanished?' (*TY*, p. 312) – indicates this perpetual renewal, and it is no accident that the final words spoken in the novel are her simple 'And now?' (*TY*, p. 318), which again emphasises her commitment to the 'here and now' of one of the novel's discarded titles. Her powers of renewal do not, however, signify a simple discarding of the past, although at one point she does think to herself 'I've only the present moment', a notion immediately qualified in the text by memories of 'millions of things' prompted by the sight of her siblings at the party (*TY*, p. 268). We are further told near the end of the novel that 'she wanted to enclose the present moment; to make it stay; to fill it fuller and fuller, with the past, the present and the future, until it shone, whole, bright, deep with understanding' (*TY*, p. 313).

Even so, compared with much of Woolf's other writing the Victorian past informs the present far less positively in *The Years*. Eleanor's desire to embrace the present moment is stressed in a way that differs markedly from the presentation of that moment in *Orlando*:

> what more terrifying revelation can there be than that it is the present moment? That we survive the shock at all is only possible because the past shelters us on one side and the future on another. (*O*, p. 206)

As the 1930s wore on, however, both past and future seemed to offer increasingly less 'shelter', forcing Woolf 'to hug the present moment' even more: 'If one does not lie back & sum up & say to the moment, this very moment, stay you are so fair, what will be one's gain, dying? No: stay, this moment. No one ever says that enough' (*D* IV. 135). This response not unnaturally intensified with the approach of the war (see *D* V. 262, 346). Woolf's noting that after writing *To the Lighthouse* her father 'comes back now more as a contemporary' when she thinks of him (*D* III. 208) ties in with the emphasis in *The Years* on not succumbing to what she had earlier described as 'the enkindling effect of the past' (*E* III. 299 — the context within which *Night and Day* was written, as we have seen) simply in so far as it is the past, but to live it, so to speak, as a contemporary experience free from any glamour of retrospect. We might also contrast *Orlando*'s ideal of the successful synchronising of 'the ... different times which beat simultaneously in every normal human system' (*O*, p. 211) with Rose's being made to feel 'puzzled' at 'living at two different times at the same moment' (*TY*, p. 123). It is as if the moment needs to concentrate its resources on itself.

When Martin answers Peggy's question about whether the youthful Delia and Patrick were in love: ' "We were all in love", he said, glancing sideways at Peggy. The younger generation were so serious' (*TY*, p. 260), the romancing of the past carries much less weight than in *Mrs Dalloway*, or *To the Lighthouse* or even *Orlando*, where Victorian love and courtship are a significant theme. We see nothing of this grand passion in *The Years*, whereas the episode of 'street love' remains from *The Pargiters*, and Martin himself, as the spokesperson of 'love', is shown experiencing only casual flirtations (*TY*, pp. 94–5, 182ff). Nor does Woolf indulge in the novel her admiration for 'old coronets' (*MOB*, p. 208) and aristocratic tradition – Martin salutes those at Lady Lasswade's dinner-party in '1914' ('it's a good world ... he added; large; generous; hospitable. And very nice-looking' (*TY*, p. 186)), but Martin is not someone the reader is encouraged to identify with and Eleanor's declining to attend the party can be seen, as Lady Lasswade herself feels, as a more significant moral judgement (*TY*, p. 190). Lady Warburton, whose slow, crabbed exit from the party prompts Martin's observation 'the nineteenth century going to bed' (*TY*, p. 195), displays 'beautiful breeding that simulated at least human charity' (*TY*, p. 190), but Woolf's remarks on 'breeding' have not hitherto been qualified in such a way.

When, in comparing her Victorian past with her present, Eleanor declares 'We're happier – we're freer ...' (*TY*, p. 283), our instant assent is qualified by Peggy's bitter reaction to the proposition. Woolf's own claim that the moderns have 'a keener appetite for happiness' than the Victorians (*E* II. 37) illustrates her obsessive measuring of present experience against that of the previous era. Thus a fancy-dress party of 1923 prompts the observation: 'We were all easy & gifted & friendly & like good children rewarded by having the capacity for enjoying ourselves thus. Could our fathers? I, wearing my mothers laces, looked at Mary [MacCarthy]'s little soft Jerboa face in the old looking glass – & wondered' (*D* II. 223).[15] But the point is that any judgement of the comparative benefits of the Victorian and the modern requires that one has experienced both, as Eleanor has. Peggy may be sardonic about the latter's belief in progress, but she herself belongs to the next generation who, from childhood on, have experienced greater freedom (her night-time escapade is referred to in '1911' (*TY*, p. 154)); she is not a product of Abercorn Terrace but was brought up in a spacious house in

Dorset where 'it was always the eighteenth century' and 'the past seemed near, domestic, friendly' (*TY*, p. 144). The 'portrait of a Victorian spinster', which Peggy is concocting in order to describe Eleanor to a friend may, as she recognises, be totally false (*TY*, p. 245), but the Victorian remains a critical part of Eleanor's experience, enabling her to estimate the value of modernity in a way that Peggy, who takes its privileges for granted, cannot. This is also the justification in *The Years* for historical memory, and a reminder of Woolf's constant theme that to live 'most fully in the present' – to fully embrace the moment as Eleanor does – still requires that present to be 'backed by the past' (*MOB*, p. 98), even if that backing is now a much darker one. Part of Eleanor's greater freedom (a term, like 'happiness', that Peggy also queries) is the freedom of expression, and it is here that 'we steal a march upon the Victorians' in Woolf's eyes (*E* IV. 451): 'how much that we talk of openly was wrapped up in brown paper and hidden away behind plush curtains'.[16] As far as the private life is concerned Woolf could congratulate her own generation thus: 'No doubt we have re-arranged life almost completely. Our parents were mere triflers at the game – went to the grave with all the secret <drawers> springs unpressed ... we have all mastered the art of life, & very fascinating it is' (*D* II. 199). If *The Years* gave Woolf the opportunity to express beliefs in a modern emancipation that are here not complicated by being entwined with a powerful nostalgia now laid to rest, it reminds us through Peggy, in a way *Three Guineas* will develop, that that emancipation should not lead to a new captivity. And the way to prevent this, as we shall see, is paradoxically to maintain and transform other aspects of the Victorian heritage.

And even in *The Years* this heritage is not in any case completely thrown off; it would be surprising if it ever could be, given what we have seen thus far. When Eleanor attacks the photograph in the evening paper of 'a fat man gesticulating' (who is likely to be Mussolini) – 'She tore the paper across with one sweep of her hand and flung it on the floor' – Peggy is 'shocked' and impressed by the expression on Eleanor's lips ('Damned ... bully!') that accompanies the gesture: 'It was as if she still believed with passion – she, old

Eleanor – in the things that man had destroyed. A wonderful generation, [Peggy] thought, as they drove off. Believers ...' (*TY*, pp. 242–3). Apart from emphasising the constant renewal of Eleanor's commitment, and thus ironising Peggy's use of the term 'old', the episode confirms Woolf's belief that the Victorians possessed an energy and engagement which for the next generation, experiencing more directly the destruction of the First World War, had disappeared, instanced by Peggy's weariness and pessimism (though Eleanor's action, however admirable, is not politic, as we shall see). The point is underlined when the two women pass the statue of Edith Cavell on the way to the party, and Eleanor reflects on how Peggy's bitterness results from her brother's death in the war (*TY*, pp. 246–7). As early as 1915 as we have seen (above, p. 17) Woolf was comparing a contemporary apathy which 'sought for nothing, believed in nothing' adversely with the Victorians. In commenting on a biography of Alice Meynell (1847–1922) in her diary in 1929, Woolf noted how 'When one reads a life one often compares one's own life with it', and in the comparison of Victorian and modern attitudes she is led to suggest inter alia how 'They believed in things & we didn't' (*D* III. 250). Another area where the Victorians may be said to 'steal a march' in Woolf's term over their successors is in their expression of individualism; thus *The Years* sketches some worries about those 'who had not even the courage to be themselves', prompted by the spectacle of 'faces mobbed at the door of a picture palace; apathetic, passive faces; the faces of people drugged with cheap pleasures' (*TY*, p. 284). Here worry over a modern apathy and a disdain for mass entertainment come together. In one of the essays from her series *The London Scene* (1931–2) Woolf contrasts the past of the House of Commons when 'Individuality was allowed to unfold itself' in the oratory of exceptional figures like Gladstone, Disraeli and Palmerston with the sight of the minister of today, who is a 'common hard-worked man of business', stamped by a 'huge machine' rendering him 'plain, featureless, impersonal'. In 'speaking to all men everywhere', via media like the radio, his speeches too take on an impersonality in which 'Wit, invective, passion, are no longer called for'. Woolf equates this down-sizing of the individual, so to speak, with democracy, and declares her own contrary love of 'the abnormal, the particular, the splendid human being', adding 'let us hope that democracy will come, but only a hundred years hence, when we are beneath the grass' (*LS*, pp. 42–4).[17]

In her Victorian retrospect Woolf frequently notes how 'any sort of distinction or eminence' was promoted 'in a way no longer so carefully arranged for, or so unquestionably accepted ... Personality ... seems to have been accorded a licence for the expression of itself for which we can find no parallel in the present day' (*E* II. 172). Woolf adds 'Tennyson, of course, is the supreme example of what we mean'. If in *The Years* itself the Victorian is not conspicuously saluted for its 'individuality' any more than for its romance, the sense of a 'featureless' modernity is certainly present in the text, and it is the 'old brothers and sisters' gathered in the window who form the final spectacle in the novel:

> The group in the window, the men in their black-and white evening dress, the women in their crimsons, golds and silvers, wore a statuesque air for a moment, as if they were carved in stone. Their dresses fell in stiff sculptured folds. Then they moved; they changed their attitudes; they began to talk. (*TY*, p. 316)

In her essay on the House of Commons, Woolf indeed notes that the days of statuary are over, and how absurd it would be to commemorate the plain and 'featureless' moderns in this manner – 'the transition into marble is unthinkable' (*LS*, p. 40). Our 'little men and women' move about on the floor of a vast 'splendid hall', an architectural image of the global reach of the new communications, as opposed to the Victorian sculptural image of individuality and personal projection. Although Woolf asks for a deferment of democracy, rather than its rejection, she does end this essay with the hope that 'by some stupendous stroke of genius' we might see combined 'the vast hall and the small, the particular, the individual human being' (*LS*, pp. 43–4). The desire to salvage individuality within an inevitably 'impersonal' future, to retain particularity however much it is writ 'small', recalls North's image of 'the bubble and the stream, the stream and the bubble' above. The trace of individualism as a key Victorian legacy survives then into *The Years*, as it does elsewhere more insistently: Tennyson, as its supreme exemple, features in the project Woolf finally realised in January 1935, while she was 'in the thick' of writing *The Years* (*D* IV. 264), the revision and staging of her play *Freshwater*, with its cast of eccentrics that includes Julia Margaret Cameron, Ellen Terry and G. F. Watts. Woolf did have some doubts about the licence she argued the Victorian age ('which for all its faults was prolific of genius') accorded to 'personality', in so far as it encouraged 'the great men [who] were secluded and worshipped' to write 'twice as much as they ought to have written' (*E* II. 81), but whatever her ambivalence about Victorian 'greatness' she remained fascinated by it, and it is significant that *The London Scene* series should include an essay on 'Great Men's Houses', sites of irresistible attraction to Woolf whatever she may have thought of some of their inhabitants like Carlyle (*LS*, pp. 23–9). One such house she visited (while its incumbent was still alive) was Max Gate in Dorchester, at Hardy's invitation, an invitation she scorned in a letter to Janet Case ('we don't do it ... as I hate great men', *L* III. 202). This didn't stop the visit (in 1926) being written up in the diary, however, at great (and glowing) length – 'What impressed me was his freedom, ease, & vitality. He seemed very "Great Victorian" doing the whole thing with a sweep of his hand ...' (*D* III. 100).

Throughout the 1930s Woolf was worried about the specialisation and professionalisation that she saw overtaking the world of letters, raising the problem in her essay 'All About Books' in 1931. After praising Trollope, Dickens, Carlyle and Macaulay for 'all providing that solace, that security, that sense that the human heart does not change which our miserable age requires and our living authors so woefully fail to provide' (*CDB*, p. 112), Woolf considers 'a collection of critical essays by various writers' entitled *Scrutinies* (*CDB*, p. 114) and laments the evidence there of 'a uniformity and a drill and a discretion unknown before' in critical writing, produced by the university system of teaching and examining English literature (*CDB*, p. 116).[18] Individuality in this sphere too seems doomed to die out among this 'erudite and eugenic offspring' (*CDB*, p. 117): 'Where is the adventurous, the intolerant, the immensely foolish young man or woman who dares to be himself?' (*CDB*, p. 115).

Woolf ends the essay 'turning over the honest, the admirable, the entirely sensible and unsentimental pages' of *Scrutinies* and asking herself, 'where is love? . . . where is the sound of the sea and the red of the rose; where is music, imagery, and a voice speaking from the heart?' (*CDB*, p. 117).[19] This returns us to the start of the essay, where the 'human heart' is seen as always in Woolf as a particularly Victorian feature.

Woolf continued to attack the university degree in English literature in essays like 'Why?' of 1934 and in *Three Guineas*, and her contrary approach to the subject ('why learn English literature at universities when you can read it for yourselves in books?', 'Why?', *DM*, p. 147) returns us to earlier essays like 'Reading', and to Woolf's retrospective model of a literary education. In the obituary on Lady Strachey Woolf notes how 'She was an omnivorous reader. She had her hands upon the whole body of English literature, from Shakespeare to Tennyson, with the large loose grasp that was so characteristic of the cultivated Victorian' (*E* IV. 575). Here we have something approaching Woolf's ideal of the common reader, obviously not 'common' here in terms of social class, but rather in the sense of 'omnivorous', non-specialised. But the Victorian legacy here – 'those old books which she could no longer read herself, but almost commanded the younger generation to love as she had loved them' (*E* IV. p. 576) – is certainly under threat, and *Three Guineas* will be among other things a manifesto on behalf of this threatened way of reading.[20] The terms in which Woolf described Augustine Birrell, whom she met in 1923 – 'a good Victorian all round humane literary type, sunned by various kinds of life, as we aren't now – barrister, politician, essayist' (*D* II. 256) – similarly reveal a figure threatened by an increasingly specialised and professionalised way of life, and even his son Francis, born in 1889 and a close friend of Woolf's in the 1920s and 30s, qualifies for the label 'Victorian' on account of, among other qualities, his 'random energy' (*D* III. 61). Here the adjective and noun are of equal importance in Birrell's being thus labelled.[21]

Returning to *The Years*, we can see how in aspects of her temperament and personality, and in her upbringing, Eleanor displays her

Victorian pedigree, a figure whose endowment of energy and resoluteness paradoxically allows her to cast off the age that thus endowed her. In this, she anticipates Woolf's portrayal of Roger Fry in the biography of 1940, discussed below. But *The Years* no longer aims at the cultural and historical mediation we find in Woolf's earlier novels, and in the absence of any such project inclines towards finding order and pattern in realms that lie 'outside' history altogether. Thus the older generation's desire to escape from its past and the younger generation's being baffled and disaffected by its present, as with North and Peggy, ensure that neither modernity nor the Victorian seems a particularly hospitable era, and the contrast between them (for good and bad) not as productive a subject as hitherto for Woolf. Eleanor is in the best position, and has the most receptiveness as a character, to make that contrast, and although this receptiveness – involving passion, family loyalty, the power to 'believe', the possession of a 'heart' – may be a Victorian birthright, she shows, as remarked, little sympathy with the century of her birth. If 'history' thus seems inhospitable, the refuge the natural world provides is mediated again, in part, through the receptivity of Eleanor, but however much she is attuned to that world and its pigeons (and in this possesses an unmistakeable Wordsworthian resonance: compare the 'miracle' of her spirit which in old age is unchanged from 'So when I was a child; so when I was a girl' (*TY*, p. 280) with Wordsworth's poem 'My heart leaps up') we still have to see her within a social and historical context. Within this context, Eleanor, for all her 'commitment', can seem at times benignly vaporous in a stereotypically 'elderly' way: 'I'm not despondent, no, because people are so kind, so good at heart ... So that if only ordinary people, ordinary people like ourselves ...' (*TY*, p. 247). Like many statements of belief and proposals of action in the novel, the sentence remains unfinished, a little speech without a peroration, picking up one of the novel's recurrent themes (*TY*, pp. 236, 316).[22] Eleanor sets the reader similar problems, in fact, to Mrs Swithin in Woolf's final novel, *Between the Acts*, a character whose elderly benignity and vision of wholeness ('one-making', *BA*, p. 104) are both undimmed and ineffectual.

'Nox est perpetua una dormienda', North reads by chance browsing in a book at the party. The words of Catullus occupy him as he watches the guests go downstairs to eat, with the older members of the party going first:

> The others began to follow them. The younger generation following in the wake of the old, North said to himself as he put the book back on the shelf and followed. Only, he observed, they were not so very young; Peggy – there were white hairs on Peggy's head – she must be thirty-seven, thirty-eight? (*TY*, p. 288)

It would be easy to argue from this and other instances in the novel that its fundamental theme is transience, the succession of the 'hungry' generations treading one another down, as in Keats's famous ode – see also Kitty's meditation at the end of '1914', referred to above. The only sure peroration is death. This would bear out the idea of there being a deliberate reference in the novel's title to the refrain of Hardy's poem 'During Wind and Rain', 'Ah, no; the years, the years', with its lament that all leads but to the grave. Although Eleanor does experience a sense of the 'endless night' awaiting her at the end of the novel, confirming the undeniable emphasis on the 'nox perpetua' theme, her experience is immediately countered by the arrival of the dawn and all it signifies. But whether we prioritise the 'Hardyesque' mood of *The Years*, or prefer a more Wordsworthian emphasis on renewal in the face of time passing, or indeed a mixture of both elements, we are led towards age-old issues of life striving with death that have the effect of reducing the significance of the specific historical context, the years 1880 to the 'present day', and with this the Victorian–modern 'debate'. In this, the unadorned title *The Years* shows a minor but telling contrast with a memoir Woolf refers to in *Three Guineas* (p. 274, n. 1) that covers a similar time span, the Countess of Lovelace's *Fifty Years, 1882–1932*. The debate does not disappear in Woolf, but concentrates itself elsewhere, in the non-fiction works discussed in the following chapter.

The fictional withdrawal from this debate, after its centrality to the earlier novels, is announced in *The Waves* of 1931; *The Pargiters* in its original novel-essay form would inevitably have reintroduced it, but Woolf's abandoning this project testifies to her seeming desire for the fiction to address more 'elemental' considerations and a less determining time-span, so that if *The Years* is to be seen as a combination of *The Waves* and *Night and Day*, it is the former text which arguably represents the dominant discourse. Although *The Waves* does contain some specific historical referents — for example the picture of Queen Alexandra at the school the girls attend (*W*, pp. 16, 23) — it follows a series of lives attuned to an ahistorical natural cycle of birth, growth, maturity and death rather than one defined by temporal events.[23] Thus the six figures are introduced to us in infancy with personalities already determined and distinguished from one another, and the rest of their lives, as the novel traces the cycle towards death, is an unfolding of these original states. Critics such as Lyndall Gordon have been quick to note the Wordsworthian scheme here, prompted by Woolf's transcribing in her diary lines from Book 7 of the 1850 *Prelude* (458–66), which talk of documenting the passage of a life by 'attention to inner as opposed to external event' *D* III. 247).[24] As Gordon also notes, Wordsworth's 'Immortality Ode', especially lines 164–70, is an 'obvious *donneé* for *The Waves*' (p. 237) in its suggestion of life's issuing from an 'immortal sea', as also in the idea of childhood as the authentic site of being and identity.[25] In *A Sketch of the Past* Woolf will open by recording 'the most important of all my memories', hearing the waves breaking over the beach at St Ives from her nursery, suggesting that 'If life has a base that it stands upon, if it is a bowl that one fills and fills and fills — then my bowl without a doubt stands upon this memory' (*MOB*, p. 64) – a moment of being that, in the perpetual renewal it offers, corresponds precisely to Wordsworth's 'spots of time' famously described in Book 12 of the 1850 *Prelude* (lines 208–335).

If *The Waves* and *The Years* insist on an elemental framework to human existence that subordinates historical context, thus anticipating a similar emphasis in *Between the Acts* illustrated in Mrs Swithin's declaration that 'the Victorians' never existed – 'only you and me and William dressed differently' (*BA*, p. 104) – they also confirm Woolf's fascination with retrospect, with a past that, however defined, can never be left behind: we may not know where we are going, but we know the crucial and determining importance of where we have come from. And the continuing importance of that past, both as historically defined and yet essentially ahistorical, is as marked in Woolf's writing of the 1930s as it was previously – though here the unresolved debate between these two positions, returned to below, is a further factor in that 'unravelling' of the Post-Victorian synthesis with which we began this chapter.

CHAPTER 5

Incoherence: the final works

Woolf regarded *Three Guineas* (1938) as forming 'one book' with *The Years* (*D* v. 148), in the sense that the frustrated yearnings of the novel – 'she saw, not a place, but a state of being, in which there was real laughter, real happiness, and this fractured world was whole; whole, and free. But how could she say it?' (*TY*, p. 285) – are here addressed through a programme of action whereby freedom and wholeness – key terms in *Three Guineas* – might be achieved. A statement in the early part of the book – 'The years change things; slightly but imperceptibly they change them' (*TG*, p. 151) – heralds both progress for women in the educational and professional spheres in the last hundred years or so, and also a rate of change that is slow and grudging and qualified by the persistence of age-old problems, sometimes in a new guise. Thus 1919, 'the sacred year', saw the opening up of several of the professions to women previously barred to them, and is a clear marker of historical progress (*TG*, p. 141); but if, as Woolf goes on to insist, the professions in question inculcate a masculine competitiveness, slavery to money-making and addiction to ambition that are inimical to health and humanity, what is the value of these so-called new freedoms? (*TG*, p. 197). This question was raised in relation to Peggy in *The Years*, who, in spite of Eleanor's declaration that 'We're happier – we're freer', seems to enjoy neither state in herself, or see them in others, but the debate about progress, which is left in something of an impasse in the novel, is analysed in detail in *Three Guineas* and solutions are proposed.

In short, the educational and professional freedoms now starting to open up to women cannot be embraced without some fundamental change to the entire system, a system that, in 1938, is still denying female access, or, where access is permitted, is introducing women to a public world which, 'with its possessiveness, its jealousy, its pugnacity, its greed', is a counterpart to the war-mongering of continental Fascism (*TG*, p. 199). In the former case, 1938 is still playing out the battles of the age of Queen Victoria, when the professional men were such 'great fighters': 'the battle of Harley Street in the year 1869 [seeking to deny women entrance to the medical profession] might well be the battle of Cambridge University at the present moment [denying women's colleges membership of the university] . . . It seems as if there were no progress in the human race, but only repetition' (*TG*, p. 190). Nevertheless, the great patriarchal fighters of the Victorian age did meet their match, and the 'force of the fathers' had to yield to an opposing force 'of tremendous power' unleashed by the desires of the daughters to escape their confinement (*TG*, p. 266). The biography of the previous century ('once more we will have recourse to Victorian biography because it is only in the Victorian age that biography becomes rich and representative', *TG*, p. 258), is a major resource for Woolf throughout *Three Guineas* in documenting what she calls 'the great Victorian fight between the victims of the patriarchal system and the patriarchs, of the daughters against the fathers' (*TG*, pp. 188–9). This fighting quality, found in fathers and daughters alike, represents another symptom of Victorian 'heart' or passion which characterises Eleanor in *The Years*, and the 'force' of her invective against Mussolini as she tears the newspaper photograph across exemplifies a passion which Peggy admires as a feature of that 'wonderful generation' but which she cannot find in herself: 'What a queer set they are, she thought . . . So she had seen her father crumple *The Times* and sit trembling with rage because somebody had said something in a newspaper. How odd!' (*TY*, p. 242). Woolf's celebrating the female protagonists of 'the great Victorian fight' in *Three Guineas* invests the Victorian period as a more 'heroic age' than her own, but it is important to stress that for her the continuation of the 'fight' has now to develop a very different strategy.

In chapter 4 of *A Room of One's Own* Woolf ponders the harm that being caught up in a climate of 'fight' did to the Victorian woman writer; how for example 'anger was tampering with the integrity of Charlotte Brontë the novelist' (*RO*, p. 66). In *Three Guineas* Woolf maintains this attitude by outlining, in the quest to stave off war, a strategy of 'indifference' rather than opposition – if the educational system and professional life both promote a competitiveness and pugnacity that contribute to the likelihood of war, woman's battle for access, however necessary and admirable, now takes second place to a 'battle' for reform of these spheres that needs to work with other tools and approaches than those of Victorian militancy. This is a more urgent and difficult task than continuing the battle for access, which has not been won in all areas, as in the case of the Church, to which Woolf turns her attention in Part 3. 'Fighting' being 'a sex characteristic which she cannot share' (*TG*, p. 232), the 'educated man's daughter' must work to subvert war through, for example, promoting colleges where 'competition would be abolished' (*TG*, p. 155), or games leagues where 'there could be no cup or award of any kind' (*TG*, p. 242). Where militarism is met with, the response should not be the 'excited emotion' (*TG*, p. 235) of either assent or protest but 'an attitude of complete indifference' (*TG*, p. 232). Even Eleanor's attack on Mussolini's photograph, however admirable in its passion, is an instance of force provoking force that accordingly feeds into the enemy's hands, and is reminiscent of the famous episode in Chaucer where the Wife of Bath tears pages out of Jankyn's book – an episode frequently seen as replicating antifeminist aggression rather than countering it effectively.[1] When Woolf introduces the picture of the *Duce* at the end of *Three Guineas* it is not, she says, to 'excite once more the sterile emotion of hate', but to emphasise the need to reflect upon the fact that tyranny and servility are present in our own institutions and our own responses no less than in the Fascist system (*TG*, pp. 270–1).

But Woolf does not simply go back to the Victorian period for the historical record of the great father–daughter fight, and to consider its implications; the extent to which *Three Guineas* is dyed in

Victorian biography indicates that that record has a more extensive use than this. Woolf sees in the Victorian past not only the tradition of militancy she admires but departs from, but also the inspiration for her own position as 'outsider', which enables her to establish ancestries. If the biographies of figures like Gertrude Bell and Mary Kingsley confirm the sparseness of women's education in conventional terms, and the 'horrors' of this deprivation, the record also gives, in their undertaking of domestic and public work without opportunity for advancement or professional recognition, a model for the 'outsider' position Woolf promotes: 'not to be recognized; not to be egotistical; to do the work for the sake of doing the work' (*TG*, p. 201). Victorian women had what Woolf terms an 'unpaid-for education', in which their teachers were, famously, 'poverty, chastity, derision and freedom from unreal loyalties' (that is, 'loyalty to old schools, old colleges, old churches, old ceremonies, old countries') (*TG*, p. 203), and it is this tradition of outsiderness that modern women should bear with them into the professions, enabling them to escape the risks that professional life brings with it: excessive and self-crippling concerns with money-making, self-promotion, professional pride and exclusiveness. With this, the reform of those professions, and an end of fostering belligerence in all its forms, could be achieved. The same might be hoped from a college system free from degrees, distinctions and prizes, 'the old poisoned vanities and parades which breed competition and jealousy' (*TG*, p. 156).

As with *A Room of One's Own*, therefore, Woof outlines a female ancestry to be recognised and adopted by modern women and put to use: a recuperation of age-old denials. Just as it would be 'a thousand pities' in *A Room* if women's confinement indoors 'all these millions of years' were 'wasted' as an aesthetic heritage, so the deprivations inflicted not only on the celebrated women of the Victorian age but on all 'our uneducated mothers and grandmothers' can be used to enable a reform of public life: 'the traditions of the private house, that ancestral memory which lies behind the present moment, are there to help' (*TG*, p. 207). Thus the 'private house', the scene of immemorial repression, is transformed into an image of a new, non-competitive public world – the quest is 'not to burn the house down, but to make its windows blaze':

And let the daughters of uneducated women dance round the new house, the poor house ... and let them sing, 'We have done with war! We have done with tyranny!' And their mothers will laugh from their graves, 'It was for this that we suffered obloquy and contempt!' (*TG*, p. 208)

Woolf's call 'not to burn the house down' is consistent with her literary reservations elsewhere about a rampant modernity bent on 'smashing and crashing', and her need to set the explosive energies of the new within the perspective of historical ancestry, as in *The Common Reader*. And indeed, *Three Guineas* as a whole, bent on maximising the value of Victorian biography both for its evidence of injustice and for a proper response to that injustice that can be adopted today ('biography is many-sided; biography never returns a single and simple answer to any question that is asked of it', *TG*, p. 204), has another crucial element making up its Post-Victorianism, namely its critical and investigative method, where the practice of the 'common reader' is again to the fore.

Early on in the book Woolf returns to her criticism, referred to in the previous chapter, of the 'vain and vicious' practice of studying English literature at university level (*TG*, p. 158), while her call for a reform of the university system argues that its aim 'should be not to segregate and specialize, but to combine ... [to] discover what new combinations make good wholes in human life' (*TG*, p. 155). As we have seen, she presents university teaching in English as promoting a critical 'uniformity and a drill' that threatens to convert what is traditionally the most liberal of the professions, that of literature, where the entry requirements are simply pen and paper ('Pianos and models, Paris, Vienna and Berlin, masters and mistresses, are not needed by a writer', 'Professions for Women', *DM*, p. 149), into another unit of that competitive procession where all must keep 'in step' (*TG*, pp. 137, 183). Throughout *Three Guineas* Woolf is seen practising (and promoting) a literally untutored approach to her subject, insisting that the evidence for her argument and for its conclusions is directly available to anyone on the library shelves:

'The answer to that question is scattered all about these volumes; and is legible to anyone who can read plain English' (*TG*, pp. 187–8); 'let us go into greater detail and consult the facts which are nowadays open to the inspection of all who can read their mother tongue in biography' (*TG*, p. 195). Here 'the traditions of the private house' are again operative, more specifically deriving from the education afforded Woolf by access to her father's library and the reading habits this facilitated, a similar opportunity now, she argues, being universally available, whatever problems with access continue elsewhere – 'enter any of the public libraries which are now free to all' (*TG*, p. 206). By the time of *Three Guineas*, we might say, Woolf has definitively crossed the threshold from the maternal garden of her 1920s nostalgia to the paternal study as the key Victorian locale (retracing Cam's passage from one to the other in *To the Lighthouse*, p. 205) in her quest for fact and documentation rather than romance.

This resistance to modern educational developments, and desire to promote and extend her own readerly upbringing and practice, is a central theme in *Three Guineas*, and is consistent with an observation Woolf made as early as 1906 that 'there is much to be said surely for that respectable custom which allows the daughter to educate herself at home, while the son is educated by others abroad', an early recuperation of the unequal restrictions the daughters of educated men suffer.[2] In Part 3 of *Three Guineas* she again resorts to biography to dig out cases of 'Victorian psychology' in which fathers assert ownership over daughters, motivated as they were by a 'very strong emotion [of jealousy] which has its origin below the levels of conscious thought' (*TG*, pp. 260–1). Woolf rejects the claim that the discussion of 'the psychology of the sexes is "... a matter for specialists" ':

we cannot leave the psychology of the sexes to the charge of specialists . . . Let us then grope our way amateurishly enough among these very ancient and obscure emotions which we have known ever since the time of Antigone and Ismene and Creon at least . . . which the Professors have only lately brought to the surface and named 'infantile fixation', 'Oedipus complex', and the rest. (*TG*, pp. 257–8)

Again, what the academics would appropriate and veil in professional obscurity is there in the literary and biographical record for anyone who would consult the bookshelves, and in the evidence that 'we can collect from history, biography, and from the daily paper' (*TG*, p. 258), evidence that is plentiful and not at all obscure. Woolf's position as a common reader and not a 'specialist', her belief that 'if common men and women are to be free they must learn to speak freely' about areas the specialist would lay claim to (*TG*, p. 257), see specialism and the professionalisation of study as bad for the specialist and the public alike. In the former case it carries all the dangers that lead to the life of a 'cripple in a cave' – lack of time for other things, lack of a sense of proportion, lack of humanity, competitiveness and so on (*TG*, p. 197). The 'wish to withdraw and study, as theology with its refinements, and scholarship with its subtleties' show, 'all those meaningless but highly ingenious turnings and twistings into which the intellect ties itself', results no less in 'the immense elaboration of modern instruments and methods of war' than in 'the vast deposit of notes at the bottom of Greek, Latin and *even* English texts' (*TG*, pp. 256, 315 n. 31, my emphasis). The outcome is 'that separation between the Church and the people; between literature and the people; between the husband and the wife which has had its part in putting the whole of our Commonwealth out of gear' (*TG*, p. 256).

The reference to the separation between husband and wife reminds us that the opportunity 'to withdraw and study' has hitherto been largely provided for men; the life of the scholar (or the cleric) being sustainable because 'his wife can undertake the care of the household and the family' (*TG*, p. 256). This is of course as much or more true of the Victorian cleric or scholar as of the modern, and it has long been an insistence of Woolf's that the 'great men' of the Victorian age, being 'secluded and worshipped ... wrote twice as much as they ought to have written' (*E* II. 81), and that 'devis[ing] a method by which men may bear children' might be one way of checking this 'unbridled' writing activity ('A Society', *CSF*, p. 135). The first quotation here is taken from a review of 1917, in which Woolf protests at the implied idea in the book under review of a 'priesthood' of writers and artists 'properly pensioned and quartered in comfortable rooms in Oxford and Cambridge, where so long as they live the masses shall do them honour' – 'Was there ever a plan better calculated to freeze literature at the root ...?' she asks, an enquiry that indicates how long some of the ideas in *Three Guineas* had been brewing (*E* II. 81).

In *Three Guineas*, then, Woolf takes her own upbringing and experience as a reader and promotes it as a model for all, a renewal of the relation 'between literature and the people' which will be destroyed if literature is left to 'the charge of the specialists'. A similar emphasis is found in 'The Leaning Tower', a lecture delivered in the wake of *Three Guineas* to the Brighton branch of the Workers' Educational Association (WEA) in April 1940, where Woolf claims a shared status with her audience – 'are we not commoners, outsiders?' (*M*, p. 125) – on the grounds of belonging to that 'immense class to which almost all of us must belong' who have been largely excluded from formal education, and left 'to pick up what we can in village schools; in factories; in workshops; behind counters; and at home' (*M*, p. 123). In looking forward to a post-War future Woolf advances the hope of 'a world without classes' (*M*, pp. 121–2), though this is presented almost exclusively in terms of a democratisation of reading, writing and literary study based once more on the development of the public library system:

This book ... was borrowed from a public library. England lent it to a common reader, saying 'It is time that even you, whom I have shut out from all my universities for centuries, should learn to read your mother tongue. I will help you'. (*M*, p. 124)

'We have got to *teach ourselves* to understand literature', she adds (my emphasis), the development of the critical sense being also crucial for the enfranchisement of writing which Woolf's lecture envisages: 'in future we are not going to leave writing to be done for us by a small class of well-to-do young men ... We are going ... to make our own contribution' (*M*, p. 124). The lecture ends significantly with Woolf's prospecting the future by returning explicitly to the past, invoking the words of her own father, 'an eminent Victorian', who consistently encouraged walkers to trespass on private ground: 'Literature is no one's private ground' (*M*, p. 125).[3]

Critics who have claimed what Anna Snaith has called this 'thoroughly democratic' position – one which evidences Woolf's interest 'in the ordinary, the common and the communal, particularly as regards literature, readers and writers' – as 'an extended rebuttal to claims about Woolf's elitism', have ignored I believe several of the problems thrown up by Woolf's rhetoric here in their eagerness to embrace her democratic positioning.[4] As Snaith points out, Woolf may be responding to Leavisite attitudes involving the 'denigration of the capabilities of the reading public' that she was conscious of in the 1930s, but the fact that Woolf's position is such a volte-face from the situation we considered earlier, in comments like that on *Ulysses* from 1922 – 'the book of a self taught working man, & we all know how distressing they are, how ... ultimately nauseating' (*D* II. 189) – might be one factor in making us pause. In *The Pargiters* Woolf applauds in the person of Sam Brook the 'working man' who rises up through the educational establishment to secure a university post, thanks to his own efforts and those of his mother, whom he regards as worth all 'the Masters & Mistresses in Oxford' (*P*, p. 146 – Sam's career is based on that of Joseph Wright, for whom Woolf's admiration is expressed in her diary, IV. 115–6). But as with 'The Leaning Tower' it is not clear how far this 'turn' to the working man is motivated by Woolf's casting for allies against university education; that is, how far the 'democratisation' of literature is a tactical weapon in such an attack, as opposed to representing any 'thorough' ideal of common solidarity.

Thus the provision of public libraries where 'nothing is chained down and nothing is locked up' (*TG*, p. 187), contrasting so markedly with the college library and its vetoes recorded at the start of *A Room of One's Own* (pp. 6–7), is welcomed by Woolf at the same time as she maintains explicitly anti-democratic prejudices outside the sphere of reading. Thus in 1937 she recorded a visit she made to her great-grandfather's dwelling in Clissold Park – 'one of those white pillared houses in which Grandpapa [sic] studied The Times while She cut roses' – which, now it had become a public park, 'smelt of Clissold Park mothers; & cakes & tea; the smell – unpleasant to the nose – of democracy' (*D* V. 102).[5] Ideas of common access here seem rather less inviting, though perhaps had the house been converted into a library, and hence catered for the type of common activity Woolf did approve of – the extension to all of what Melba Cuddy-Keane has called her 'ideal' of 'democratic highbrowism' – she would have been less scornful.[6] If in *Three Guineas* Woolf is careful to confine her exhortations to 'the very class which should have learnt to read at home – the educated' (*TG*, p. 286, n. 30), in 'The Leaning Tower' her enthusiasm for the practice of reading and animus against its specialist confinement lead to a visionary exhortation that, in effacing crucial practical and economic questions, needs to be tested further by those critics who have celebrated it unreservedly. A stimulus in Woolf's politics of reading was her correspondence with Agnes Smith, a Yorkshire mill-worker who wrote to her about *Three Guineas* and showed herself to be a committed public library user. But when Woolf insists in her lecture to the WEA that we must 'teach ourselves' by reading as much and as widely as we can, 'omnivorously ... It never does to be a nice feeder' (*M*, p. 125), she totally ignores the fact that resources available for such 'feeding' are likely to be sparse for many working people, however unlocked the public libraries are, most obviously the leisure time and energy available for this consumption, even if fares are available to get to the library in the first place and it is adequately stocked. Indeed, Agnes Smith's letters to Woolf at this very time draw attention to such problems even as she praises the library service: 'Yes, I can get books, the trouble is the shortage of time, when one is working, the shortage of money when one is not'; two weeks later she notes, 'I could use Huddersfield [Library] for 5/- yearly, but it costs me eightpence return and takes twenty minutes each way to get there.'[7] In *A Room* Woolf does insist that economic support is crucial for the writer, which makes the omission here of considerations of such support for the reader the more conspicuous. When she suggests above that those denied formal education have had to 'pick up what we can' in various venues including the factory and the home, she elides critical differences between her own 'home' opportunities and those of people at work, a real problem in her quest to carry forward and socially extend the practice of the 'eminent Victorian' reader – her father, Augustine Birrell, Lady Strachey – in the teeth of an age of specialist literary study. The enterprise founders in the gulf between say Lady Strachey, 'an omnivorous reader' indeed, as noted in Woolf's obituary on her, and members of the WEA which is hardly concealed by the ambiguities of the word 'common', encompassing both Woolf's non-specialist ('omnivorous') programme and, as the dictionary defines it, 'without rank or position'.

Desmond MacCarthy noted in his review of 'The Leaning Tower' that Woolf herself 'owes everything as a writer to having seen the world from a tower which did not lean, and I think that, except as a sign of sympathy, she ought not to have used the pronoun "we" in addressing an audience of working-men', a comment that Woolf challenged in a letter to him (L VI. 467–8).[8] The undeniable substance of MacCarthy's charge has been written off rather summarily I believe by Cuddy-Keane, whose detailed and vigorous defence of Woolf's democratisation of reading does not consider the questions of access and implementation referred to above. She argues, ironically, that MacCarthy is 'forgetting that [Woolf] had argued for the comfortable though not exorbitant wage of £500 per year' (*Virginia Woolf*, p. 111), though it is not clear why Woolf's attention to the writer's needs in *A Room* palliates the absence of any attention to the economic situation of the worker-reader in her lecture. MacCarthy is also accused of 'forgetting that Woolf was rejecting privilege not money', a problematic distinction illuminated perhaps in Cuddy-Keane's summary of Woolf's position:

> Woolf was a highbrow and to be a highbrow was – and still is to a large extent – to have benefited from certain kinds of privilege, if nothing more than the privilege of having had the time to learn to read books. But rather than disdaining the results of privilege, Woolf modeled a future world in which the attainments traditionally reserved for a privileged few would be available for all. Democratic highbrowism was her ideal ... making books and knowledge accessible to all on an equitable basis ... (pp. 110–11)

'If nothing more than the privilege of having had the time ...'. But what sounds here like a minor 'privilege' is in fact critical – and of course having the time to do anything depends on an income that can provide that time. Moreover, even Cuddy-Keane's detailed study of 'democratic highbrowism' can find little evidence that Woolf anywhere '*modeled* a future' for her extension of reading; a model implies a plan or programme that might be put into practice, and in 'The Leaning Tower' we have rather a powerful Woolfian rhetoric of exhortation and encouragement.[9] Anna Snaith has called attention to work Woolf did do in raising funds and stock for what was to become the Fawcett Library, but the tone of identification with the audience in 'The Leaning Tower' might have been less disarming had there been some acknowledgement of practical concerns that need addressing.[10] Cuddy-Keane does not quote the passage from the lecture that occasioned MacCarthy's scepticism about Woolf's class-affiliation, where 'England' is blamed in that 'she has left the other [uneducated] class, the immense class to which almost all of us must belong, to pick up what we can in village schools; in factories; in workshops; behind counters; and at home' (*M*, p. 123). Here opposition to the privilege of university education leads to the construction of a simple binary, an 'immense' other class, which elides the enormous differences between the reading opportunities of the factory worker and of someone from Woolf's 'home' background, as noted above.[11] And the curious collective voice — 'We have got to teach ourselves to understand literature', 'in future we are not going to leave writing to be done for us by a small class of well-to-do young men … We are going … to make our own contribution' — cements the identification between speaker and audience by implying that all are at a similar starting-point, where Woolf's own work has yet, so to speak, to be written or her eminence attained, such statements setting the seal on that 'remarkable, and quite unconvincing, declaration of solidarity, of community, with the underprivileged and uneducated', in John Mepham's words.[12]

In 'How Should One Read a Book?', originally a lecture delivered to schoolgirls in 1926, Woolf's memorable peroration suggests that progress from barbarism to civilisation (including the practices of giving to the poor and helping the sick) results from 'nothing but this: we have loved reading' (*E* IV. 399). The activity and love of reading is here the beginning and end of civilisation, the passport, one might say, to full and free entry into society, and throughout Woolf's writing the key 'right' in social participation. In this sense, 'democratisation' for Woolf is indeed equated with the right to read, far more, one might say, than ensuring legal rights or the right to vote. In *Three Guineas* there is passionate resistance to any encroachment on this right. 'Private judgement', Woolf argues, 'is still free in private; and that freedom is the essence of freedom' – and here the reading self, alone with a book, is the embodiment of that essence, so that to read the *Antigone*, for example, is a better instruction in psychology, politics and sociology than any professional in these disciplines can offer (*TG*, pp. 206–7). But in proclaiming this basic right in 'The Leaning Tower', especially from the position of 'outsiderness' that encapsulates Woolf's resistance to all organisations, committees, governing bodies and so forth, this ideal of freedom – the self alone with a book – becomes universalised, mystified, decontextualised, subject to no economic or educational frameworks – 'I expect you to make yourselves critics' (*M*, p. 124). The problems in a position that rejects the mundane traffic of practical organisation are perfectly apparent here. And like other transcendental entities this ideal is in 'The Leaning Tower' defined by nothing beyond itself, is its own alpha and omega, so that one can only learn to read by reading, and indeed by 'reading omnivorously, simultaneously, poems, plays, novels, histories, biographies, the old and the new' (*M*, pp. 124–5), in a kind of eternity of time and provision where the heavenly library never closes and no-one is denied a reader's ticket or has a limit on the number of items he or she can borrow. But this vision does, I would suggest, originate in actual time and place, the keeper of that library being the 'eminent Victorian' invoked at the end of Woolf's lecture, who invites his readers to range or 'trespass' where they will, the new dispensation being thus the realisation of the old. In a letter to Lady Tweedsmuir of 1938, Woolf discloses this Post-Victorian mysticism: 'I owe all the education I ever had to my father's library, and so perhaps endow libraries with more divinity than I should' (*L* VI. 234). And she also became aware retrospectively, more than some of her recent critics perhaps, of the limitations of her vision in 'The Leaning Tower', as suggested in a letter to Benedict Nicolson describing 'the other day when I lectured the WEA on poetry at Brighton':

> It seemed to me useless to tell people who left school at 14 and were earning their livings in shops and factories that they ought to enjoy Shakespeare. But how can we, if we remain artists, give them that education, or change their conditions? (*L* VI. 421)

In the letter the question of how the artist can change such 'conditions' is left despairingly unanswered. What is not in doubt, however, is that the lecture shows a Victorian affiliation still powerfully at work in Woolf, offset by notes of rejection that make up an increasingly conflicted attitude towards the Victorian past, which has intensified with the approach of war.

In *Three Guineas*, the immediate threat to and encroachment on the freedom discussed above is not Hitler nor Mussolini, but our own systems of education, professional practice and public reward and recognition, 'the limelight which paralyses the free action of the human faculties and inhibits the human power to change and create new wholes ... ease and freedom, the power to change and the power to grow, can only be preserved by obscurity' (*TG*, p. 240). We must remain 'outsiders' as far as these public spheres are concerned, even if we enter them, for only then can we achieve wholeness. 'Whole' is another key term throughout *Three Guineas*, as also in *The Years* – 'when will this new world come? When shall we be free? When shall we live adventurously, wholly, not like cripples in a cave?' (*TY*, p. 217) – and *Three Guineas* specifies that such wholeness consists in resisting any slavery to money-making, scholarship, writing, ambition or indeed rearing children that would confine all the varied potential of the self to one role, task or obsession, wherein people 'lose their sense of proportion – the relations between one thing and another' (*TG*, p. 197). In *Three Guineas* Woolf recognises that 'obscurity' can now be a deliberate choice of professional women, including writers, and distinguishes it from the forced obscurity of the Victorian woman (*TG*, p. 201) which nevertheless forms an exemplary part of the modern woman's heritage. The need to promote this heritage is ever more pressing in the twentieth century, with its growth in professionalisation, specialised education and the publicity machine, which encourages a competitiveness nourished by an environment of endemic acclaim.

In 1933 Woolf's letter to the *New Statesman* on 'The Protection of Privacy' offered to subscribe not one guinea but five guineas annually 'to any society that will rid us of these pests', these pests being newspaper photographers and all the associated clamour of interview- and autograph-hunters and 'unknown admirers': 'members of the literary profession . . . might take an oath not to allow any photograph, drawing or caricature of themselves to appear in the papers without their consent . . .'; ironically, the same issue of the *New Statesman* contained the famous Low caricature of Keynes.[13] The proliferation of a celebrity culture, in which the photographer and the picture press play a key role, is a feature of modernity for which Woolf used a characteristic image of exposure in *Three Guineas* – 'a rabbit caught in the glare of a head-lamp', with its 'glazed eyes' and 'rigid paws' (*TG*, p. 240), an image that recalls our previous discussions of the alienating effect of modern lighting and the shelter of shadow, as well as the 'fixing' effect of photography.[14] The 'ease and freedom' that Woolf celebrates in *Three Guineas* updates her Victorian experience of literary self-reliance and retirement, 'dream[ing] quietly in the shade with a book' (*E* III. 435), which has now become an active polemic as she speaks out from that shade. Hermione Lee remarks on how, 'like all [Woolf's] central preoccupations, the idea of "the common reader" is rooted in her childhood and adolescence', and in her introduction to *Three Guineas* she suggests that Woolf's 'own upbringing is the concealed subject' of the book.[15] But in arguing that that upbringing only enters *Three Guineas* as matter for Woolf's anti-patriarchal 'anger', and in elsewhere drawing a distinction between it and works close in time that contain more approving responses to the Victorian period, like *A Sketch of the Past* (*Virginia Woolf*, pp. 85–6), Lee neglects the sheer extent to which in *Three Guineas* Woolf continues to fill her urn, for good and ill, at the Victorian well. Indeed, *Three Guineas* could well be a candidate for the title of most 'Post-Victorian' of

Woolf's works, in the strategies with which it aims to redress the direction of modernity.

A Sketch of the Past (1939–40), the memoir left unfinished at her death, represents the end of Woolf's Post-Victorian journey, a journey that concludes by taking her not away from her past but emphatically back round towards it, as if, in the words from Eliot's near-contemporary 'Little Gidding', she might arrive where she started and 'know the place for the first time'. It must be admitted, however, that in the memoir this knowledge remains less rather than more certain. The number of times we have seen *A Sketch* anticipated by statements in Woolf's earlier work indicates, perhaps, how long a gestation period the memoir had, and how inevitable its production was. Though the ending is abrupt and accidental, and though it is impossible to know what insights into the Victorian period in its relation to modernity might have developed had Woolf continued it (especially given that the past 'is much affected by the present moment. What I write today I should not write in a year's time', *MOB*, p. 75), it seems entirely appropriate that we finally have no definitive 'summing up' of Woolf's Victorian inheritance but a position that is contradictory and indeed inconclusive. On the one hand the tribute to Henry James in the penultimate paragraph shows a marked nostalgia informed by filial piety:

> I remember the hesitations and adumbrations with which Henry James made the drawing room seem rich and dusky. Greatness still seems to me a positive possession; booming; eccentric; set apart; something to which I am led up dutifully by my parents. It is a bodily presence; it has nothing to do with anything said. It exists in certain people. But it never exists now. I cannot remember ever to have felt greatness since I was a child. (*MOB*, p. 158)

On the other hand the final paragraph takes us away from such 'great men' back to Woolf's Duckworth half-brothers ('No more perfect fossil of the Victorian age could exist' than George) and the far from numinous 'patriarchal machine' (*MOB*, pp. 151–3) of the Victorian public world which Woolf felt so 'distant' from (*MOB*, p. 158). In short, her retrospect embraces 'so many different worlds', worlds which she cannot make 'cohere': the world of her own reading and study, the public world, the world of domestic duty, the social world (*MOB*, pp. 158–9). Hyde Park Gate embodied them all, in a starkly demarcated way that did not assist the achievement of 'wholeness': 'The division in our lives was curious. Downstairs there was pure convention; upstairs pure intellect' (*MOB*, p. 157).

We have seen that where Woolf's experience of life at Hyde Park Gate enters her fiction most directly, that is in the Hilbery household of *Night and Day* and that of the Pargiters in *The Years*, a curious editing takes place. The former home, ruled over by a spirited and 'literary' mother and emptied of any tyrannical half-brothers, paints a much rosier picture of the domestic environment, while Abercorn Terrace, governed by a father with no pretensions to 'intellect' or literature, conspicuously denies its inhabitants a cultural legacy that was so important to Woolf herself. Both transformations serve Woolf's purposes, as we have seen, of a recuperation of the past on the one hand or a forceful critique on the other. In *A Sketch of the Past* there is both recuperation and critique to an extent that goes beyond any possibility of synthesising them, and the full impact of Hyde Park Gate's contradictory significance for Woolf is admitted and explored, and centres on her father, in her feelings for whom 'rage alternated with love'. Here she distinguishes herself from her sister Vanessa, who seems to have experienced a much more straightforward rejection of the father, and Woolf admits to having found a word in Freud that is too useful in describing the situation to be mocked (as generally happens when she comes across psychoanalytic terminology, like 'infantile fixation' above), namely 'ambivalence' (*MOB*, p. 108). And ambivalence towards 'the alternately loved and hated father' (*MOB*, p. 116) characterises Woolf's response to the Victorian period as a whole in *A Sketch*. The essay is thus full of questioning, qualification, speculation, contradiction and inconclusiveness, aspects of which find their way into the contemporary *Between the Acts*, as we shall see. Whatever the 'Victorian' finally was to Woolf, it remained a source of complex fascination, and it is not clear how far the memoir would have continued into later periods with the same engagement, even if Woolf had lived to pursue it.

Some things, however, Woolf was decided about, such as her long-standing conviction that to speak 'openly, frankly, without prudery' is a great advance on Victorian suppression (*E*. IV. 451). Any reservations about this seem to have lessened by the close of her life, to judge from 'The Leaning Tower', where the modern autobiographer's ability to tell 'the unpleasant truth' about the self contrasts with a reticence that explains 'why so much of the nineteenth-century writing is worthless' (*M*, p. 120). *A Sketch of the Past* begins with a reference to 'the unhappy case of Lady Strachey', too old and impaired in memory to produce anything other than a very patchy memoir in 1924, though Woolf may also have had in mind the fact that Lady Strachey writes solely of events and personages in the public world, and that her memoir reads simply like a brief Victorian *Who's Who*. We learn nothing of her private life, of her marriage or her relations with her children, whereas *A Sketch* concentrates on the intimacies of domestic experience, including, of course, its disclosures of incest.[16]

We also see, in Woolf's comparative evocation of her mother and father, a confirmation of the roles allotted them in *To the Lighthouse*. The rational father, 'like a steel engraving, without colour, or warmth or body; but with an infinity of precise clear lines', and in whom 'there are no crannies or corners to catch my imagination' (*MOB*, p. 109), contrasts with the 'vision' of the mother as Woolf's imagination creates her standing in the garden of Little Holland House – 'I dream; I make up pictures of a summer's afternoon' (*MOB*, p. 87), a figure emblematic of the romance and beauty of the Victorian past. Akin to this is the effect of Stella's engagement to Jack Hills as the 'standard of love' – 'a sense that nothing in the whole world is so lyrical, so musical, as a young man and a young woman in their first love for each other' (*MOB*, p. 105). The fact that her mother died when Woolf was young, and that with her death came the sense of a door being 'shut for ever' on 'the merry, various family life which she had held in being' (*MOB*, p. 93), together with the fact that Woolf has since 'never seen anyone who reminded me' of her (or of Stella – 'They do not blend in the world of the living at all', *MOB*, p. 97), enables a definitive placement of her within the

Victorian past, and confirms the imagination as the essential means of access to her. (Unlike Woolf's father, she left no mass of writing behind her.)[17] As Woolf says, up until completing *To the Lighthouse* she constantly communed with her mother in this way – 'I could hear her voice, see her, imagine what she would do or say as I went about my day's doings' (*MOB*, p. 80), whilst the writing of that novel is seen as possibly answering the question 'Why ... should my vision of her and my feeling for her become so much dimmer and weaker?' (*MOB*, p. 81).

And it is true that in *A Sketch* it is the father who tends to dominate, a father who, as noted above, represents in a number of ways the antithesis to the mother, never having stimulated Woolf's 'imagination' – a fact we see rehearsed in the memoir itself, where she confesses her failure to picture someone of his intellectual nature taking part, alongside her mother, in 'that well to do sociable late Victorian world' – 'I cannot conceive my father in evening dress' (*MOB*, p. 114). Here it is also more difficult to create pictures that definitively 'frame' the father partly because he inhabits the several 'different worlds' that make up the retrospect, as also because he lived on into Woolf's early adulthood and has left so many traces behind him: 'The sociable father then I never knew. Father as a writer I can get of course in his books ...' (*MOB*, p. 115). It also adds to the difficulty of seeing the father as a Victorian period-piece that, unlike the mother, who resembles no-one she has seen since, he had a plentiful succession, being 'the very type, or mould, of so many Cambridge intellectuals – like George Trevelyan, like Charlie Sanger, like Goldie Dickinson – whom I knew later' (*MOB*, pp. 108–9). In short, the father is always threatening to escape, or at least disrupt, the Victorian frame, in spite of Woolf's desire that he remain there – 'Father himself was a typical Victorian' (*MOB*, p. 147). Yet at other times she had regarded him as 'more as a contemporary' (*D* III. 208).

Many of the more categorical statements made about her father in *A Sketch* she is, in fact, forced to modify. Although Woolf's imagination is not stimulated – it 'bores me to write of him' (*MOB*, p. 109) – she fills many pages of the memoir with his portrait, warming indeed to her theme, finding that 'I am introducing a picturesque element into the steel engraving; something that one cannot analyse' (*MOB*, p. 111), an enigmatic note which is related to his many different facets and roles – 'He had clearly that – something – which is not this quality or that quality, but all sorts of qualities summed up into what one calls "character" . . .' (*MOB*, p. 110). In seeking to represent him as a 'typical' Victorian Woolf emphasises the designation by pushing him further back into the period as a grandfather-figure rather than father, seeing him in 'the framework of 1860' even as his children were living in that of 1910, though she also modifies this typicality: 'he smoothed out the petty details of the Victorian code with his admirable intellect, with his respect for reason – no one was less snobbish than he, no one cared less for rank or luxury' (*MOB*, pp. 147, 151–2). There is, however, no modifying or mitigation of Woolf's attack on the indulgence of her father's own upbringing, and particularly on the early Victorian cult of 'genius' which Leslie was encouraged to identify with and which, in the 'violent outbursts' it licensed, could make him so 'brutal' with his daughters (*MOB*, pp. 109–10, 145–6). Again, however, Woolf expresses her admiration for his refusal to play the authoritarian paterfamilias, recording various examples of his liberalism; for example, though he thought fishing cruel he would not ban his daughter from doing it: 'It was a perfect lesson. It was not a rebuke; not a forbidding; simply a statement of his own feeling, about which I could think and decide for myself' (*MOB*, p. 135). And more significantly, in the matter of Nessa's relations with Jack Hills, 'she must do as she liked; he was not going to interfere. That was what I admire in him; his dignity and sanity in the larger affairs; so often covered up by his irritations and vanities and egotisms' (*MOB*, p. 142).

This last statement summarises the conflicting elements in the father that produced the ambivalence, the 'violently disturbing conflict of love and hate' in his youngest daughter (*MOB*, p. 108).[18] In *A Sketch*, this ambivalence extends to the Victorian age itself in a series of questions and uncertainties. Thus her undoubted pleasure in recalling 'that crowded merry world which spun so gaily in the centre of my childhood' (*MOB*, p. 84), a world of 'parties', 'young men and women laughing', 'flashing visions of white summer dresses and hansoms dashing off to private views and dinner parties', 'that natural life and gaiety which my mother had created' (*MOB*, p. 94), leads her to ponder whether the continuation of such an existence would have been more productive for her than the education in the 'insecurity of life' provided by her mother and Stella's deaths: 'Perhaps to have remained in the family, believing in it, accepting it, as we should, without those two deaths, would have given us greater scope, greater variety, and certainly greater confidence. On the other hand, I can put another question . . .' (*MOB*, p. 137). And indeed Woolf puts a whole series of 'on the other hands' about the relative value of the experience that came when the door 'shut for ever' on the merry world of childhood, and about whether the fall was a fortunate one. This reminds us it would be a mistake to regard Martin's horror at Victorian family life in *The Years* as simply Woolf's own (or indeed Delia's – 'It was Hell!' – who is more a representation of Vanessa). Woolf's strictures elsewhere ('I felt the horror of family life, & the terrible threat to one's liberty that I used to feel with father, Aunt Mary or George', *D* III. 194) refer to the family as it became after her mother's death, and though in the same diary entry she goes on to exclaim against the 'tyranny of mother over daughter' this is not occasioned by her own mother's controls but by those of her mother-in-law. Her mother's legacy to Woolf was not a mood of brooding resentment but a social merriment as important in its way as the literary legacy of her father: 'This social side is very genuine in me . . . It is a piece of jewellery I inherit from my mother' (*D* II. 250).

At the same time the continuing presence of Woolf's mother would hardly have prevented the social difficulties Woolf began to experience during her adolescence, however much nostalgia she shows for her family childhood. Over George Duckworth's hounding of Woolf 'into society' 'the ghosts of mother and Stella presided', however much they may have (in the flesh) cushioned and alleviated the experience (*MOB*, p. 156). Social duties required of women both outside and inside the home imposed a conventional behaviour which Julia Stephen, who was no radical and showed no support for women's emancipation, firmly upheld: 'the Victorian manner ... was not natural for Vanessa or myself. We learned it. We learned it partly from memory: and mother had that manner ... Nobody ever broke the convention', the convention being the participation in polite and ceremonious 'light discussion' around the tea table (*MOB*, pp. 149–50). Woolf goes on to expand upon this 'manner' and its effect on her and Vanessa:

> We both learnt the rules of the game of Victorian society so thoroughly that we have never forgotten them. We still play the game. It is useful. It has also its beauty, for it is founded upon restraint, sympathy, unselfishness – all civilized qualities. It is helpful in making something seemly out of raw odds and ends ... But the Victorian manner is perhaps – I am not sure – a disadvantage in writing. When I read my old *Literary Supplement* articles, I lay the blame for their suavity, their politeness, their sidelong approach, to my tea-table training. I see myself, not reviewing a book, but handing plates of buns to shy young men and asking them: do they take cream and sugar? On the other hand, the surface manner allows one, as I have found, to slip in things that would be inaudible if one marched straight up and spoke out loud. (*MOB*, p. 150)

Here, the idea that things can be better heard if not spoken out loud corresponds with the sense that they can be better 'discerned' if not flooded with the 'glare of day', as in the review of James's *The Middle Years*, a parallel image of the discretion of the 'Victorian manner'.[19] It is remarkable how little this manner is excoriated here as an instance of servitude but is rather salvaged for its civilised and 'seemly' qualities, and even in Woolf's consideration of its value in writing there is an inconclusive verdict: 'perhaps – I am not sure'.[20] The idea that one can say things that 'would be inaudible if one marched straight up and spoke out loud' emphasises the method of *Three Guineas*, a polemic conducted in a tone of formal and even elaborate 'politeness' – 'That passage, Sir, is not empty rhetoric, for it is based upon the respectable opinion of the late head master of Eton, the present Dean of Durham' (*TG*, p. 157) and one that resists on every level, as we have seen, the martial 'march' and the loudspeaker tone as symptoms of the situation it wants to resist, preferring to present itself in the form of a series of private letters.[21] This civilised quality that 'is helpful in making something seemly out of raw odds and ends' is saluted at a time when the violence of the Second World War is intruding into the writing of the memoir: 'Yesterday ... five German raiders passed so close over Monks House ...', *MOB*, p. 124). If producing *A Sketch of the Past* is something of a refuge for Woolf, the past that is transcribed is not idealised into a refuge per se, and Woolf makes a deliberate decision to also 'include the present' (*MOB*, p. 75), indeed at times converting the memoir into a war diary. The quest is not nostalgically to evade the present but to try and find some anchorage in the past that will enable Woolf to cling on to a sense of reality: 'I write this partly in order to recover my sense of the present by getting the past to shadow this broken surface' (*MOB*, p. 98).

In the novel Woolf was writing contemporaneously with the memoir, *Between the Acts*, there is again the sense of the wartime present as a 'broken surface' with the final scene of the pageant putting the question to the audience of how civilisation is 'to be built by ... orts, scraps and fragments like ourselves?' (*BA*, p. 111). If the pageant's Victorian scenes portray a period by contrast of settled order and rule under the sway of Mr Budge's truncheon, this is clearly treated satirically, and even those in the audience like Mrs Lynn Jones, who do feel a powerful attachment towards their Victorian upbringing, recognise its possible defects (*BA*, p. 103). In the earlier typescript of the novel the Victorian scenes were followed by an exchange between Isa and Mrs Swithin which does not survive unaltered in the published version:

'The Victorians', said Isa, for now that the actors had gone, the scene came back to her much more completely than when they were acting it. 'The Victorians had that – a pattern. The old mother; the old father; and all going home in a donkey cart'.

'I don't believe there ever were such people', said Mrs Swithin. 'No, no. Only you and me and William dressed up'. She patted her niece on the knee.[22]

As with Peggy and Eleanor in *The Years*, it is the younger, modern woman (characterised throughout *Between the Acts* as notably dissatisfied and displaced) who feels the attraction of a past that is 'patterned' rather than splintered (significantly this response arises 'now that the actors had gone', a metaphor for the workings of retrospect), while her elderly aunt (who shares something of the character of Eleanor, as we have noted) shows no tendency to idealise the era in which she grew up. In declaring there never 'were such people', but rather their own selves 'dressed up', Woolf through her speaker suggests again the fiction of an attitude to the past that would empty it of problems and emotions that people experience in the present (as with Peggy's desire to resort to its 'safe' quality, *TY*, p. 244). If Mrs Swithin's attitude in turn is described by William in terms that suggest its own myopia – 'You don't believe in history' (*BA*, p. 104) – it has long been an attitude of Woolf's that 'history' needs to be rerouted from the record of great public events to consideration of everyday lives whose qualities do not change greatly from age to age: 'our passions and despairs have nothing to do with trade; our virtues and vices flourish under all governments impartially . . . At any rate, we are left out, and history, in our opinion, lacks an eye' (*E* 1. 331).

As with *The Years*, there is no refuge in periodisation, particularly that which would 'compose' the past, and the unsettling aspect of this in *Between the Acts* is felt particularly with regard to the Victorian period, which many in the audience have themselves experienced. Although Etty Springett joins with Mrs Lynn Jones in disapproving of the satire on her father's generation, she is forced to recognise in part its justice: 'How difficult to come to any conclusion!' And it is at this point that the disorientating effect of the pageant is first felt, given that 'She liked to leave a theatre knowing exactly what was meant' (*BA*, p. 98).

This loss of period identity or refuge for the audience then proceeds apace, and is particularly felt in the intervals of stage action, 'between the acts', as if identity and historical belonging are particularly about 'doing' and action: 'All their nerves were on edge. They sat exposed . . . They were neither one thing nor the other; neither Victorians nor themselves. They were suspended, without being, in limbo. Tick, tick, tick, went the machine' (*BA*, p. 106). Here the 'limbo', with the gramophone 'ticking' like a bomb waiting to explode, refers of course to the unnerving eve-of-war waiting for the action to start. In *A Sketch of the Past* Woolf notes how 'peace is necessary' to feel 'the present sliding over the depths of the past'; in times of upheaval not only is the present a 'broken surface' but in its turn it obliterates a sense of those depths: 'it shallows; it turns the depth into hard thin splinters' (*BA*, p. 98). The effect of the broken surface of the present in *Between the Acts* is not only to turn the past into splinters (all the bits of speeches mixed together in the pageant's final scene, *BA*, p. 110), but indeed to turn it into fiction – everything becomes unreal, parodic, pastiche, with an audience who are themselves actors on a stage watching in the interval others of their number producing a play within a play.

The effect in the novel is to create a curiously suspended dream/nightmare state occasioned by the present's heightened but inactive alert, an occasion that permits Woolf a whole range of effects, including some superb comedy. But in *A Sketch of the Past* she complains about this reduction of 'the fullness of life' to shallows, splinters and indeed fiction: 'As I say to L[eonard]: "What's there real about this? Shall we ever live a real life again?" ', and the scope of the memoir, of 'getting the past to shadow this broken surface' (*MOB*, p. 98), is to find an alternative but genuine world of 'reality', one that is available to the memory indeed in such intensely realised detail that it is 'more real than the present moment':

is it not possible – I often wonder – that things we have felt with great intensity have an existence independent of our minds; are in fact still in existence? ... I feel that strong emotion must leave its trace; and it is only a question of discovering how we can get ourselves again attached to it, so that we shall be able to live our lives through from the start. (*MOB*, p. 67)

A Sketch of the Past insists on this reality in defiance of the state of war that threatens to destroy it, and as part of that enterprise it holds onto a sense of period identity and 'placement' as a means of structuring and making sense of history. The Victorian period, however ambivalent in Woolf's eyes, is undeniably 'there', and evidence of the human ability indeed to make civilisation 'out of raw odds and ends'. There is a good deal of nostalgia for it in the memoir, mixed with a good deal of criticism – but perhaps the nostalgia it mainly evokes lies in the assurance it gives that it simply did, and does, exist, and that we can 'get ourselves again attached to it'.[23]

But it still presents its own problems in the memoir, which ends with Woolf's reliving her inability to make it 'cohere'. Seen purely in terms of a bullying patriarchy, it can be rendered unitary and stable, one of the 'Two different ages [that] confronted each other in the drawing room at Hyde Park Gate. The Victorian age and the Edwardian age ... We were living say in 1910; they were living in 1860' (*MOB*, p. 147). Here the freedoms Woolf was to gain on her father's death are used in a period antithesis that stabilises her historiography, but outside the drawing room – in the garden say, or study – the Victorian period has a much more potent appeal. If Woolf anticipates and re-enacts in the above comment the Edwardian liberation of her youth, once released from the immediate experience of this she spends the rest of her life taking a longer and more considered view of the world of her upbringing, and is generally dismissive of the Edwardian era when taking that view. Here it is instructive to consider *A Sketch* alongside its counterpart of 1907, the memoir *Reminiscences*, to see how it differs in terms of historical periodisation. As we saw, the later memoir confesses its inability to retain the memory of Julia Stephen who has been lost to the past, so to speak, inhabiting the Victorian dreamscape of the 'summer afternoon world' of Little Holland House (*MOB*, pp. 86–7); with her death part of Woolf's world 'shut for ever' (*MOB*, p. 93), and 'Victorian' is used in part as a term and a context for that which lies irretrievably on the other side of this door. In *Reminiscences*, written a little over a decade after Julia's death, we have by contrast the powerfully continuing presence of the mother through doors that can still be opened:

on more occasions than I can number ... as I come into the room, there she is; beautiful, emphatic, with her familiar phrase and her laugh; closer than any of the living are, lighting our random lives as with a burning torch, infinitely noble and delightful to her children. (*MOB*, p. 40).

The survival of 'a true and most vivid mother' (*MOB*, p. 45) in *Reminiscences* is one reason why period demarcation, and any Victorian–modern antithesis, is out of place in this early text. Whereas in *A Sketch* mother and father tend to be seen and examined separately, in *Reminiscences* there is fervent talk about the parental union – 'no match was more truly equal, or more ceaselessly valiant . . . a triumphant life, consistently aiming at high things' (*MOB*, pp. 33–4), with each partner finding 'in the other the highest and most perfect harmony which their natures could respond to' (*MOB*, p. 37). This idealising of the marital relationship shows the influence of Leslie Stephen's own *Mausoleum Book*, to which *Reminiscences* is very near both in time and genre. The lack of period consciousness in *Reminiscences* – the word 'Victorian' is never used, nor is there any sense of seeing the family in such a context – is also explicable in terms of that nearness in time to the events Woolf was writing about; the Victorian period may have ended technically with the Queen's death in 1901, but until modernity started to define itself in differential terms the earlier period awaited its definition too. As Woolf says, it is only with *A Sketch* that we get the idea of two different dates and periods confronting each other in her family life, 1860 and 1910, explained as an effect of how 'from my present distance of time I see too what we could not then see' (*MOB*, p. 147).[24]

In promising to send Clive Bell some chapters from *Reminiscences* in a letter of 1908, Woolf notes how 'It might have been so good! As it is, I am too near, and too far; and it seems to be blurred, and I ask myself why write it at all?' (*L* 1. 325). Here the clear relations of past and present are not yet in place, leading to the 'blurred' effect. In a review of 1908 Woolf describes the early Victorian period as 'just distant enough to be old-fashioned', with the sense that the later period has not yet assumed this distance (*E* 1. 241). In this sense, Woolf is still 'too near' to her past (and to her mother). On the other hand, Leslie Stephen's death in 1904 and the move to Bloomsbury did enable the present to press its claims in the shape of a new beginning, and the early journals and *The Voyage Out* are largely devoid of a sense of the past impinging, for good or ill, on the present. Even the Cornwall journal of 1905, though declaredly a return to the scene of the childhood past, finds much to attend to in the events and experiences of the present, including the sight of the famous pilchard-catch (*PA* pp. 291–4), an event which never occurred in Woolf's childhood. Being caught up in the present, the sense as Woolf puts it in a 1906 review that 'the nineteenth century is already yesterday' (*E* 1. 83), suggests the converse position that Woolf is 'too far' from her past.

But being too near and too far represents, of course, two sides of the same coin. There is little nostalgia, indeed little retrospect (*Reminiscences* aside), in Woolf's early writing. Describing some children playing in the Wells and Manorbier journal of 1908 she asks herself, 'Did I ever play all day when I was a child? I cant remember it' (*PA*, p. 379). This observation from one who, in *A Sketch of the Past*, talks of 'the enormous number of things I can remember' (*MOB*, p. 64), strikes one as surprising in the extreme. One of the candidates for Woolf's 'first memory' in *A Sketch* is 'of feeling the purest ecstasy I can conceive' while lying in the nursery at St Ives, listening to the waves and 'the blind draw its little acorn across the floor as the wind blew the blind out' (*MOB*, pp. 64–5). This memory is used in *The Voyage Out*, but here as part of Rachel's terminal fever: 'The movement of the blind as it filled with air and blew slowly out, drawing the cord with a little trailing sound along the floor, seemed to her terrifying, as if it were the movement of an animal in the room' (*VO*, p. 310). Given the disturbing events of Woolf's adolescence, the family deaths, her own breakdowns, it is hardly surprising that the early writing shows so little inclination towards retrospect, nostalgic or otherwise; at the same time, the past remained so close as to make retrospect unnecessary, if nostalgia is prompted by that which is felt to be beyond reach. Thus the Cornish section of *A Sketch* is far more nostalgic than the 1905 Cornwall journal.

In *A Sketch* the significant Post-Impressionist date of 1910 is used to represent Woolf and her sister's modernity, and in considering her father's limitations – 'never used his hands . . . congenitally unaware of music, of art' – she immediately refers to the contrasting figure of Roger Fry, for whom 'civilisation means awareness' (*MOB*, p. 146).

Her biography of Fry, published in 1940 while she was writing *A Sketch*, arguably reveals a model for Woolf of what it is to be fully human, given the range of his interests – painting, poetry, science, medicine (*RF*, pp. 86–8), abhorrence of specialisation (*RF*, p. 116), rejection of 'the idea of official life and titles and honours' (*RF*, p. 165) and constant receptivity to 'new ideas' and passions (*RF*, p. 183). Fry's 'lifelong antagonism to all public schools and their ideals' (*RF*, p. 43) also shows how much his attitudes may have inspired Woolf when she was working on *Three Guineas*. But where she differs from Fry is over a critical blind spot that featured among all his interests, the fact that, as she claims, he was 'very little interested in the past compared with the present' (*RF*, p. 289), very little interested in his own memories, that is. His attitude to the Victorian period, as it comes across in Woolf's biography, is one of an unrelenting stigmatising of its 'hypocrisy' (*RF*, p. 184), 'fantastic puritanism' (*RF*, p. 255) and suppressions (*RF*, pp. 260–1), a passion of rejection that makes Fry perhaps a more dramatic version of Eleanor in *The Years*, an anti-Victorian Victorian.[25] Though Woolf herself also espoused such criticisms, she does this, as we have seen, as part of a mixed and much more complicated retrospect, and could hardly have simply rejoiced with Fry that 'Victorianism was evaporating' (*RF*, p. 261). Nor could she summarily identify the enemy as her own husband did in his battle 'against what for short one may call Victorianism' (*Sowing*, p. 102). In distinction to some of her peers, she not only had a family background composed of and intimately familiar with eminent writers and artists, but her recognition of the achievements of Victorian fiction and poetry ensured that Fry's dismissal of the Victorians in another field – British art of the nineteenth century being 'coarse, turbulent, clumsy', and under the sway of a plutocratic regime that encouraged 'pseudo-artists' to prostitute their talents in 'the orgy of Victorian philistinism' – was impossible for her to emulate.[26] And Woolf's feminism, as we have seen, is not so much about embracing a visionary future as of attending to the past, of listening to the voices that compose the 'ancestral memory' and of allowing these to permeate into the present.

As Woolf grew further in time from her Victorian past, her interest in it intensified, resulting in a paradoxical mixture of enchantment and (disillusioned) clarity, the clarity contrasting with the 'blurring' of close-up: 'from my present distance of time I see too what we could not then see'. We have traced a trajectory in Woolf's Post-Victorianism in this study from an over-compensating nostalgia in *Night and Day*, to a romanticism that becomes increasingly alert to patriarchal injustice, to something approaching disillusion in *The Years*. At the same time, the results of that injustice, the heritage of deprivation, are put to productive use in *Three Guineas*, where the Victorian legacy also continues to be upheld in other ways. These different responses do not cleanly succeed each other, but always coexist to a greater or lesser degree, and all find increasingly 'incoherent' expression as we approach the Second World War, and above all, in *A Sketch* itself, Woolf's fullest and most detailed exploration of her own responses. The picture here may not be 'blurred', but not surprisingly it is very complicated. In contemporary pieces like 'The Leaning Tower' we have Woolf's own educational upbringing offered as a model for all, but alongside what is arguably Woolf's most caustic dismissal of the past. Here the ruthless, truth-telling auto-analysis of the new generation of writers contrasts with the evasions and suppressions which make so much nineteenth-century writing 'worthless' (*M*, pp. 120–1); here, August 1914 is indeed seen as a watershed before which the 'steady tower' of class division unjustly guaranteed the writer's sense of security (*M*, pp. 112–3); and here Woolf does embrace a post-War vision of 'a world without classes or towers .... the classless and towerless society of the future' (*M*, pp. 121–3). I have indicated my doubts about Woolf's response to the First World War as an opportunity to welcome unreservedly the 'new', and about Woolf's commitment to the idea of a classless society, given her obsession with retrospect, but there is undoubtedly a sense in 'The Leaning Tower' that a second war can only be borne as a prelude to complete and necessary change.[27] Yet the vision that expresses that future was hatched in her father's library, and thus brings with it the problems discussed above, in its allegiance to a past that, as *A Sketch* confirms, is in many ways never outgrown.

And if finally we did ever understand more than Woolf herself her response to the 'Victorian', and hence the precise value of the Post-Victorian, there is still Mrs Swithin to contend with:

'The Victorians', Mrs Swithin mused. 'I don't believe', she said with her odd little smile, 'that there ever were such people. Only you and me and William dressed differently'. (*BA*, p. 104)

This further complication, with which Woolf certainly had some sympathy, will be addressed in my conclusion.

CONCLUSION

Reclaiming the shadows

Woolf's inability to make her picture of the Victorian 'cohere' at the end of her life is a final and more intense statement of contradictory responses apparent throughout her life and career. Woolf recognised these contradictions, and even got a certain amount of fun out of them, as in her characteristic device of introducing the term 'Victorian' as a kind of shorthand for conclusions that cannot be concluded; see for example the end of 'A Talk About Memoirs' ('He enjoyed life; that's what the Victorians – but, go on – tell me how Orme was poisoned', *E* III. 184), or Orlando's 'conclusion' about Victorian literature ('which was of the highest importance but which ... we must omit', *O*, pp. 201–2), or the essay on the 'genius' of B. R. Haydon ('not the Shakespearean but the Victorian genius ... not the true, but – let us pause, however ...', *E* IV. 406). If Victorian 'genius' is never precisely defined in this last essay, it seems to be associated with the extravagance of a passionate temperament or temper, as Woolf later confirmed in relation to Leslie Stephen and the licence 'the "genius" legend' seemed to permit him (*A Sketch*, *MOB*, pp. 121, 158). One of the paradoxical relations of Victorian culture is precisely that between 'passion' and volubility and 'suppression' and reserve, which has been touched on previously. There may have been many areas of Victorian life where 'things could never be said'; on the other hand, Woolf constantly suggests a higher emotional temper to Victorian life – 'their passionate loves and hates' (above, p. 18), a life dominated by the heart rather than the head – than she recognised in modern behaviour.

But a broader Woolfian inconclusiveness about the Victorians is summed up in the exchange from *Between the Acts*, involving

Mrs Swithin's scepticism that 'there ever were such people' and William's reply, 'You don't believe in history' (*BA*, p. 104). Throughout Woolf's writing there is a debate between these two positions. If the Victorian is undeniably 'there' in Woolf's writing, as in *A Sketch*, as part of her attempt to understand history and historical change, there are many other instances where she resists periodisation (as in *The Years*) in holding to an idea of the essential constants of human nature, which are the novelist's prime material: 'Mrs Brown is eternal, Mrs Brown is human nature, Mrs Brown changes only on the surface, it is the novelists who get in and out ...' (*E* III. 430).[1] *Orlando*, which delights in the exaggeration of period effects, as in its discussion of 'Elizabethan' weather – 'The brilliant amorous day was divided as sheerly from the night as land from water. Sunsets were redder and more intense; dawns were whiter and more auroral' (*O*, pp. 19–20) – is the fullest debate between these ideas of fundamental identity and a surface 'history' ('Nick Greene had not changed ... And yet, some change there was', *O*, p. 194). Even when Woolf is in the thick of constructing the Victorian–modern partnership, as in *Night and Day*, she can agree with Frederic Harrison's observation that 'There is no Victorian era at all ... great as the changes have been [from William IV to George V], both material and spiritual, there has been little spasmodic in it at any time. From 1789 to 1918 there has been a continuous post-revolutionary stream' (*Obiter Scripta*, p. 145, quoted *E* III. 65). The idea of the continuous stream is reconfigured in Woolf as a river, with its depths and smoothly flowing surface (*A Sketch*, *MOB*, p. 98), or else at the conclusion of *The Common Reader* as the sea, where 'the storm and the drenching are on the surface; continuity and calm are in the depths' (*E* IV. 241).

'Only you and me and William dressed differently', Mrs Swithin goes on to explain. In her 1910 review of a translation of Max Ulrich von Boehn's *Modes and Manners of the Nineteenth Century* Woolf sees the type of social history there performed as 'not a history of ourselves, but of our disguises. The poets and the novelists are the only people from whom we cannot hide' (*E* I. 334). The suggestion that historians deal with a more superficial, transitory order of things – necessarily attend to 'period' in fact – while literature probes to an elemental core – 'get[s] in and out' – is affirmed in the same review even when history deals with matters of greater moment than modes and manners: 'our passions and despairs have nothing to do with trade; our virtues and vices flourish under all governments impartially ... At any rate, we are left out, and history, in our opinion, lacks an eye' (*E* I. 331). The retrieval of the human, and of human kinship across the ages, is seen as the novelist's duty towards the past, and Woolf's frequent quarrel with that hybrid form the 'historical novel' is that it avoids this duty by letting itself be distracted by a lesser 'period' discourse. Thus we have her attack on Maria Edgeworth's novels in 1909, picturesquely 'charming' treatments of our ancestors that refuse to accept that they were 'as ugly, as complex, and as emotional as we are' – 'turbans and chariots with nothing inside them' is her summary of Edgeworth's work (*E* I. 318, 316). In Mary Debenham's *A Flood Tide* (1907), 'superficial distinctions of custom and manner' lead the novelist to 'forget that even in that picturesque age men and women were made of something more substantial than powder' (*E* I. 70). As we saw in *The Years*, Woolf is keen to avoid conflating the past with the picturesque.

Something of this sense of what history 'leaves out' explains Woolf's lifelong fascination with the 'lives of the obscure':

It is one of the attractions of the unknown, their multitude, their vastness; for, instead of keeping their identity separate, as remarkable people do, they seem to merge into one another ... melting into continuous years so that we can lie back and look up into the fine mist-like substance of countless lives, and pass unhindered from century to century, from life to life. (*E* IV. 120)

'The dim light is exquisitely refreshing to the eyes', Woolf adds (*E* IV. 121), as opposed to the spotlight that invests celebrity. As we go deeper into the core of the 'common', the everyday, the distinctions that exist between 'remarkable people' as well as the sense of historical difference subside. It is a figure like James Woodforde – 'nothing in particular ... had no special gift ... no oddity or infirmity' – who 'does not die', who 'goes on', while we 'change and perish': 'It is the

Kings and Queens who lie in prison' (*E* IV. 442–3, 445). This review of 1927 is significantly entitled 'Life Itself'. In a review of twenty years earlier Woolf salutes the 'obscure' but persistent generations of the Fanshawe family, 'a family history running alongside of all seasons of English life, inconspicuously, as a murmured accompaniment. So set humming, the whole land seems to swim in a pleasant kind of harmony, in which no age is more present than another, and all are of the one piece' (*E* I. 144). At the end of her life, in the anonymous 'Chaucerian' pilgrims who thread through the various ages of the pageant in *Between the Acts*, and in contemporary essays like 'Anon', where traditions of anonymity are saluted, Woolf will return to this musical sense of the *continuo* as the fundamental site of Englishness, constant from age to age, or, to change the metaphor, to the 'mist-like substance' that links the centuries together rather than sectioning them off. This deep sense of the unchanging overarches any Woolfian embrace of the 'new' and of modernity.

One of the most conspicuous links between Woolf and George Eliot is thus being drawn to 'the pathos to be found in commonplace lives', to use a phrase from Leslie Stephen's study of the latter.[2] At times Woolf's own political gradualism, notable at the end of *A Room*, where Judith Shakespeare will come in 'another century or so . . . if we worked for her . . . even in poverty and obscurity' (*RO*, pp. 102–3), is highly reminiscent of George Eliot's, as in the finale of *Middlemarch*, where 'the growing good of the world . . . is half owing to the number who lived faithfully a hidden life'.[3] Leslie Stephen himself clearly echoes these words and sentiments in describing one such exemplary life and its beneficent influence – that of Woolf's mother – in a passage from the *Mausoleum Book* (p. 96), and elsewhere, again with Julia Stephen in mind, he acknowledges the 'ennobling influence' of 'men and women who lived in obscurity' and 'who never had a thought of emerging out of obscurity'.[4] If Woolf inherited, so to speak, this emphasis, she also had an embodiment in her parents of female obscurity and male visibility; thus Stephen's light was still burning in the twentieth century, and various aspects of his thought and writing, as we have seen, could be put to contemporary use.

But so paradoxically could the precious heritage of female obscurity and anonymity, reworked in *Three Guineas* as we saw, and there handed down from the Victorians (and its apologists like George Eliot) to offset the masculine competitiveness of modern culture. 'Obscurity' as a particularly female quality also bears fruit on a personal level; thus in a letter to Jacques Raverat in 1925 Woolf intends 'to cultivate women's society entirely in future. Men are all in the light always: with women you swim at once into the silent dusk' (*L* III. 164). Here the silent dusk, like the 'dim light' of obscurity above, describes the refuge, repose and 'suggestive power' (*RO*, p. 92) provided by women, just as similar tropes of lighting describe the shelter from the exposing present the past provides. As I have argued, it is a mistake to seek to put the shadows to flight in Woolf, given their status as her major imaginative resort in reaction to the Stracheyan 'shaft of white light' that images an invasive, iconoclastic, unromantic and masculine modernity. In *Night and Day*, the portrait of Alardyce – 'The paint had so faded that very little but the beautiful large eyes were left, dark in the surrounding dimness' (*ND*, p. 8) – not only suggests a Victorian androgyny, but is an icon of the inevitable fading, and of the enticing chiaroscuro, of the past. The further we go back, the more obscure the light becomes; the Victorian period, vanished but remaining, retains, however, its play of light and shade, the retrospect that James experiences in 'turning back among the many leaves which the past had folded in him, peering into the heart of that forest where light and shade so chequer each other . . .' (*TL*, p. 200).[5]

Janis M. Paul has argued that in Woolf's fiction 'the insistent opposition between the material world and the world of consciousness is the literary manifestation of the conflict between the Victorian and the Modern sensibilities that shaped Woolf's life'.[6] For Paul this Victorian materialism 'celebrated externality and factuality, subjected the needs of the individual to the needs of society, denied thoughts and feelings, and placed value mainly on outward appearances and empirical facts' (p. 9). Woolf's novels, in their fascination with consciousness and individuality, are yet seen as wedded to this traditional 'externality': 'the forays into imagination take as their point of departure and return a Victorian sense of solidity and factuality which is vested in the English world of time, place, and society' (p. 37). But to restrict the Victorian, and the Victorian element in Woolf, to (novelistic) realism in this way seems to exactly misrepresent the retrospect we have been tracing, which frequently focuses on the poetic heritage of romance, individualism and passion, and in which the so-called 'Victorian sense of solidity' melts into a shadow that precisely prompts 'forays into imagination', or 'dissolves in an iridescent mist', to borrow once more Woolf's phrase on Anne Ritchie. In the drafts of the much-revised story 'A Scene from the Past' (parts of which were salvaged and published as 'The Searchlight'), such elements are there to a parodic degree:

The scene was Freshwater; the date 1860; the month June. Outside the studio all the birds were singing as birds sang then – the lark, the thrush, and the blackbird. All together, all day, they sang in the sun-flecked brilliant garden; and when the moon rose [,] nightingales vociferated their eternal sorrow from trembling sprays. As for the flowers [,] the hollyhocks grew in that wind warm hollow to twenty feet or more.[7]

Freshwater, as Woolf's other representations of it confirm (including her play of that name) was a scene of the exotic and the hyperbolic, with its extraordinary cast of characters: 'Is there *nobody* commonplace?' she reports a bewildered aunt 'lamenting' in her essay on Julia Margaret Cameron (*E* IV. 381), and it is no surprise that 'A Scene from the Past' develops from the above opening into a story of passion and romance – 'He kissed me . . .' – underwritten by references to Tennyson's *Maud* and 'The Lady of Shalott' (p. 7). 'Everything there was different from what it is today' (p. 6), and if at the end of the story Woolf acknowledges her exaggerated romancing of the scene and of its 'noble' protagonist, Sir Henry Taylor, she also satirises the denigration of such susceptibility in 'our oblivious age':

Should any one object; the story here given is not to be found in the Dictionary of National Biography, and is therefore untrue; should they say birds never sang so loud; hollyhocks never grew so high, it is impossible now to contradict them. For ... the book in which this story is told, and the album in which you could see [Sir Henry] draped in a shawl posed as King Arthur were destroyed only the other day 'by enemy action'. ('A Scene from the Past', p. 9)

'By enemy action' here has a wider significance than the reference to the wartime situation of 1941, when the draft was written; it also represents the hostility of the modern era towards the lyricism and sentiment of Victorian romance which has been discussed in this study. And as the only 'true' record of Sir Henry, the DNB testifies to a breadth of talent as statesman and writer – the ability to inhabit several worlds – that Woolf responded positively to as a Victorian endowment, as we have seen.

If Woolf seems to contradict in this her own reservations above about picturesque writing – our ancestors were in fact 'as ugly, as complex, and as emotional as we are', or rather, we are as ugly, emotional and complex as they – 'A Scene from the Past', which exists in many drafts written over a twelve-year period from 1929–41, recalled a specific scene that particularly engrossed Woolf, and that, in its published form 'The Searchlight' (which omits the Freshwater setting), continues to address several issues discussed in previous chapters. This scene is one Taylor recalled very much in passing in describing a solitary stretch of his youthful life in his *Autobiography* (1885), where, happening to look through a telescope, 'I saw once a young daughter of the farmer rush into the arms of her brother, on his arrival after an absence, radiant with joy. I think this was the only phenomenon of human emotion which I had witnessed for three years ....'[8] On this hint, Woolf builds up a tale of bold passion in 'The Searchlight', where the spectator of this kiss (the great-grandfather of the tale's narrator) runs for 'miles and miles' across the moor to claim the girl as his own (*CSF*, p. 272), while the kiss itself is plainly more passionate that that between a sister and brother: 'And then ... look ... A man ... A man! He came round the corner. He seized her in his arms! They kissed ... they kissed!' (*CSF*, p. 272, ellipses in original). The audience at the end of the story, who have listened to Mrs Ivimey telling it while a searchlight on manoeuvres scans the sky, is just as interested in the untold narrative that has slipped back into the shadows:

> 'But tell us – what about the other man, the man who came round the corner?' they asked.
> 'That man? That man', Mrs Ivimey murmured, stooping to fumble with her cloak, (the searchlight had left the balcony), 'he, I suppose, vanished'.
> 'The light', she added, gathering her things about her, 'only falls here and there'. (*CSF*, p. 272)

I do not read the audience's reaction here as J. W. Graham does, who sees a failure to understand the story as tantamount to an entire civilisation's 'blindness' as it embarks on war.[9] This ending rather relates to Woolf's own practice as a writer, and treats the necessary tact and limitations of the writer's art as its 'searchlight' enters the obscure depths of history. On the one hand the intrusive military light, a vehicle for revelation and destruction, is a parallel to Woolf's fictional explorations of a night sky 'thick with the star dust of innumerable lives' as she puts it in 'The Lives of the Obscure' (*E* IV. 121), this very innumerability being both an enticement and a frustration. Thus in the early short story 'Memoirs of a Novelist' (1909), where she exposes the 'platitudes' of Victorian biography to search out with what she called the 'greater . . . truth of fiction' (*E* IV. 395) the biographer's subject, Miss Willatt, she notes how the latter's everyday companions are lost to recognition – 'all these people . . . tempt us almost intolerably to know more about them . . . but we shall never know, or hear of them again. They have been rolled into the earth irrecoverably' (*CSF*, p. 72). Woolf again agonises about the sheer multiplicity of life-stories in *Jacob's Room*, where the opera-house audience, with each person offering the temptation to 'know more about them', provokes a situation where 'the observer is choked with observations': 'wherever I seat myself, I die in exile' (*JR*, p. 57).

Woolf as a writer cannot but identify herself with procedures that not only illuminate but 'expose' the past; if the searchlight is an image of reclaiming stories from oblivion, it also confesses the guilt of the writerly intruder. Woolf's constant resort to her familial past as a source for her writing, the fact that, as Hermione Lee notes, her family life gave rise to 'her most passionate, profound and humane art',[10] sits uncomfortably alongside her constant fears of her own privacy being exposed, her dislike of publicity and public appearances, and the agony that the publication of her work always caused. Thus as noted earlier, when *The Years* was about to appear she records feeling 'As if I were exposed on a high ledge in full light' (*D* v. 63). But Henry James, who made the drawing room at Hyde Park Gate seem 'rich and dusky', offered an alternative model of literary lighting, mellow, discreet, 'shading, suggesting' (*D* v. 215), that revives, even as it respects, the shades of the past. The contrast with Strachey, discussed in chapter 1, is enforced by Strachey's own militaristic metaphors in the Preface to *Eminent Victorians*: the biographer 'will attack his subject in unexpected places: he will fall upon the flank, or the rear; he will shoot a sudden, revealing searchlight into obscure recesses, hitherto undivined'.[11] Although Strachey admits the impossibility of any total knowledge of the past, he is far more concerned to trumpet what he finds than to yearn over and indeed lyricise what he loses, whereas Woolf's 'The Searchlight' is not only a tribute to the writer's power of imaginative retrieval but a celebration of its limitations also, in the face of more robust 'attacks' on the past, since that which is not disclosed has an equal potency and romance to that which is, preserved in respecting its elusiveness – in short, light and shadow function only in their differential relationship. This explains perhaps Woolf's recurrent use of the image of the moth in her work, the creature of shadow for whom light and brightness, however fascinating, spell danger and destruction, the light that 'dazed' Katharine Hilbery (*ND*, p. 68) or that 'dazed' Florinda in *Jacob's Room* (p. 62), or the 'full blaze of the station lamps' that dispel any mystique in the figure of Milly Masters ('The Shooting Party', *CSF*, p. 260). Such figures, as with many others in Woolf's work, are little served by the alienating habitat of modernity. Her brief essay 'The Death of the Moth', first published in 1942, is an elegy for a creature caught up by 'an oncoming doom', threatening 'not merely a city, but masses of human beings', the climax of an aggressive modernity leading logically, as *Three Guineas* warned, to war (*DM*, p. 11).

In *A Sketch of the Past* Woolf notes the scanty details of the climactic event of her mother's life, her falling in love and marrying her first husband, simply adding, 'That is all I know, perhaps all that anyone now knows, of the most important thing that ever happened to her' (*MOB*, p. 89). Some stories will never be told; 'the light ... only falls here and there'. While Strachey talks about lowering his 'bucket' into the great ocean of the Victorian to 'bring up to the light of day some characteristic specimen' (*Eminent Victorians*, p. 19), Woolf, to maintain the metaphor, rejoices in the vast stocks that can and should never be over-fished, the preservation of which intensifies the pleasure of the catch itself when it does occur, even on a solely 'visual' level: 'Then she had a glimpse of silver – the great carp himself, who came to the surface so very seldom' (*BA*, p. 121).[12] It is the inexhaustible wealth of 'countless lives', the chequer-work of both the lit and the lost, which informs Woolf's imaginative engagement with the past.

Notes

Place of publication is London, unless otherwise stated.

INTRODUCTION: POST-VICTORIAN WOOLF

1. On the relationship of rupture and continuity between postmodernism and modernism, see Linda Hutcheon, *The Politics of Postmodernism*, 2nd edn (Routledge, 2002), pp. 26–8.
2. H. H. Asquith, *Some Aspects of the Victorian Age*, Romanes Lecture (Oxford: Clarendon, 1918), p. 28.
3. *The Post Victorians* (Ivor Nicholson & Watson, 1933), pp. vii, ix.
4. See for example the Earl of Midleton's essay on Lord Balfour, in *The Post Victorians*, p. 3.
5. T. S. Eliot, 'Reminiscences of Virginia Woolf', *Horizon*, 3 (Jan.–June 1941), 316; rpt in Robin Majumdar and Allen McLaurin, eds., *Virginia Woolf: the Critical Heritage* (Routledge & Kegan Paul, 1975), p. 431.
6. Elizabeth French Boyd, *Bloomsbury Heritage: their Mothers and their Aunts* (Hamish Hamilton, 1976), p. 77.
7. Leonard Woolf, *Sowing*, in *An Autobiography*, vol. 1: *1880–1911*, introd. Quentin Bell (Oxford: Oxford University Press, 1980), p. 102. S. P. Rosenbaum's *Victorian Bloomsbury* (Macmillan, 1987), as its title suggests, shows how this 'battle' conceals literary and philosophical debts to a series of Victorian writers, but it has very little on Woolf herself as opposed to the male and Cambridge-educated members of the group. On Leonard Woolf's work maintaining the moral code of his Victorian upbringing, see F. M. Leventhal, 'Leonard Woolf 1880–1969: the Conscience of a Bloomsbury Socialist', in Susan Pedersen and Peter Mandler, eds., *After the Victorians: Private Conscience and Public Duty in Modern Britain: Essays in Memory of John Clive* (Routledge, 1994), pp. 149–68.
8. Introduction to *The Voyage Out*, ed. and introd. Jane Wheare (Penguin, 1992), p. xii.
9. Hermione Lee, *Virginia Woolf* (Chatto & Windus, 1996), p. 55.

10. 'The Great Victorian Myth' as expressed by the *Evening News* (London), quoted in Guy Barefoot, '*East Lynne* to *Gas Light*: Hollywood, Melodrama and Twentieth-Century Notions of the Victorian', in Jacky Bratton, Jim Cook and Christine Gledhill, eds., *Melodrama: Stage, Picture, Screen*, (British Film Institute, 1994), p. 98. One might note as another and more recent element added to this myth the presence of pervasive and systematic household incest proposed by Louise DeSalvo, *Virginia Woolf: the Impact of Childhood Sexual Abuse on her Life and Work* (The Women's Press, 1989).
11. Quentin Bell, *Virginia Woolf: a Biography*, 2 vols. (Hogarth, 1972), II. 186. See also I. 80, II. 44, 95–6.
12. As in her essay 'Storming the Toolshed': Woolf 'was arguing for a total subversion of the world of empire, class, and privilege'. Jane Marcus, *Art and Anger: Reading Like a Woman* (Columbus: Ohio State University Press, 1988), p. 195.
13. Jane Marcus, *Virginia Woolf and the Languages of Patriarchy* (Bloomington: Indiana University Press, 1987), p. 5.
14. Exemplary in their refusal to polarise Woolf within a Victorian–modernist antithesis are several of the contributions to *Virginia Woolf and the Essay*, ed. Beth Carole Rosenberg and Jeanne Dubino (Basingstoke: Macmillan, 1997); see in particular Eleanor McNees, 'Colonizing Virginia Woolf: *Scrutiny* and Contemporary Cultural Views', pp. 41–58 and Melba Cuddy-Keane, 'Virginia Woolf and the Varieties of Historicist Experience', pp. 59–77.
15. Victoria Rosner, *Modernism and the Architecture of Private Life* (New York: Columbia University Press, 2005), p. 61 (see also pp. 84, 90).
16. Jane de Gay, *Virginia Woolf's Novels and the Literary Past* (Edinburgh: Edinburgh University Press, 2006), pp. 215–16.
17. Carola M. Kaplan and Anne B. Simpson, 'Introduction: Edwardians and Modernists: Literary Evaluation and the Problem of History', *Seeing Double: Revisioning Edwardian and Modernist Literature* (Basingstoke: Macmillan, 1996), pp. xii–xiii.
18. 'Introduction: the British Intelligentsia after the Victorians', in Pedersen and Mandler, eds., *After the Victorians*, p. 1.
19. Matthew Sweet, *Inventing the Victorians* (Faber, 2001), p. xxii. In fact Sweet deserves some credit for not parading the Woolfian cliché of December 1910, though he does attack *Three Guineas* for its demonizing of a proto-Fascist Victorian patriarchy, given that masculinity in the period was 'beset by the knowledge of its own weakness and incoherence' (pp. 175, 189). He also documents Victorian sexual freedoms that give the lie to Bloomsbury claims of a sexual liberation from the past (pp. 207–21). The 1910 quotation is a customary prop of convenience in the 'Anti-Victorianism' chapter of John Gardiner, *The Victorians: an Age in Retrospect* (Hambledon & London,

2002), p. 26, and in Christopher Herbert, 'The Golden Bough and the Unknowable', in Suzy Anger, ed., *Knowing the Past: Victorian Literature and Culture* (Ithaca: Cornell University Press, 2001), p. 33.
20. Peter Stansky, *On or About December 1910: Early Bloomsbury and its Intimate World* (Cambridge, Mass.: Harvard University Press, 1996); Ann Banfield, *The Phantom Table: Woolf, Fry, Russell and the Epistemology of Modernism* (Cambridge: Cambridge University Press, 2000). See also Edwin J. Kenney, Jr, 'The Moment, 1910: Virginia Woolf, Arnold Bennett, and Turn of the Century Consciousness', *Colby Library Quarterly*, 13 (1977), 42–66, which reminds us what a long critical history Woolf's 'moment' has had as 'a convenient point of departure' (p. 42, a 'point' which Kenney then proceeds to endorse himself).
21. Perry Meisel, *The Absent Father: Virginia Woolf and Walter Pater* (New Haven: Yale University Press, 1980); Alison Booth, *Greatness Engendered: George Eliot and Virginia Woolf* (Ithaca: Cornell University Press, 1992).
22. Woolf already defends the 'perfect sincerity and good faith' of Victorian sentimentality in a review of 1917 – 'It is an art known to the Victorians. They heard a sad story; they were genuinely moved by it; they wrote it down straightforwardly, asking no questions and without a trace of self-consciousness; and this is what we cannot do, and this is what we find most strange in them' (*E* II. 150).
23. Leslie Kathleen Hankins, 'A Splice of Reel Life in Virginia Woolf's "Time Passes": Censorship, Cinema and "the usual battlefield of emotions" ', *Criticism*, 35 (1993), 95. The 'modernist revulsion against sentimentality' is explored in Suzanne Clark, *Sentimental Modernism: Women Writers and the Revolution of the Word* (Bloomington: Indiana University Press, 1991) (quotation p. 5).
24. See for example *In Memoriam* section xxi, in *Tennyson: a Selected Edition*, ed. Christopher Ricks (Harlow: Longman, 1989), pp. 365–6.
25. See for example Carol T. Christ, *Victorian and Modern Poetics* (Chicago: University of Chicago Press, 1984). More recent work continues along similar lines to chip away at the notion of modernist 'rupture' in claiming 'often unexpected and unacknowledged continuities between early twentieth-century writers and their Victorian precursors' (Giovanni Cianci and Peter Nicholls, eds., Introduction to *Ruskin and Modernism* (Basingstoke: Palgrave, 2001), p. xvi).
26. 'A Retrospect', in *Literary Essays of Ezra Pound*, ed. and introd. T. S. Eliot (Faber, 1960), p. 11.
27. T. S. Eliot, 'Andrew Marvell', 'The Metaphysical Poets', 'Swinburne as Poet', all in *Selected Essays*, 3rd edn (Faber, 1951), pp. 299, 288, 327 respectively.
28. 'Dante', in *Selected Essays*, p. 262.

29. 'Tradition and the Individual Talent', in *Selected Essays*, p. 16.
30. Pound, 'Cavalcanti', in *Literary Essays*, p. 150. On the coolness of Woolf's response to the Middle Ages in contrast to that of other modernists, see my 'Framing the Father: Chaucer and Virginia Woolf', in Wendy Scase, Rita Copeland and David Lawton, eds., *New Medieval Literatures*, 7 (2005), 42–3. We shall see that Woolf did have her own interest in Dante, however, though this often focuses on the Dante–Beatrice relationship as mediated through Victorian romance, a conflation that Eliot specifically repudiates: see his 'Dante', p. 262.
31. Sir Leslie Stephen, *Mausoleum Book*, introd. Alan Bell (Oxford: Clarendon, 1977), p. 42.

1 RECLAMATION: *NIGHT AND DAY*

1. The book under review was John F. Harris, *Samuel Butler: Author of 'Erewhon', the Man and his Work* (Grant Richards, 1916), quotation p. 16.
2. Elinor Mordaunt, *The Park Wall* (Cassell, 1916), p. 186.
3. 'Adventures in Books', *Athenaeum*, 18 August 1918, p. 351. Books Woolf reviewed included Ernest Belfort Bax, *Reminiscences and Reflexions of a Mid and Late Victorian* (George Allen & Unwin, 1918) and J. A. Bridges, *Victorian Recollections* (G. Bell & Sons, 1919) – see *E* II. 261–4, *E* III. 180–6.
4. Katherine Mansfield, 'A Ship Comes into Harbour', *Athenaeum*, 21 November 1919, p. 1227, rpt in Robin Majumdar and Allen McLaurin, eds., *Virginia Woolf: the Critical Heritage* (Routledge & Kegan Paul, 1975), p. 82.
5. Harrison's strictures on 'The New Woman' include his observation, 'as a veteran', of 'a grievous falling off in manners of our girls' (*Obiter Scripta* (Chapman & Hall, 1919), pp. 39–40).
6. Phyllis Rose, *Woman of Letters: a Life of Virginia Woolf* (Routledge & Kegan Paul, 1978), p. 161; 'A Great Man', unsigned review of Lord Fisher, *Memories* (Hodder & Stoughton, 1919), *Athenaeum*, 21 November 1919, p. 1225.
7. *Virginia Woolf and Lytton Strachey: Letters*, ed. Leonard Woolf and James Strachey (Hogarth, 1956), pp. 43, 45, hereafter abbreviated to *Letters*. Woolf's letter is also in *L* II. 12–14. Alex Zwerdling, *Virginia Woolf and the Real World* (Berkeley: University of California Press, 1986), quotes Strachey's comment in this exchange twice, omitting Woolf's reply on both occasions (pp. 41, 149), in keeping with what he claims as the 'programmatic anti-Victorianism' that the early Woolf shared with the rest of Bloomsbury (p. 202).
8. The idea that *Eminent Victorians* is solely an assault on the Victorians is, as Simon Joyce points out, a curious simplification, even if this has been and continues to be the primary response of many of Strachey's readers. For Joyce, Strachey uncovers in his subjects a fascinating proto-modern

psychological complexity, at odds, however, with a simplistic moral creed which Strachey does treat with a good deal of irony. But Joyce uses the rest of 'Bloomsbury', including Woolf herself, as a foil for Strachey's less dismissive evaluation, relying once again on the 'on or about December 1910' formulation to establish this position. See Simon Joyce, 'On or About 1901: the Bloomsbury Group Looks Back at the Victorians', *Victorian Studies*, 46 (2004), 631–54; a similar argument is found in his 'The Victorians in the Rearview Mirror', in Christine L. Krueger, ed., *Functions of Victorian Culture at the Present Time* (Athens: Ohio University Press, 2002), pp. 3–17. Whatever degree of sympathy with his subjects Strachey may or may not have, Samuel Hynes regards *Eminent Victorians* as 'the first important post-war book' in that it presents the Victorians as belonging to 'a remote and distant time, separated from the present by a great chasm'; indeed, 'the book is a paradigm of the common post-war sense that the war had made history discontinuous . . . .' (*A War Imagined: the First World War and English Culture* (Bodley Head, 1990), pp. 244–5).

9. Lytton Strachey, Preface to *Eminent Victorians: the Definitive Edition*, introd. Paul Levy (Continuum, 2002), p. 3.
10. By contrast with her remarks on James, Woolf would later say of Strachey's *Queen Victoria* that it lacked the '*depth or richness* which it would have had if it had been written [in] an age like the Victorian age' (*E* III. 516, my emphasis). Her observation on James here informs Lyndall Gordon's description of how his works 'enter the shadow' to seek a truth eclipsed by 'glare-of-day facts' in *A Private Life of Henry James: Two Women and His Art* (Chatto &Windus, 1998), p. 135.
11. On the influence of James's fiction on *Night and Day*, see Daniel Mark Fogel, *Covert Relations: James Joyce, Virginia Woolf, and Henry James* (Charlottesville: University Press of Virginia, 1990), pp. 130–7. Fogel also notes the extraordinarily 'celebratory pitch' of Woolf's review of *The Middle Years* (p. 83), without, however, contextualising this within the debate aroused by the Victorians around the end of the First World War. A good summary of the 'strongly ambivalent feelings' Woolf felt towards James's work is provided by Carol M. Dole, 'Oppression, Obsession: Virginia Woolf and Henry James', *Southern Review*, 24 (1988), 253–71 (quotation p. 257).
12. See Elizabeth Heine, 'Postscript to the Diary of Virginia Woolf, Vol. I: "Effie's Story" and *Night and Day*', *Virginia Woolf Miscellany*, 9 (Winter 1977), 6.
13. Laura Troubridge, *Memories and Reflections* (Heinemann, 1925), p. 38.
14. J. W. N. Sullivan, 'Victorian Heroes', *Athenaeum*, 14 May 1920, p. 634.
15. Gillian Beer, 'The Victorians in Virginia Woolf: 1832–1941', in *Virginia Woolf: the Common Ground* (Edinburgh: Edinburgh University Press, 1996), p. 97.

16. *Freshwater: a Comedy*, ed. Lucio P. Ruotolo (Hogarth, 1976).
17. Woolf indulges what she calls 'our natural instinct of reverence' for 'great men' in a 1917 review of Coulson Kernahan's memoir of Swinburne and his circle, *In Good Company* (*E* II. 109).
18. Elena Gualtieri, *Virginia Woolf's Essays: Sketching the Past* (Macmillan, 2000), p. 123.
19. In her review of Hugh Walpole's novel *The Green Mirror* (1918), Woolf is clearly critical of Walpole's conventional treatment of what she calls 'the family theme' in contemporary fiction, whereby 'another English family has been smashed to splinters and freedom is stealing over the roof-tops', ironically offering to rewrite the novel to avoid the 'hysterical' and melodramatic outcomes Walpole describes, and insisting that 'there is no need for [him] to apologise for what is slow, uneventful, and old-fashioned in the world which he portrays' (*E* II. 214–17). This 'rewrite' can be seen as what she then offers in *Night and Day*. Jane Marcus takes the review in an opposing sense (wrongly I believe) that confirms Woolf's own participation in the destruction-of-family movement in *Virginia Woolf and the Languages of Patriarchy* (Bloomington: Indiana University Press, 1987), p. 9.
20. Unsigned review of Samuel Butler, *Notebooks*, *Athenaeum*, 29 August 1919, pp. 808–9. The sentiment of an 'insurmountable barrier' dividing Victorians and moderns was often accompanied by a trenchant anti-Victorianism – see John Middleton Murry, 'The Victorian Solitude', *Nation*, 2 November 1918, p. 136.
21. E. M. Forster, *A Room with a View*, ed. Oliver Stallybrass (1908; rpt Penguin, 1978), p. 23. Subsequent page references to this edition are cited parenthetically in the text.
22. Towards the end of her life Woolf was similarly doubtful about a 'future ... ruled & guided by these active & ambitious & after all competent, & I suppose able, Fabians – oh why dont they any of them embrace something – but what? Poetry, I suppose, the sensuous, the musical?' (*D* v. 265).
23. The prioritising of 'night' over 'day', rather than a 'union of the eternal opposites' as Jane Marcus argues (*Virginia Woolf and the Languages of Patriarchy*, p. 25), might suggest that Woolf saw herself as a novelist of the 'dark' rather than 'light' side of 'the human soul', an antithesis outlined in 'How Should One Read a Book?', where 'a novelist will always tend to expose one rather than the other' (*E* IV. 392).
24. It is extremely difficult to read this passage from *Orlando*, and the wider context in which it is set, and say as Jane de Gay does that here 'modernity is welcomed in the form of the motor car and electric lighting, and celebrated for breaking through the gloom of Victoriana' (*Virginia Woolf's Novels and the Literary Past* (Edinburgh: Edinburgh University

Press), p. 141). In fact, the development of electric lighting in the late nineteenth century led many commentators to bemoan what R. L. Stevenson called its 'ugly blinding glare' in comparison with the 'warm domestic radiance' and 'old mild lustre' of the lighting it superseded. See 'A Plea for Gas Lamps', in *Virginibus Puerisque*, *Works*, vol. II (Cassell, 1906), p 443.
25. Domestic electric lighting was common in well-to-do households by the end of the nineteenth century, including 22 Hyde Park Gate, where Woolf noted that George Duckworth 'kept a store of old electric light bulbs which he shied at cats' (*MOB*, p. 123). In 1903 she reports on writing a letter 'under great difficulties' because 'my electric light is seized with a sort of Vitus's dance' (*L* I. 99). This is contradicted by Vanessa Bell's memoir 'Life at Hyde Park Gate after 1897' – 'we had no electric light anywhere' – a contribution to (or symptom of?) her sense that 'Darkness and silence seem to me to have been the chief characteristics of the house in Hyde Park Gate'. See *Sketches in Pen and Ink*, ed. Lia Giachero (Pimlico, 1998), pp. 70–1, 81.
26. On the 'absorption' of Ralph, see Zwerdling, *Virginia Woolf and the Real World*, p. 60. It is easy to over-estimate Ralph's status as a 'liberating spirit' (Marcus, *Virginia Woolf and the Languages of Patriarchy*, p. 30), or even as 'a spokesman for modernism, who will enable [Katharine] to move into the twentieth century' (Hermione Lee, *The Novels of Virginia Woolf* (Methuen, 1977), p. 63).
27. In a letter to Strachey of 1922 Woolf admitted to a 'romanticism' in her writing that might have been 'caught' from her Great Aunts (*L* II. 568–9).
28. For recent discussion of the Woolf photograph albums, see Maggie Humm, *Modernist Women and Visual Cultures: Virginia Woolf, Vanessa Bell, Photography and Cinema* (Edinburgh: Edinburgh University Press, 2002). Humm remarks on the non-chronological organisation of the albums: 'The Woolfs' preference for contiguity over chronology suggests a past which haunts the present rather than a past which precedes the present' (p. 57); thus 'past photographs impact on contemporary scenes' (p. 59).
29. Jane Goldman, *The Feminist Aesthetics of Virginia Woolf: Modernism, Post-Impressionism and the Politics of the Visual* (Cambridge: Cambridge University Press, 1998), p. 93.
30. Anne Ritchie's volumes of memoirs include *Chapters from Some Memoirs* (1894) and *From Friend to Friend* (1919), but Woolf was mainly influenced in *Night and Day* by the 'Reminiscences' of Freshwater, attached to a volume of photographs, that inform Mrs Hilbery's rhapsodising over the photograph album in chapter 9, and that indeed invest the past with, in Ritchie's own phrase, a 'friendly radiance'. She goes on to discuss

Cameron's photographs in terms of the light and shade effects that are one of their conspicuous features: 'The sun paints the shadow of life, and the human instinct and intelligence bestowed upon this shadow create in it that essence of light and life which is so priceless in a picture'. See *Alfred, Lord Tennyson and His Friends: a Series of 25 Portraits and Frontispiece in Photogravure from the Negatives of Julia Margaret Cameron ... [with] Reminiscences* by Anne Thackeray Ritchie ... (T. Fisher Unwin: 1893), p. 11. Woolf emulated this volume by publishing *Victorian Photographs of Famous Men and Fair Women* (Hogarth, 1926), for which she wrote the prefatory essay on Julia Margaret Cameron (*E* IV. 369–86). See further Carol Hanbery MacKay, 'The Thackeray Connection: Virginia Woolf's Aunt Anny', in Jane Marcus, ed., *Virginia Woolf and Bloomsbury: a Centenary Celebration* (Basingstoke: Macmillan, 1987), pp. 68–95, esp. 73–6.

31. Janis M. Paul, *The Victorian Heritage of Virginia Woolf: the External World in her Novels* (Norman, Okla: Pilgrim Books, 1987), p. 84.
32. Paul's contrast between 'stuffy, overcrowded rooms' and 'open gardens and streets' has recently been developed by Victoria Rosner, who sees the Hilbery house as 'dark, heavy, and even foggy' (in defiance of the very passages describing the interior that she quotes) in her pursuit of antitheses between confinement/freedom, past/present and so forth ('On the other hand, Katharine's experience of the city is joyous ....'). Interpretations that convert the 'fine mist' hanging in the Hilbery drawing-room – 'mist' tending to have a positive valency in Woolf as we have seen – into 'fog', and those that imply that the narrative ends at Mary's flat rather than the family house, are part of the equation between modernity and female flânerie that rejects any positive values in Woolf's Victorianism, estimating the 'backward-looking' solely in terms of critique. See Victoria Rosner, *Modernism and the Architecture of Private Life* (New York: Columbia University Press, 2005), pp. 155, 159.
33. See the Introduction to Virginia Woolf, *Melymbrosia: an Early Version of 'The Voyage Out'*, ed. and introd. Louise A. DeSalvo (New York: New York Public Library, 1982), pp. xxxiii–v.
34. John Ruskin, 'The First Morning', in *Mornings in Florence, Works*, ed. E. T. Cook and Alexander Wedderburn, 39 vols. (George Allen, 1903–12), XXIII. 295–311.
35. Woolf's picture of the English colony in Santa Marina is indeed based on people she met in Italy as described in her Florence diary of 1909 (*PA*, pp. 395–401) – see DeSalvo, Introduction, pp. xxxiv–vi.
36. On Vanessa Bell as a 'model' for Helen, see Peter Stansky, *On or About December 1910: Early Bloomsbury and its Intimate World* (Cambridge, Mass.: Harvard University Press, 1996), p. 247.

37. Hermione Lee, *Virginia Woolf* (Chatto & Windus, 1996), pp. 206–8. Quentin Bell agrees with Lee's distinction; see *Virginia Woolf: a Biography*, 2 vols. (Hogarth, 1972), I. 121.
38. Though I would not concur with Sonya Rudikoff's claim that George Duckworth's physical approaches to Woolf described in '22 Hyde Park Gate' (p. 177) were a fantasy born out of her need for outrageous sexual experience to match that of other members of her Bloomsbury audience. See *Ancestral Houses: Virginia Woolf and the Aristocracy* (Palo Alto, Calif.: The Society for the Promotion of Science and Scholarship, 1999), pp. 174–9.
39. *Athenaeum*, 20 February 1920, pp. 234–5.
40. Elizabeth Abel, *Virginia Woolf and the Fictions of Psychoanalysis* (Chicago: University of Chicago Press, 1989), p. 157, n. 12.
41. James's upholding the validity of the 'misty' retrospect might lend support to the suggestion that he is meant to chime with his namesake Henry James; see Fogel, *Covert Relations*, p. 151.

2 SYNCHRONICITY: *MRS DALLOWAY*

1. The new novel would arise from 'Conceiv[ing] mark on the wall, K[ew]. G[ardens]. & unwritten novel taking hands & dancing in unity' (*D* II. 14).
2. The visitors to Kew in Woolf's story are compared with 'white and blue butterflies' in their 'irregular movements', and also seen as 'dissolving like drops of water in the yellow and green atmosphere, staining it faintly with red and blue' – both images of fleeting and insubstantial beauty (*CSF*, pp. 90, 95).
3. Compare Woolf's remarks in a letter of 1919 on her sister-in-law Karin Stephen's taste for brightly coloured clothes, resulting in an effect 'like that of some debauched parrot' (*L* II. 369).
4. Some of the echoes from Eliot are pointed out in Sue Roe's notes to the novel, for example nn. 16, 22, pp. 173–4.
5. In a much later piece of writing Woolf returns fiercely to the visual stridency she accosts in *Jacob's Room*: 'We can see shop windows blazing; and women gazing; painted women; dressed-up women; women with crimson lips and crimson fingernails. They are slaves who are trying to enslave. If we could free ourselves from slavery we should free men from tyranny. Hitlers are bred by slaves' ('Thoughts on Peace in an Air Raid', *DM*, p. 155).
6. Mrs Ramsay compares her exhilarating sense of the permanence of the dinner scene in *To the Lighthouse* to a ruby (*TL*, p. 114), while in her essay on the Brontës Woolf quotes a passage from *Jane Eyre* featuring the 'ruby red' glassware that was conspicuous in Victorian decoration (*E* IV. 166).

7. John Mepham, *Virginia Woolf: a Literary Life* (Basingstoke: Palgrave, 1991), pp. 71–6.
8. Alex Zwerdling, in his tendency to subsume early Woolf within a general Bloomsbury 'anti-Victorianism', posits her 'easy concourse with Bohemia' in a manner that is clearly not reflected in *Jacob's Room*, noting that 'though she herself was not really bohemian, her sister, Duncan Grant, and many of their friends certainly were' (*Virginia Woolf and the Real World* (Berkeley: University of California Press, 1986), pp. 115–16). But arguably the first part of this formulation is more significant than the second.
9. Vanessa Bell, *Sketches in Pen and Ink*, ed. Lia Giachero (Pimlico, 1998), pp. 127–34. Contemporary connections made between Post-Impressionism and sexual 'irregularity' are noted by Hermione Lee, in *Virginia Woolf* (Chatto & Windus, 1996), p. 291.
10. Later antipathies between Woolf and Rebecca West lead to her imaging the latter as 'a lit up modern block, floodlit by electricity' (*D* IV. 327). Woolf's evaluation of landscape can take on similar tones, as with the countryside round Bayreuth: 'I don't much admire the country, because it is very florid and without shadow ...' (*L* I. 405).
11. As in establishing contact with her departed mother in *Reminiscences*: 'now and again on more occasions than I can number ... as I come into the room, there she is' (*MOB*, p. 40). Woolf's short story 'A Haunted House' is full of doors opening and shutting to admit the ghosts of the past, and the familiar 'house of fiction' metaphor she often uses to represent the literary tradition is a chronological rather than spatial structure.
12. Suzette A. Henke, '*Mrs Dalloway*: the Communion of Saints', in Jane Marcus, ed., *New Feminist Essays on Virginia Woolf* (Lincoln: University of Nebraska Press, 1981), n. 30, pp. 146–7.
13. Dante, *Purg*. 30. 39, 46–8; translation by John D. Sinclair, *The Divine Comedy of Dante Alighieri, II Purgatorio*, rev. edn (1948; rpt Oxford: Oxford University Press, 1971).
14. As in the line from Cavalcanti's sonnet 'Chi è questa che vien' beloved of Ezra Pound – 'Che fa di clarità l'aer tremare' ('makyng the air to tremble with a bright clearenesse'). See *The Translations of Ezra Pound*, introd. Hugh Kenner, new edn (Faber, 1970), pp. 24, 38–9. As Beverly Ann Schlack observes, there seem to be no significant correspondences between the protagonists of Woolf's novel and Richardson's; see *Continuing Presences: Virginia Woolf's Use of Literary Allusion* (University Park: Pennsylvania State University Press, 1979), p. 143. Schlack also makes a detailed case for Woolf's drawing on Dante's *Inferno* in stressing the 'damnation' Septimus suffers (pp. 69–72), though she misses the corresponding purgatorial 'resurrection' of Peter through Clarissa's agency.

15. J. Hillis Miller has noted in a well-known reading how *Mrs Dalloway* 'has the form of an All Souls' Day' in which figures from her past 'rise from the dead to come to Clarissa's party', but this resurrection motif is immeasurably strengthened by the parallel with Beatrice's rescuing Dante from the spiritual death of *presenti cose*. See 'Virginia Woolf's All Souls' Day: the Omniscient Narrator in *Mrs Dalloway*', in Melvin J. Friedman and John B. Vickery, eds., *The Shaken Realist: Essays in Modern Literature in Honor of Frederick J. Hoffman* (Baton Rouge: Louisiana State University Press, 1970), p. 115.
16. Perry Meisel, *The Absent Father: Virginia Woolf and Walter Pater* (New York: Yale University Press, 1980), pp. 36, 48.
17. It is significant that David Weir's *Decadence and the Making of Modernism* (Amherst: University of Massachusetts Press, 1995), which argues that decadence is 'crucial to the development of the modern novel' (p. xvii), can do nothing with Woolf, who is not mentioned at all in Weir's study. His adoption of the term decadence in preference to any 'period concept' as the 'common denominator underlying the extremely complex and diverse literary activities in the mid- to late nineteenth century' (p. xvii) provides an alternative map to Woolf's investment in the 'great Victorians', and points up how *relatively* little Weir's key French figures – Baudelaire, Flaubert, Mallarmé, Zola, and so forth – are mentioned in Woolf's criticism.
18. See her diary comment following a visit to the novelist Lucy Lane: 'large codfish eyes & the whole figure of the nineties – black velvet – morbid – intense, jolly, vulgar – a hack to her tips, with a dash of the stage' (24 January 1920, *D* II. 12). See also the satire on superannuated aesthetes in numbers 6 and 7 of the 'Portraits' ('Yes, I knew Vernon Lee'), *CSF*, p. 245. For Woolf's effacing of important literary debts to Vernon Lee and to Alice Meynell, see Dennis Denisoff, 'The Forest Beyond the Frame: Picturing Women's Desires in Vernon Lee and Virginia Woolf', in Talia Schaffer and Kathy Alexis Psomiades, eds., *Women and British Aestheticism* (Charlottesville: University Press of Virginia, 1999), pp. 251–69, and 'The Angel in Hyde Park: Alice Meynell's "Unstable Equilibrium"', chapter 5 of Talia Schaffer, *The Forgotten Female Aesthetes: Literary Culture in Late-Victorian England* (Charlottesville: University Press of Virginia, 2000), pp. 159–96.
19. Woolf was inspired in her picture of modern vandalism by the second instalment of Mary MacCarthy's memoir *A Nineteenth-Century Childhood* (*Nation & Athenaeum*, 8 September 1923): 'For a long time now the sound of crashing and smashing of glass has been in my ears. It is the strong, rose-coloured glass of the nineteenth-century conservatories cracking up.

Now the wrecking is over. There is a great mass everywhere about, and something perhaps of the early morning misgiving after the spree ...' (p. 713). Woolf reviewed the memoir when it was published in volume form in 1924 (*E* III. 443–5). The passage is quoted by S. P. Rosenbaum, *Victorian Bloomsbury* (Macmillan, 1987), pp. 105–6, but with the suggestion that Woolf had no sympathy with MacCarthy's regret, and by Zwerdling, *Virginia Woolf and the Real World*, p. 201, who links it with his idea of Woolf's later revisionism (see below, pp. 115–16) rather than with these earlier essays where it obviously belongs.

20. The title was doubly loaned by the Victorians, so to speak, having featured in Leslie Stephen's obituary essay on George Eliot; see *Hours in a Library*, new edn (1892), II. 208.
21. A comment of 1917 to the effect that 'much of Thackeray and Dickens seems to us far away and obsolete' (*E* II. 77) predates of course the arrival of the modernist 'squall' that might now make these writers seem a safe haven.
22. The moderns, Woolf notes in the essay, 'cannot generalise', only individualise (p. 359). In 'The Mark on the Wall', one of the short stories written 'all in a flash' and heralding the new approach of *Jacob's Room* (*L* IV. 231), the narrator attacks 'generalization' – 'the military sound of the word is enough' – as a feature of Victorian coercion and discipline (*CSF*, p. 86). In 'How It Strikes a Contemporary', however, the merits of generalization have become more apparent.
23. Allen McLaurin, *Virginia Woolf: the Echoes Enslaved* (Cambridge: Cambridge University Press, 1973), p. 40, quoting *Mrs Dalloway*, p. 8.
24. Augustine Birrell, *Frederick Locker-Lampson: a Character Sketch* (Constable, 1920), p. 67, quoted in Woolf, *E* III. 255–6. In the essay 'Miss Ormerod' (1924), Woolf again satirises the idea that 'life' can be represented by being divided into a series of chapters and chapter headings, *E* IV. 140.
25. Zwerdling, in quoting Woolf's diary entry on criticising the social system, notes how the statement 'has regularly been ignored', himself ironically ignoring (in not quoting) Woolf's afterthought on the possibility of her here 'posing' (*Virginia Woolf and the Real World*, p. 120).
26. Lyndall Gordon, *Virginia Woolf: a Writer's Life*, rev. edn (Oxford: Oxford University Press, 1991), p. 164.
27. For a discussion of Septimus not as a war case but as personifying Woolf's own early trauma, see Mark Spilka, *Virginia Woolf's Quarrel with Grieving* (Lincoln: University of Nebraska Press, 1980), pp. 62–4.
28. In her essay 'The Niece of an Earl' Woolf attacks the 'offensive' use of lower-class characters as 'objects of pity' or 'examples of curiosity' to 'show up the rich' or 'point the evils of the social system' (*E* IV. 562).

29. Sonya Rudikoff, *Ancestral Houses: Virginia Woolf and the Aristocracy* (Palo Alto, Calif.: The Society for the Promotion of Science and Scholarship, 1999), p. 230.
30. Compare 'Vita [Sackville-West] as usual like a lamp or torch in all this petty bourgeoisdom; a tribute to the breeding of the Sackvilles ...' (*D* III. 204).
31. MS of *Mrs Dalloway*, Berg M19. Woolf herself admitted to being a party animal, or even what she called a 'social festivity snob': 'Any group of people if they are well dressed, and socially sparkling and unfamiliar will do the trick; sends up that fountain of gold and diamond dust which I suppose obscures the solid truth' ('Am I a Snob?', *MOB*, p. 210). She saw her 'social side' as 'a piece of jewellery I inherit from my mother' (*D* II. 250).
32. In referring back to this worry about Clarissa in her diary for 18 June 1925, Woolf notes how she offset this 'tinsely' effect: 'Then I invented her memories' (III. 32), another indication of how the 'backing' of the past can substantiate the thinness of the present in Woolf.
33. Trudi Tate also talks of the novel being 'judgemental of [Clarissa] and of her entire class' in a discussion heavily indebted to Zwerdling; see *Modernism, History and the First World War* (Manchester: Manchester University Press, 1998), p. 167.
34. This is not, of course, to make Richard Dalloway the 'hero' of the novel, as Jane Marcus reprimanded Jeremy Hawthorn for doing in his *Virginia Woolf's 'Mrs Dalloway': a Study in Alienation* (Eastbourne: Sussex University Press, 1975) – see Marcus, 'Middlebrow Marxism: *Mrs Dalloway* and the Masses', *Virginia Woolf Miscellany*, 5 (Spring–Summer 1976), 5. Marcus's dismissal of Dalloway seems not only prompted by the class he belongs to, but also by the 'stiff upper lip' mentality which is seen as characterising that class, an emotional reticence at odds with the directness of Marcus's own textual encounters. Thus she writes as one who has 'learned to grasp the radical nature of Woolf's political ideas' by 'trust[ing] the text alone' (in distinction to Hawthorn's reading that is 'biased by class and sex', pp. 4–5), adding 'North Americans like Woolf straight', an alarming use of one of the last adjectives, one would have thought, that should be applied to Woolf. Something of this attitude persists in Zwerdling's (often repeated) claim that Richard's inability to tell Clarissa he loves her represents the emotional 'atrophy' of an entire class (*Virginia Woolf and the Real World*, p. 124), a fantastic exaggeration given Woolf's insistence throughout her work on means of communication other than speech alone; see below, p. 100.
35. Showalter, Introduction, p. xxiv, quoting Maureen Howard's Introduction to *Mrs Dalloway* (New York: Harcourt Brace Jovanovich, 1981), p. viii.

36. It is noteworthy that Zwerdling's comment on the social order depicted in *Mrs Dalloway* – 'the calm is only on the surface; there is turbulence beneath' (*Virginia Woolf and the Real World*, p. 124) – precisely inverts Woolf's insistence in 'How It Strikes': 'The storm and the drenching are on the surface; continuity and calm are in the depths' (*E* IV. 241).
37. Sandra M. Gilbert and Susan Gubar, *No Man's Land: the Place of the Woman Writer in the Twentieth Century*, 3 vols. (New Haven: Yale University Press, 1988–94), III. 55.
38. Elizabeth Abel, *Virginia Woolf and the Fictions of Psychoanalysis* (Chicago: University of Chicago Press, 1989), p. 43.
39. Michael H. Whitworth calls Walsh a 'Uranian', whose 'distinctly unmanly' qualities 'blur the boundaries' of gender. *Virginia Woolf* (Oxford: Oxford University Press, 2005), pp. 138–40.

3 INTEGRATION: *TO THE LIGHTHOUSE*

1. 'We Nominate for the Hall of Fame', *Vogue*, late May 1924, p. 49.
2. Jane Garrity, 'Virginia Woolf, Intellectual Harlotry, and 1920s British *Vogue*', in Pamela L. Caughie, ed., *Virginia Woolf in the Age of Mechanical Reproduction* (New York: Garland, 2000), p. 202. The photograph accompanies Garrity's essay, and has been reproduced many times elsewhere, as for example in Christopher Reed, *Bloomsbury Rooms: Modernism, Subculture, and Domesticity* (New Haven: Yale University Press, 2004), p. 25.
3. Compare her comment on Karin Stephen, p. 189 n. 3 above, with her remark to Vanessa Bell in a letter of 1916: 'My God! What colours you are responsible for! Karins clothes almost wrenched my eyes from the sockets – a skirt barred with reds and yellows of the vilest kind, and a pea green blouse on top, with a gaudy handkerchief on her head, supposed to be the very boldest taste. I shall retire into dove colour and old lavender, with a lace collar, and lawn wristlets' (*L* II. 111).
4. In Suzanne Raitt's words, '*To the Lighthouse* ... is at least as nostalgic for the beauties of Victorian marriage as it is critical of its shortcomings' (*Vita and Virginia: the Work and Friendship of Vita Sackville-West and Virginia Woolf* (Oxford: Clarendon, 1993), p. 8).
5. Jane Goldman, *The Feminist Aesthetics of Virginia Woolf: Modernism, Post-Impressionism and the Politics of the Visual* (Cambridge: Cambridge University Press, 1998), p. 168.
6. Peter Knox-Shaw, '*To the Lighthouse*: the Novel as Elegy', *English Studies in Africa*, 29 (1986), 41, 50.
7. In the manuscript of *A Room*, Woolf expands on Alan's limitations: 'Imagine, romance, dream, rhapsodise he cannot ....' *Women & Fiction:*

the *Manuscript Versions of 'A Room of One's Own'*, ed. S. P. Rosenbaum (Oxford: Blackwell, 1992), p. 154.
8. But this is very far from saying, as Jane Marcus claims, that it 'mock[s] Tennyson and Rossetti's lovey-doveyness as obsolete' (*Virginia Woolf and the Languages of Patriarchy* (Bloomington: Indiana University Press, 1987), p. 160).
9. Dante Alighieri, *La vita nuova*, trans. Barbara Reynolds (Penguin, 1969), pp. 45–7.
10. 'Al cor gentil rempaira sempre amore / come l'ausello in selva a la verdura....' *Poeti del duecento*, ed. Gianfranco Contini, 2 vols. (Milan: Ricciardi, 1960), II. 460.
11. Sir Leslie Stephen, *Mausoleum Book*, introd. Alan Bell (Oxford: Clarendon, 1977), p. 31. On the Victorian fascination with Beatrice and the *Vita nuova*, see Steve Ellis, *Dante and English Poetry: Shelley to T. S. Eliot* (Cambridge: Cambridge University Press, 1983), pp. 102–39.
12. Lisa Rado, *The Modern Androgyne Imagination: a Failed Sublime* (Charlottesville: University Press of Virginia, 2000), p. 139; Ann Banfield, 'Flight and Return: the Androgynous Mind', in *The Phantom Table: Woolf, Fry, Russell and the Epistemology of Modernism* (Cambridge: Cambridge University Press, 2000), pp. 196–200, which sees androgyny as a trope for the 'union of mysticism and logic' in Woolf (see also p. 386).
13. John W. Bicknell, 'Mr Ramsay was Young Once', in Jane Marcus ed., *Virginia Woolf and Bloomsbury: a Centenary Celebration* (Basingstoke: Macmillan, 1987), p. 63.
14. As Zwerdling notes, Woolf 'had much less faith in the triumph of reason than most of her Bloomsbury colleagues', including Leonard Woolf (*Virginia Woolf and the Real World* (Berkeley: University of California Press, 1986), p. 294). For a picture of Leonard as 'an often intolerant rationalist' perpetuating the line of the Victorian patriarch, see Perry Meisel, *The Absent Father: Virginia Woolf and Walter Pater* (New York: Yale University Press, 1980), p. 35.
15. Leslie Kathleen Hankins, 'A Splice of Reel Life in Virginia Woolf's "Time Passes": Censorship, Cinema and "the usual battlefield of emotions"', *Criticism*, 35 (1993), 111.
16. On psychoanalytic theories suggesting women have more 'permeable ego boundaries' than men, see Elizabeth Abel, *Virginia Woolf and the Fictions of Psychoanalysis* (Chicago: University of Chicago Press), p. 71.
17. *The Storm-Cloud of the Nineteenth Century* (1884), in *Works*, XXXIV. 5–80. On Woolf and Ruskin, see Gillian Beer, 'The Victorians in Virginia Woolf', in *Virginia Woolf: The Common Ground* (Edinburgh: Edinburgh University

Press, 1996), pp. 98–101, where Woolf's appreciation of the 'androgynous' in Ruskin is discussed.
18. Sandra Gilbert (in keeping with my observations at the end of chapter 2) assumes Woolf's unreserved embrace of the modern in this description, an instance of 'the radiant intensity of the temporal experience – the "moment of being" ... that this writer continually sought to capture'; see her Introduction to *Orlando*, p. xxxiii.
19. The letters are reproduced in 'Virginia Woolf's *Orlando*: an Edition of the Manuscript', ed. Madeline Moore, Appendix A, *Twentieth Century Literature*, 25 (1979), 349.
20. Elena Gualtieri, *Virginia Woolf's Essays: Sketching the Past* (Macmillan, 2000), p. 82.
21. *Orlando*'s obsessive insistence on past–present relations in the final section makes Gilbert's claim that the ending of the text is radically future-oriented deeply problematic – there seems no warrant to believe that by the conclusion of the book 'Woolf did begin to imagine at least the inception of a future that would be radically different from the past she had so yearningly revised' (Introduction, *O*, p. xxxvii).
22. Goldman's argument recalls Meisel's phrasing on Woolf and Pater's shared commitment to 'the luminous immediacy of the present moment' (*Absent Father*, p. 104) as though (the shades of) the past were not an equally critical investment for her.
23. Woolf's heroine's tastes here differ markedly from Roger Fry's: 'There was a magnificence about the Turkish hills that gave him immense satisfaction. They were not romantic. The light was real light, not pea-soup dissolved in vapour. One could see the structure of the hills' (*RF*, p. 171).
24. In a review of 1916 Woolf had called attention to a desire to combine new realism with old romance in writing as 'our modern problem' (*E* II. 53).
25. Lynda Nead, *Victorian Babylon: People, Streets and Images in Nineteenth-Century London* (New Haven: Yale University Press, 2000), p. 83.
26. The mutual 'telepathic insight' between characters as a feature of Woolf's work is dicussed by J. Hillis Miller, in 'Virginia Woolf's All Souls' Day: the Omniscient Narrator in *Mrs Dalloway*', in Melvin J. Friedman and John B. Vickery, eds., *The Shaken Realist: Essays in Honor of Frederick J. Hoffman* (Baton Rouge: Louisiana State University Press, 1970), p. 116. Leslie Stephen himself declared of his second wife 'I loved even her reticence. In truth, husband and wife, living together as we did in the most unreserved intimacy, confiding to each other every thought and feeling as it arises, do not require the language of words' (*Mausoleum Book*, p. 90).
27. Allen McLaurin, *Virginia Woolf: the Echoes Enslaved* (Cambridge: Cambridge University Press, 1973); Diane Filby Gillespie, *The Sisters'*

Arts: the Writing and Painting of Virginia Woolf and Vanessa Bell (Syracuse: Syracuse University Press, 1988); Ann Banfield, The Phantom Table: Woolf, Fry, Russell and the Epistemology of Modernism (Cambridge: Cambridge University Press, 2000) passim, but especially pp. 260–73. Although Gillespie does note the rivalry between the sisters which led Woolf to make 'many condescending remarks about the visual arts' (p. 10, see also p. 46), she stresses throughout her study how 'Woolf's equation of the world with color is close to the view of modern painters like her sister and like Cézanne' (p. 282), and how 'color was central to both sisters when they looked at the world around them' (p. 305).

28. Roger Fry, 'The Art of Florence', in Vision and Design (1920; rpt Harmondsworth: Penguin, 1937), pp. 154–5. For Fry's insistence on gradations of colour as a characteristically modern form of modelling that has replaced the 'plastic' function of chiaroscuro, see 'Plastic Colour', in Transformations: Critical and Speculative Essays on Art (Chatto & Windus, 1926), pp. 213–24.

29. Vanessa Bell, 'Memories of Roger Fry', in Sketches in Pen and Ink, ed. Lia Giachero (Pimlico, 1998), p. 128. Woolf's contrary enthusiasm for 'the Victorian passion for getting Nature perfectly accurately, for her own sake, into poetry' is illustrated in a 1917 review of Thomas Gordon Hake's Parables and Tales, where the stanza she quotes approvingly is full of the effects of sunlit clouds and 'wild shadows' (E. II. 150–1).

30. 'Lecture Given at Leighton Park School', in Sketches, p. 155.

31. Commenting on the passage Goldman argues that Woolf sees this movement only 'in terms of "new colour". It is this prismatic exploration of the newly illuminated feminine that marks Woolf's innovatory feminist aesthetic' (Feminist Aesthetics, p. 22).

32. The other noted use of the memento mori in Woolf is of course Jacob's finding the sheep's skull at the opening of Jacob's Room, an episode that sets the tone for the novel's elegiac discourse.

33. Tennyson: a Selected Edition, ed. Christopher Ricks (Harlow: Longman, 1989), p. 158. For Hermione Lee, To the Lighthouse as a whole 'has the emotions of a Victorian pastoral elegy. There is a Tennysonian mood to it' (Introduction, TL, p. xxxvi); see also Knox-Shaw's discussion of Tennyson's presence in the novel in 'To the Lighthouse: the Novel as Elegy', especially p. 50. The response to Percival's death in The Waves echoes In Memoriam at several points, as in the 'despicable' street Bernard observes with 'disillusioned clarity' (p. 204); compare 'On the bald street breaks the blank day', etc., In Memoriam VII. Jane Wheare has argued, though exaggeratedly in my view, for important correspondences between

In Memoriam and *The Voyage Out* – see her Introduction to the novel, *VO*, pp. xvi–xix.

34. On the interest of modernist writers in Queen Victoria, see Margaret Homans and Adrienne Munich, eds., *Remaking Queen Victoria* (Cambridge: Cambridge University Press, 1997), and Jay Dickson, 'Surviving Victoria', in Maria Di Battista and Lucy McDiarmid, eds., *High and Low Moderns: Literature and Culture, 1889–1939* (Oxford: Oxford University Press, 1996), pp. 23–46.
35. For a psychoanalytical account of Woolf's 'turning from the mother to the father' in the 1930s, see Abel, *Virginia Woolf and the Fictions of Psychoanalysis*, p. 112 (also p. 102).

4 DISILLUSION: *THE YEARS*

1. Alex Zwerdling, *Virginia Woolf and the Real World* (Berkeley: University of California Press, 1986), pp. 284–6.
2. *To the Lighthouse: the Original Holograph Draft*, ed. Susan Dick (Hogarth, 1983), pp. 251, 315.
3. *The Common Reader*, new edn (Hogarth, 1929), p. 299.
4. John Gardiner, *The Victorians: an Age in Retrospect* (Hambleton & London, 2002), p. 53.
5. Julian Hawthorne, *Shapes that Pass: Memories of Old Days* (John Murray, 1928), pp. 347–8.
6. Thus she mined *Fifty Years: Memories and Contrasts: a Composite Picture of the Period 1882–1932 by Twenty-Seven Contributors to 'The Times'*, foreword George Macaulay Trevelyan (Thornton Butterworth, 1932), for evidence of the restrictions the Countess of Lovelace lived under (*Three Guineas*, p. 166, n. 1) rather than for the 'gilded youth' reminiscences of Sir Ian Malcolm or Sir Arthur Quiller-Couch. See *Fifty Years*, pp. 24–30, 38–45, 54–5.
7. The 'tightness' Peggy feels 'round her lips and eyes' (*TY*, p. 252) is a recurring Woolfian sign of the pressures of modernity, as discussed previously with *Orlando* and *Jacob's Room*.
8. The generational discomforts of *The Years* have some basis in Woolf's own sense in the 1930s of 'the feeling of age coming over us: & the hardship of losing friends; & my dislike of the younger generation' (*D.* IV. 55).
9. Compare Woolf's craving in the Greece journal of 1906 for 'a great London square, where the lamps are just lit, & all the windows stand out red for the virtuous evening' (*PA*, p. 346).
10. Mitchell A. Leaska, Introduction to *The Pargiters*, p. xix.

11. Peggy's sense of isolation from her grandmother, and indeed from her own mother, is in stark contrast to the mother–daughter celebrations as the old college and the old house of professional confinement 'blaze' in *Three Guineas* (*TG*, pp. 157, 208), and represents her entrapment in such a house.
12. Sandra M. Gilbert and Susan Gubar's over-estimation of Woolf's political optimism leads them in their discussion of *The Years* and its 'new world' theme to pay no attention to Eleanor's own misgivings, nor to Woolf's disillusion with such 'wind blown' rhetoric; see *No Man's Land: the Place of the Woman Writer in the Twentieth Century* (New Haven: Yale University Press, 1988–94), II. 304–5, III. 50–1.
13. Although Woolf consistently uses electric light as an index of modern exposure and alienation, this never stopped her from appreciating it in practical terms, along with modern fridges and ovens, as a 'material blessing' and 'luxury' – see *D* IV. 27–8, 36. In passages excised from the final version of *The Years*, Eleanor enthuses over modern amenities while feeling 'bewildered' by an urban environment 'glaring with light' (Appendix: 'Two Enormous Chunks', *TY*, pp. 370, 372, 366).
14. Compare Jed Esty's discussion of *Between the Acts* as Woolf's 'classically liberal (and English) notion of social cohesion based on the promotion of individual freedom' in *A Shrinking Island: Modernism and National Culture in England* (Princeton: Princeton University Press, 2004), p. 98.
15. The enigmatic final observation here suggests perhaps that Victorian children had their own rich worlds of fantasy and adventure, in looking-glasses and elsewhere.
16. 'The Essays of Augustine Birrell', *Life & Letters*, 5 (1930), 32.
17. The disappointing status of the modern politician is also embodied in the Prime Minister who attends Clarissa's party – 'He looked so ordinary. You might have stood him behind a counter and bought biscuits – poor chap, all rigged up in gold lace' (*MD*, p. 188). Shortly before beginning *Mrs Dalloway* Woolf records meeting Lady Gwendolen Cecil and their exchange of views: 'Gladstone was a dishonest man if you like – but he was a great man. He had a policy. This man [Lloyd George] has nothing ... there's no politics now as there was in our youth' (*D* II. 176).
18. *Scrutinies*, vol. 2, ed. Edgell Rickword (Wishart, 1931).
19. Compare her complaint in 'A Letter to a Young Poet' of 1932 on the absence of 'beauty' in contemporary verse (*DM*, pp. 141–2)
20. Q. D. Leavis's fierce review of *Three Guineas* ended with the statement, 'Certainly there is no longer any use in this field of speculation for the non-specialist like Mrs Woolf' in 'Caterpillars of the Commonwealth Unite!', *Scrutiny*, 7 (1938–9), 214; rpt in Robin Majumdar and Allen

McLaurin, eds., *Virginia Woolf: the Critical Heritage* (Routledge & Kegan Paul, 1975), p. 419.
21. Compare Woolf's comment on Lord Robert Cecil, whom she entertained to tea in 1936: 'Best type of Eng. Governing class I suppose: the flower of 19th Century civilization: urbane, broadminded, kind & hopeful' (*D* v. 34).
22. Turgenev's *Fathers and Sons*, discussed in an essay on Turgenev that Woolf wrote in 1933 (in *CDB*, pp. 53–60), might provide an epigraph for *The Years*, as well as a suggestion for the Russian identity of Nicholas: ' "But the trouble is, we don't know how to make speeches! Arkady, you try". "I can't, papa, I'm not prepared" ' (Ivan Turgenev, *Fathers and Sons*, trans. Rosemary Edmonds (Penguin, 1975), p. 291). The making of speeches, far less perorations, is contrary to the state of 'unfinishedness' Woolf aims at in *The Years*, as described in a diary entry of April 1933, where the novel will 'end with the press of daily normal life continuing' (*D* IV. 152). In this it shows a striking contrast with *To the Lighthouse*, even if there is a brief restatement of the androgyny theme near the very end of the novel in the vignette of the young couple leaving their taxi to stand on the threshold of their house (*TY*, p. 318), though this hardly acts as a symbolic resolution. *The Years* thus invokes the tradition of Russian fiction whereby 'if honestly examined life presents question after question which must be left to sound on and on after the story is over' (*E* III. 36), the question of where 'the years' might be taking us being certainly left open.
23. For Percival's death, however, as an index of the decline of Empire, as well as a 'socialist' interpretation of Woolf's demoting in *The Waves* (as throughout her work) 'the damned egotistical self' (*D* II. 14) in the interests of a selfhood composed inter-individually, see Michael Tratner, *Modernism and Mass Politics: Joyce, Woolf, Eliot, Yeats* (Stanford: Stanford University Press, 1995), pp. 221–40.
24. Lyndall Gordon, *Virginia Woolf: a Writer's Life*, rev. edn (Oxford: Oxford University Press, 1991), p. 204.
25. On Wordsworth and *The Waves*, see also Gillian Beer's Introduction to the novel (Oxford: Oxford University Press, 1992), p. xx. Jane de Gay provides an illuminating discussion of *The Waves* and the 'Immortality Ode' in *Virginia Woolf's Novels and the Literary Past* (Edinburgh: Edinburgh University Press, 2006) pp. 173–5.

5 INCOHERENCE: THE FINAL WORKS

1. On Woolf and Chaucer, see my 'Framing the Father: Chaucer and Virginia Woolf', in Wendy Scase, Rita Copeland and David Lawton, eds., *New Medieval Literatures*, 7 (2005), pp. 35–52.

2. 'Virginia Woolf and the Authors of *Euphrosyne*', in Quentin Bell, *Virginia Woolf* (Hogarth, 1972), 1. 205.
3. For a similar justification of Leslie Stephen's own rights as an 'amateur' philosopher/historian/critic to trespass on the 'old common-fields' that have now been enclosed by specialists, see Frederic William Maitland, *The Life and Letters of Leslie Stephen* (Duckworth, 1906), pp. 491–2. The same source reminds us that Stephen shared his daughter's reservations about lecturing being 'a vanity and a distraction', with the matter able to be 'got ... up in half the time in two or three books' (p. 382). For more on Stephen's 'sniper fire' against the universities, see John W. Bicknell, 'Mr Ramsay was Young Once', in Jane Marcus, ed., *Virginia Woolf and Bloomsbury: a Centenary Celebration* (Basingstoke: Macmillan, 1987), p. 60.
4. Anna Snaith, *Virginia Woolf: Public and Private Negotiations* (Basingstoke: Macmillan, 2000), p. 119.
5. Roses for Woolf are a prominent icon of Victorian romance (supplanted here by the different smell of modernity), featuring in the verse from Tennyson's *Maud* quoted in *A Room* (p. 11) and in the portrait of Mrs Pargiter described in *The Years* (p. 239). 'Where is ... the red of the rose ...?' she asks of the sample of the modern critical mind represented in *Scrutinies* (above, p. 135).
6. Melba Cuddy-Keane, *Virginia Woolf, the Intellectual, and the Public Sphere* (Cambridge: Cambridge University Press, 2003), p. 111.
7. Letters, 31 March 1940, 14 April 1940, Monk's House Papers, University of Sussex.
8. 'Some Literary Reviews', *Sunday Times*, 2 February 1941, p. 4. Compare Raymond Mortimer's remark that Woolf was 'very much born in the intellectual purple and keenly aware of it'; see *Recollections of Virginia Woolf*, ed. and introd. Joan Russell Noble (Athens: Ohio University Press, 1972), p. 169.
9. See Lorrie Goldensohn's thoughtful discussion of 'The Leaning Tower' and associated documents, in which 'the rhetoric is admirable, but the policy to carry it out is wanting' in 'Unburying the Statue: the Lives of Virginia Woolf', *Salmagundi*, 74–5 (Spring–Summer 1987), 1–41 (quotation p. 35).
10. Anna Snaith, 'Wide Circles: the *Three Guineas* Letters', *Woolf Studies Annual*, 6 (2000), 6.
11. In the letter to MacCarthy previously referred to, Woolf's animus against 'Eton and Cambridge' in comparison with 'my wretched little £150 education' suggests the motive that made her recoil into an identification with WEA members, but this still leaves the doubt how far feeling

excluded from one group justifies an identification with the other, as proposed in the lecture.

12. John Mepham, *Virginia Woolf: a Literary Life* (Basingstoke: Palgrave, 1991) p. 191. 'The Leaning Tower' was published in *Folios of New Writing*, 2 (Autumn 1940), 11–33. The following issue included several replies to Woolf, largely defending the 1930s poets from her charges against them rather than pursuing the issues of reading discussed above. One of these was from Louis MacNeice, and quizzes among other things 'Mrs Woolf's beloved nineteenth century' ('The Tower that Once', *Folios of New Writing*, 3 (Spring 1941), pp. 37–41. Another, from the working-class writer (and miner) B. L. Coombes ('Below the Tower', pp. 30–6) is the starting-point, together with 'The Leaning Tower' itself, for Christopher Hilliard's study *To Exercise Our Talents: the Democratization of Writing in Britain* (Cambridge, Mass.: Harvard University Press, 2006), pp. 2–3, though Hilliard does not discuss the 'democratisation of reading' in any detail. The final reply, from the volume editor, John Lehmann, suggests that Woolf's objection to the 'leaning tower' poets consisted in their would-be identification with the working class, when she herself 'was always conscious of belonging to another class', and would never 'forget or deny the advantages ... gained from the old world', though this is precisely what she does seem to deny in the lecture ('A Postscript', p. 44).

13. *New Statesman and Nation*, 28 October 1933, p. 511. On Woolf's hatred of modern publicity, see Patrick Collier, 'Woolf, Privacy, and the Press', in Ann Ardis and Bonnie Kime Scott, eds., *Virginia Woolf: Turning the Centuries: Selected Papers from the Ninth Annual Conference on Virginia Woolf* (New York: Pace University Press, 2000), pp. 223–9.

14. The image of a 'head lamp on my poor little rabbits body wh. keeps it dazed in the middle of the road' is also used in Woolf's diary to express her anxiety about the post-publication reception of *The Years*; in the same diary entry she records feeling 'exposed on a high ledge in full light' (*D* v. 63–4).

15. Hermione Lee, *Virginia Woolf* (Chatto and Windus, 1996), p. 143 and Introduction to *Three Guineas* (Hogarth, 1986), p. xi.

16. See Lady Strachey, 'Some Recollections of a Long Life', *Nation and Athenaeum*, 5 January 1924, 23 February 1924, 12 July 1924, 30 August 1924.

17. The writing she did leave is collected in *Julia Duckworth Stephen: Stories for Children, Essays for Adults*, ed. Diane F. Gillespie and Elizabeth Steele (Syracuse: Syracuse University Press, 1987).

18. Already in Woolf's 1932 essay on Stephen we find a paradoxical and contradictory figure, combining a 'power of feeling' and emotionalism

that Stephen exhibited alongside his 'cold common sense' (*CDB*, p. 70), together with a mixture of conventionality and liberal defiance of convention that we have seen Woolf explore in the later memoir. In quoting Hardy's comparison of Stephen with the Schreckhorn, 'In its quaint glooms, keen lights, and rugged trim' (p. 72), she suggests something of the enigma and turbulence of Victorian individualism, taking advantage of the figure of chiaroscuro once more to do so.

19. Critics often quote this passage on the 'Victorian manner' from *A Sketch* as if it were a wholesale repudiation of that manner, which is far from the case – see Alex Zwerdling, *Virginia Woolf and the Real World* (Berkeley: University of California Press, 1986), p. 269. Like Victoria Rosner in *Modernism and the Architecture of Private Life* (New York: Columbia University Press, 2005), p. 76, part of Zwerdling's misrepresentation involves ending the quotation at 'cream and sugar' and leaving out the final 'on the other hand' sentence. We might always in fact keep in mind with Woolf the line of Louis MacNeice: 'But, on the other hand, there is another hand' – see *Autumn Sequel: a Rhetorical Poem in XXVI Cantos* (Faber, 1954), p. 16.

20. Woolf's 'politeness' as a reviewer is particularly evident in the way that critical or lukewarm appraisals often end with a consolatory flourish; see for example, 'Two Irish Novels' (*E* 1. 79), or her review of Elizabeth Robins's novel *A Dark Lantern* (Heinemann, 1905), which after categorizing the work's 'defects' ends on the surprising note that 'there can be no doubt that few living novelists are so genuinely gifted as Miss Robins, or can produce work to match hers for strength and sincerity' (*E* 1. 43). Robins had been a friend of Woolf's parents, and later of Woolf herself.

21. Woolf noted to Lowes Dickinson about *A Room of One's Own*: 'I'm so glad you thought it good tempered', adding 'my blood is apt to boil on this one subject ... and I didnt want it to' (*L* IV. 106). Maggie Humm notes how the 'tea table' becomes the scene of Woolf's anti-war campaign in *Three Guineas* and in the essay 'Thoughts on Peace in an Air Raid', highlighting the significance of Woolf's choosing to examine the photographs of war atrocities in the former work 'on a domestic table, not in the public sphere of street or library' (*Modernist Women and Visual Cultures: Virginia Woolf, Vanessa Bell, Photography and Cinema* (Edinburgh: Edinburgh University Press, 2002), p. 22). On Woolf's salvaging the 'Victorian manner' to 'create a supple, sensitive, and responsive speaking voice' in her essays, see Cuddy-Keane, *Virginia Woolf*, p. 135.

22. *Pointz Hall: the Earlier and Later Typescripts of 'Between the Acts'*, ed. Mitchell A. Leaska (New York: University Publications, 1983), p. 159.

23. Woolf's diary at the outbreak of the war sees the war as 'bosh' compared with the 'reality' of reading and writing, or contrasts what she calls 'the reality of the mind' with 'the unreality of force'. War has created 'an empty meaningless world', whereas 'any idea is more real than any amount of war misery'. She calls this position 'my whiff of shot in the cause of freedom' (*D* v. 233–5). Compare her remark quoted above, p. 67, on the 'preposterous masculine fiction' of the First World War.
24. In *Sowing*, Leonard Woolf notes how 'the years of my generation at Cambridge ... coincided with the end and the beginning of a century which was also the end of one era and the beginning of another. When in the grim, grey, rainy January days of 1901 Queen Victoria lay dying, we already felt that we were living in an era of incipient revolt and that we ourselves were mortally involved in this revolt against a social system and code of conduct and morality which, for convenience' sake, may be referred to as bourgeois Victorianism' (*An Autobiography*, Vol. 1 (Oxford: Oxford University Press), p. 96). It is remarkable how little this sense of a new era, or of the Queen's passing or its significance, is felt in any of Virginia Woolf's essays, diaries or letters that date from the first decade of the new century.
25. There are significant differences between the two introductions Woolf and Fry wrote for the selection of Julia Margaret Cameron's photographs published by the Hogarth Press in 1926. Whereas Woolf's is an affectionate compendium of the more extravagant stories told of the Freshwater circle by Ethel Smyth, Lady Ritchie and the rest (*E* IV. 375–86), Fry's, while admitting an admiration for some of Cameron's photographs, is sardonic about the society they recorded, describing it as pompous, provincial and, in its earnest cult of beauty, skirting 'the abyss of ridicule'. *Victorian Photographs of Famous Men & Fair Women*, introd. Virginia Woolf and Roger Fry, ed. Tristram Powell, new edn (Hogarth, 1973), p. 24.
26. Roger Fry, 'Art and Socialism', in *Vision and Design* (1920; rpt Harmondsworth: Penguin, 1937) pp. 54–5. According to Simon Watney, Fry 'was totally unable to grasp any of the specific continuities which run through from late Pre-Raphaelite culture into English Post-Impressionism, or the strengths of the English *pleine-aire* tradition' (*English Post-Impressionism* (Studio Vista, 1980), p. 6). In the field of domestic design, on the other hand, as Christopher Reed has shown, Fry's work can be placed 'firmly within the legacy of Victorian radicalism manifested in the writings of Ruskin, the workshops of the Arts and Crafts Movement' and other Victorian traditions; see *Bloomsbury Rooms: Modernism, Subculture, and Domesticity* (New Haven: Yale

University Press, 2004), p. 110. Indeed, Reed sees in the later years of the First World War and the early 1920s a more retrospective and less 'provocative' Bloomsbury modernism in painting and design (p. 199) that among other things wished 'to re-investigate nineteenth-century *plein-air* precedents' (p. 215). Perhaps Woolf's own Post-Victorianism was influential here.

27. Though in a letter to Lady Simon of January 1940 Woolf's 'one hope in this war' centres on gender reform rather than reform of the class system, a clearly separable and much more characteristic project: 'do cast your mind further that way: about sharing life after the war: about pooling men's and women's work: about the possibility, if disarmament comes, of removing men's disabilities' (*L* VI. 379). I read the ending of *Between the Acts* as less hopeful in the question it leaves hanging as to whether history will ever progress beyond a recurring pattern of love–hate, peace–war, civilisation–brutality, an ending that also, in its reference to 'another life [that] might be born' (*BA*, p. 129), is Woolf's final echo of (the ending of) *In Memoriam*.

CONCLUSION: RECLAIMING THE SHADOWS

1. See Melba Cuddy-Keane on the dialogue between periodisation and the 'ahistorical consciousness' in *Virginia Woolf, the Intellectual, and the Public Sphere* (Cambridge: Cambridge University Press, 2003), pp. 154–7.
2. Leslie Stephen, *George Eliot* (Macmillan, 1902), p. 82.
3. *Middlemarch*, ed. W. J. Harvey (Harmondsworth: Penguin, 1965), p. 896.
4. Leslie Stephen, *Mausoleum Book*, introd. Alan Bell (Oxford: Clarendon, 1977); 'Forgotten Benefactors', in *Social Rights and Duties: Addresses to Ethical Societies* (1896), II. 266.
5. Writing of 'the old' in 1916, Woolf describes them as 'the deep mirrors of life, in whose depths we may see all the processions of the past, closely surrounded by the unknown, as the day by the darkness of night' (*E* II. 62).
6. Janis M. Paul, *The Victorian Heritage of Virginia Woolf: the External World in her Novels* (Norman, Okla: Pilgrim Books, 1987), p. 7.
7. 'A Scene from the Past', *Virginia Woolf Bulletin*, 1 (January, 1999), 6.
8. Sir Henry Taylor, *Autobiography*, 2 vols. (1885), I. 45.
9. J. W. Graham, 'The Drafts of Virginia Woolf's "The Searchlight"', *Twentieth Century Literature*, 22 (1976), 391. For a more recent discussion of how the story explores 'the possibility of the simultaneity of past and present' in the light of Einstein's theories, see Holly Henry, *Virginia Woolf and the Discourse of Science: the Aesthetics of Astronomy* (Cambridge: Cambridge University Press, 2003), p. 55.

10. Hermione Lee, *Virginia Woolf* (Chatto & Windus, 1996), p. 128.
11. Lytton Strachey, *Eminent Victorians*, introd. Paul Levy (Continuum, 2002), p. 3.
12. Fishing as a metaphor for writing is used in Woolf's essay 'Professions for Women', where the 'imagination had rushed away. It had sought the pools, the depths, the dark places where the largest fish slumber' (*DM*, p. 152).

Index

Abel, Elizabeth, 42, 74, 75–7, 86
Allingham, William, 13
Antigone, 145, 152
Arnold, Matthew, 10
Asquith, Herbert, 1
Athenaeum, 14, 15, 18

Banfield, Ann, 5–6, 87, 102
Beer, Gillian, 18
Bell, Clive, 166
Bell, Gertrude, 143
Bell, Julian, 38
Bell, Quentin, 3–4
Bell, Vanessa, 23, 159, 160, 161, 167, 187 n. 25, 194 n. 3
  differences with Woolf, 37, 50–1, 96, 97, 102–4, 156
Belloc, Hilaire, 29
Bennett, Arnold, 57, 58, 59, 103
Bloomsbury group, 2–3, 29, 39, 51, 71, 115, 181 n. 7, 182 n. 19, 184 n. 7, 185 n. 8
Bicknell, John, 87
Birrell, Augustine, 67, 135, 150
Birrell, Francis, 87, 135
Boehn, Max Ulrich von, 172–3
Booth, Alison, 7
Boyd, Elizabeth French, 2
Brontë, Charlotte, 142
  Jane Eyre, 91
Browning, Robert, 10, 62
Burne-Jones, Sir Edward, 85
Butler, Samuel, 7, 12, 29, 67

Cameron, Julia Margaret, 11, 18, 134, 176, 187–8 n. 30, 204 n. 25
Carlyle, Thomas, 13, 134
Case, Janet, 23, 58, 134

Catullus, 137
Chaucer, Geoffrey, 60, 110, 142, 174
Chekhov, Anton, 49
Chesterton, G. K., 29
chiaroscuro, 37, 50, 125
  and Post-Impressionism, 50, 51, 95–9, 101–4
  symbolism of 25, 26, 95–9, 101–4, 105, 107–8, 175, 203 n. 18
Christ, Jesus, 113
Church, the, 142, 146
Cole, George, 51
Cole, Margaret, 51, 98
Colefax, Lady Sibyl, 71
Coleridge, S. T., 127
Conrad, Joseph, 110
Constable, John, 36
contemporaneity, 11, 32, 44, 45, 49, 74, 94
  Woolf's response to, 4, 7, 43, 50, 52, 56, 59, 61–2, 63–6, 76
Crimean War, 110
cubism, 14
Cuddy-Keane, Melba, 149, 150–1, 182 n. 14

Dante Alighieri, 10, 55, 62, 74, 84–5, 184 n. 30, 190 n. 14
Davidson, John, 58
da Vinci, Leonardo, 102
Debenham, Mary, 173
de Gay, Jane, 4, 186 n. 24
Delane, John, 13
De Quincey, Thomas, 29
DeSalvo, Louise, 35, 182 n. 10
Dick, Susan, 102
Dickens, Charles, 13, 59, 134
Dickinson, Goldsworthy Lowes, 88, 158
Dickinson, Violet, 50
Disraeli, Benjamin, 132

208   *Index*

Dostoevsky, Fyodor, 49, 57
Dowson, Ernest, 58
Duckworth, George, 23, 155, 160
Duckworth, Stella, 23, 48, 55, 76, 84, 95, 99, 117, 157, 160

Edgeworth, Maria, 173
Eliot, George, 7, 13, 16, 18, 75, 76, 174–5
Eliot, T. S., 2, 10–11, 43, 47–8, 59–60, 63, 80, 155
Ellis, Steve, 85
Elton, Charles, 100

Fanshawe family, 174
Fawcett Library, 151
fascism, 141, 142
Fineman, Hayim, 58
First World War, 17, 44, 110–13, 125, 132, 169
    as historical divide, 22, 37, 53, 54, 65, 66, 67–70, 75, 76, 89, 115, 185 n. 8
    and the Victorian debate, 9, 13, 34
Fisher, Herbert, 1
Fisher, Mary, 1
Fogel, Daniel Mark, 185 n. 11, 189 n. 41
Forster, E. M., 22, 35, 36
Freshwater circle, 11, 18, 176–7, 187 n. 30
Freud, Sigmund, 156
Fry, Roger, 5, 51, 102, 136, 167–8, 196 n. 23, 197 n. 28, 204 nn. 25–26

Galsworthy, John, 58, 59, 71
Gardiner, John, 116
Garnett, Edward, 40
Garrity, Jane, 78
Gilbert, Sandra, 74–5, 196 n. 21, 196 n. 18
Gillespie, Diane, 102, 196 n. 27
Gladstone, W. E., 132
Goldensohn, Lorrie, 201 n. 9
Goldman, Jane, 30, 79–80, 81, 95–7, 101–2, 104–5
Gordon, Lyndall, 69, 138
Gosse, Edmund, 99
Graham, J. W., 178
Greville, Mrs Richard, 16
Gualtieri, Elena, 22, 93
Gubar, Susan, 74–5
Guinizelli, Guido, 84

Hankins, Leslie, 8, 89
Hardy, Thomas, 11, 134, 137

Harris, John F., 67
Harrison, Frederic, 14, 172
Harrison, Jane, 18, 78–9
Hawthorne, Julian, 116–17
Haydon, B. R., 171
Hemingway, Ernest, 7, 99–100
Hills, Jack, 48, 55, 76, 84, 157, 159
Hitler, Adolf, 153
Homer, 22
Horizon 2
Horner, Lady Frances, 71
Humm, Maggie, 187 n. 28, 203 n. 21
Hynes, Samuel, 185 n. 8

Ibsen, Henrik, 29
imagism, 11
Inge, W. R., 1

Jacob's Room, 9, 40, 43–52, 54, 56, 58, 61, 64, 65, 66, 68, 93, 178, 179
James, Henry, 21, 23, 30, 32, 116, 189 n. 41
    as family friend, 11, 21, 39, 155, 179
    The Middle Years, 16–17, 31, 32, 161, 185 n. 11
Johnson, Samuel, 60
Joyce, James, 43, 49, 52, 55, 57, 79
    Woolf's doubts over, 2, 26, 48, 59, 60, 61–3, 70, 83, 94, 100, 148
Joyce, Simon, 184–5 n. 8

Keats, John, 107, 137
Kemble family, 17
Keynes, John Maynard, 154
Kingsley, Mary, 143
Knox-Shaw, Peter, 80

Lawrence, D. H., 100
Leaska, Mitchell A., 29, 38
Leavis, Q. D., 148, 199 n. 20
Lee, Hermione, 3, 37–8, 41, 73, 117, 154, 179, 187 n. 26
Le Gallienne, Richard, 58–9
Lewis, Percy Wyndham, 8
light and shadow, 9–10, 46, 48–50, 51–2, 59, 81, 101–4, 107, 114, 173
    domestic and urban lighting, 33, 39, 46, 47–8, 90, 122, 125, 186–7 n. 24, 187 n. 25, 199 n. 13
    and exposure, 63, 93–9, 154, 175, 178–80
    and retrospect, 16, 19, 30, 124
    and symbolism, 25–8, 42, 86, 104, 105–6, 111

Little Holland House, 28, 77, 157, 165
Little Review, 62
London National Society for Women's Service, 113
Lovelace, Mary Countess of, 137
Low, David, 154
Lushington, Kitty, 55–6

Macaulay, Lord, 41, 134
MacCarthy, Desmond, 150–1
MacCarthy, Mary, 130, 191 n. 19
McLaurin, Allen, 66, 102
Maitland, F. W., 38, 201 n. 3
Mandler, Peter, 5
Mansfield, Katherine, 14, 33
Marcus, Jane, 3–4, 41, 186 n. 19, 187 n. 26, 193 n. 34
Marlowe, Christopher, 46
Marvell, Andrew, 10, 127
Meisel, Perry, 7, 56
Memoir Club, 38
Mepham, John, 49, 151
Meredith, George, 11, 21, 41
Meynell, Alice, 132, 191 n. 18
Middle Ages, 10
Miller, J. Hillis, 191 n. 15
Milton, John, 59
modernity, 6, 8, 9, 20, 43, 56, 67, 87, 99–100, 107–9, 117, 125, 131, 166, 167, 174, 188 n. 32
  in relation to Victorian, 4–5, 10, 24, 39, 41, 54, 56, 75, 98, 99–100, 112, 121, 154–5
  Woolf's critique of, 7, 26, 51, 65, 90, 95, 100–1, 114, 115, 133, 144, 175, 179
Mordaunt, Elinor, 12–13
Morrell, Philip, 71
Mrs Dalloway, 37, 43, 44, 48, 52–77, 81, 84, 91, 95, 100, 112, 115, 116, 124, 130, 199 n. 17
Murry, John Middleton, 186 n. 20
Mussolini, Benito, 131, 141, 142, 153

Nead, Lynda, 99
New Statesman, 154
Nicolson, Benedict, 153
Night and Day, 9, 12–34, 35, 36, 37, 39–40, 41–2, 43, 45, 46, 47, 52, 54, 76, 86, 93, 95, 115, 117–18, 126, 129, 138, 156, 169, 172, 175, 179

Orlando, 9, 20, 27, 40, 46, 52, 53, 54, 61, 79, 81, 88, 89–95, 97–8, 100, 105, 112, 113, 122, 129, 130, 171, 172

Palmerston, Lord, 132
Pater, Walter, 7, 56
Pattle sisters, 28
Paul, Janis M., 33, 39, 175–6
Pedersen, Susan, 5
Pennell, Elizabeth Robins, 58
photography, 78, 154, 187 n. 28, 187–8 n. 30, 203 n. 21, 204 n. 25
Post-Impressionism, 1, 5, 29, 45, 167
  Woolf's relations with, 5, 36, 45, 50–1, 96, 97, 101, 102–4, 105
postmodernism, 1
Post-Victorianism, 1–11, 12, 38, 66, 78, 97, 115, 139, 152, 155, 169–70
  in Woolf's writing, 1–11, 73, 75, 79, 85, 89, 93, 106, 113, 120, 144, 154
Pound, Ezra, 10–11, 89, 190 n. 14

Rado, Lisa, 87
Raverat, Jacques, 175
Reed, Christopher, 204 n. 26
Robins, Elizabeth, 203 n. 20
romance, 11, 75, 97, 145
  and Victorians, 7, 18, 95, 98, 108, 111, 157, 176–7
  in Woolf's writing, 8, 24, 29, 31, 81–4, 90–1, 107, 111, 121, 129, 133
A Room of One's Own, 8, 24, 40, 50, 65, 79, 80, 81, 82–3, 85, 87, 88, 89, 91, 92, 96, 99, 100, 105, 110–11, 112, 113, 123, 128, 142, 143, 148, 149, 150, 174
Rose, Phyllis, 15, 35
Rosenbaum, S. P., 181 n. 7
Richardson, Samuel, 55
Ritchie, Lady Anne, *née* Thackeray, 11, 18, 31, 63, 79, 116, 187–8 n. 30
  Woolf's writings on, 13, 30, 39, 40, 48, 176
Rosner, Victoria, 4, 188 n. 32, 203 n. 19
Rossetti, Christina, 50, 82–3, 84, 100, 110–11, 113
Rousseau, Jean-Jacques, 127
Rudikoff, Sonya, 70, 189 n. 38
Ruskin, John, 35, 89

Sackville-West, Vita, 70, 89, 92–3, 97, 98, 101, 105
Sand, George, 127
Sanger, Charles, 88, 158
Scrutinies, 8, 134–5
Second World War, 129, 162, 169, 204 n. 23
Shaw, Bernard, 29, 58
Shakespeare, William, 59, 73, 135, 153
Showalter, Elaine, 68, 69–71, 73
Sickert, Walter Richard, 104
A Sketch of the Past, 9, 21, 22, 28, 30–1, 32, 44, 55, 60, 61, 74, 77, 80, 84, 88, 89, 106, 117, 131, 138, 154, 155–62, 164–9, 171, 172, 180
Smith, Agnes, 149
Smyth, Ethel, 18, 31, 32, 56, 116
Snaith, Anna, 148, 151
Stansky, Peter, 5
Stephen, Harriet Marian (Minnie), 11
Stephen, Julia, 11, 23, 29, 78, 99, 106–9, 130, 160–1, 165–6, 174, 180
    as figure of romance, 39, 77, 84, 106–9, 116, 157–8, 165–6
Stephen, Sir Leslie, 6, 11, 30, 67
    and Woolf's early reading, 60, 118, 145, 147, 150, 152
    Woolf's writings on 38, 54, 80, 87–8, 89, 109, 129, 156, 157–60, 166–9, 171, 202 n. 18
    writings, 38, 54, 66, 89, 109, 174, 196 n. 26
Stephen, Thoby, 45
Sterne, Laurence, 62
Strachey, Lady Jane Maria, 4–5, 6, 7, 108, 135, 150, 157
Strachey, Lytton, 5, 14, 18, 29–30, 31, 35, 41, 99, 175, 184 n. 7, 185 n. 10
    Eminent Victorians, 13–14, 15–16, 35, 40, 57, 99, 175, 184–5 n. 8
Sweet, Matthew, 5
Swinburne, A. C., 10
Symons, Arthur, 58

Taylor, Sir Henry, 176–7
Tennyson, Alfred, Lord, 10, 13, 16, 17, 79, 87, 106, 133, 135
    and Freshwater, 11, 134
    and Victorian romance, 50, 82–3, 87, 110–11, 113, 176, 201 n. 5
    In Memoriam, 8, 197 n. 33, 205 n. 27
Terry, Ellen, 134

Thackeray, W. M., 11, 57, 59, 62, 63
Thomson, William, 15
Three Guineas, 56, 69, 109, 110, 112, 117, 125, 127, 131, 135, 137, 140–7, 148, 152–5, 161, 168, 169, 175, 179, 182 n. 19, 199 n. 11, 200 n. 22
Times Literary Supplement, 161
To the Lighthouse, 8, 9, 22, 42, 65, 66–7, 70, 73, 77, 79–81, 83–9, 91, 94–5, 96–7, 100, 101–2, 105–7, 108–9, 111–13, 114, 115–16, 118, 124, 126, 129, 130, 145, 157, 158, 175
Trevelyan, George, 158
Trollope, Anthony, 134
Troubridge, Lady Laura, 18, 116
Turgenev, Ivan, 140–7, 200 n. 22
Tweedsmuir, Lady Susan, 152

Victoria, Queen, 15, 22, 35, 72, 76, 109, 166, 204 n. 24
Vogue, 78

Walpole, Hugh, 186 n. 19
Waterford, Louisa, Marchioness of, 16
Watney, Simon, 204 n. 26
Watts, G. F., 11, 134
Webb, Beatrice and Sidney, 58
Weir, David, 191 n. 17
Wells, H. G., 58, 71, 103
Wheare, Jane, 3
Whitman, Walt, 127
Wilde, Oscar, 58
Women's Co-operative Guild, 125
Woodforde, James, 173
Woolf, Leonard, 3, 88, 164, 168, 181 n. 7, 195 n. 14, 204 n. 24
Woolf, Marie, 160
WOOLF, VIRGINIA
    and androgyny, 67, 77, 83, 87–9, 91, 93, 99, 102, 116, 175
    and the aristocracy, 52, 70–1, 97, 104–5, 126, 130
    and bohemia, 50, 58, 93
    and Cornwall, 37, 166–7
    and democracy, 3, 6, 68, 70, 133, 147–53
    and education, 78–9, 134–5, 144–53
    and fashion, 7, 50, 54, 76, 78, 123, 189 n. 5, 194 n. 3
    and feminism, 79, 81, 83, 96, 101, 104, 105, 112, 115, 168

and the historical novel, 123–4, 173
and historical periodisation, 7, 120, 124,
  163–7, 172–4
and Hyde Park Gate, 6, 23, 33, 35, 38, 39,
  118, 156, 165, 179, 187 n. 25
and the media, 92, 99
and obscurity, 11, 22, 30, 153–4, 173–5
as 'outsider', 143, 147, 152, 153
and reading, 7, 135, 146–53
and sexuality, 50, 100, 110, 121–2, 123
and specialisation, 2, 7, 134–5, 145–7, 168
and Victorian individualism, 7, 17, 19, 77,
  107, 121, 127–8, 132–4, 176, 203 n. 18
and Victorian marriage, 79, 81, 83,
  90–3, 114
and Victorian sentimentality, 7–8, 12, 18,
  75, 81, 177, 183 n. 22, 183 n. 23
Works by; *see also* individual entries for
  key works discussed
'All About Books', 134–5
'Am I a Snob?', 70, 193 n. 31
'Anon', 174
'The Art of Biography', 31, 40
Between the Acts, 136, 138, 156, 162–4, 170,
  171–2, 174, 180
'Character in Fiction', 5, 51, 57, 59–61,
  67–8, 71, 104, 123
The Common Reader, first series, 10, 22,
  60–1, 63–5, 110, 112, 144, 172
'The Death of the Moth', 179
Flush, 9, 90, 113–14
Freshwater, 19, 134, 176
'Hours in a Library', 66
'The House of Lyme', 70
'How It Strikes a Contemporary', 32, 44,
  60, 62, 63–5, 67, 68, 112
'How Should One Read a Book?', 151
'Kew Gardens', 44
'The Lady in the Looking-Glass', 103
'Lady Strachey', 4–5, 6, 108, 135
'The Leaning Tower', 147–53, 157, 169,
  202 n. 12
'Life Itself', 174
'The Lives of the Obscure', 178
The London Scene, 132–4
'The Man Who Loved His Kind', 71
'The Mark on the Wall', 103, 192 n. 22

'Memoirs of a Novelist', 15, 35, 178
Melymbrosia, 35
'Modern Novels', 49, 62, 65, 106
Monday or Tuesday, 43
'Mr Bennett and Mrs Brown', 43, 57,
  63, 103
'Mrs Dalloway in Bond Street', 76
'Old Bloomsbury', 6, 33, 38–9, 99
'The Old Order', 16–17, 19, 19, 21, 22, 26,
  31, 52, 161
'On Being Ill', 88
'On Re-reading Novels', 32, 41, 57
The Pargiters, 113, 121–3, 126, 130, 137, 148
'Pattledom', 18
'Poetry, Fiction and the Future', 107–8
'Portraits', 102–3
'Professions for Women', 85, 113, 144
'Reading', 60–1, 135
Reminiscences, 38, 48, 81, 108, 165–7
Roger Fry, 136, 168
'A Scene from the Past', 176–7
'The Searchlight', 176, 177–80
'The Shooting Party', 103, 179
'A Society', 146
'Street Haunting: a London Adventure', 122
'The Sun and the Fish', 96
'A Talk About Memoirs', 171
The Third Generation, 17
'Thoughts on Peace in an Air Raid', 189 n. 5
'An Unwritten Novel', 103
The Voyage Out, 9, 14, 15, 34–8, 97, 114,
  166–7
'A Walk by Night', 37
The Waves, 96, 112, 126, 137–9, 197 n. 33
'Why?', 135
'Women and Fiction', 105
Women & Fiction, 92, 100
'22 Hyde Park Gate', 55
Wordsworth, William, 136, 137, 138

The Years, 22, 112, 114, 117–39, 140–2, 153,
  156, 160, 162–3, 168, 169, 172, 173, 179
Yellow Book, 58

Zwerdling, Alex, 68–71, 72, 75, 111, 115–16,
  184 n. 7, 190 n. 8, 193 n. 34, 195 n. 14,
  203 n. 19

OHIO UNIVERSITY LIBRARY
Please return this book as soon as you have finished with it. In order to avoid a fine it must be returned by the latest date stamped below. All books are subject to recall after two weeks or immediately if needed for reserve.

CF